IMAGES
of America

ORLEANS COUNTY

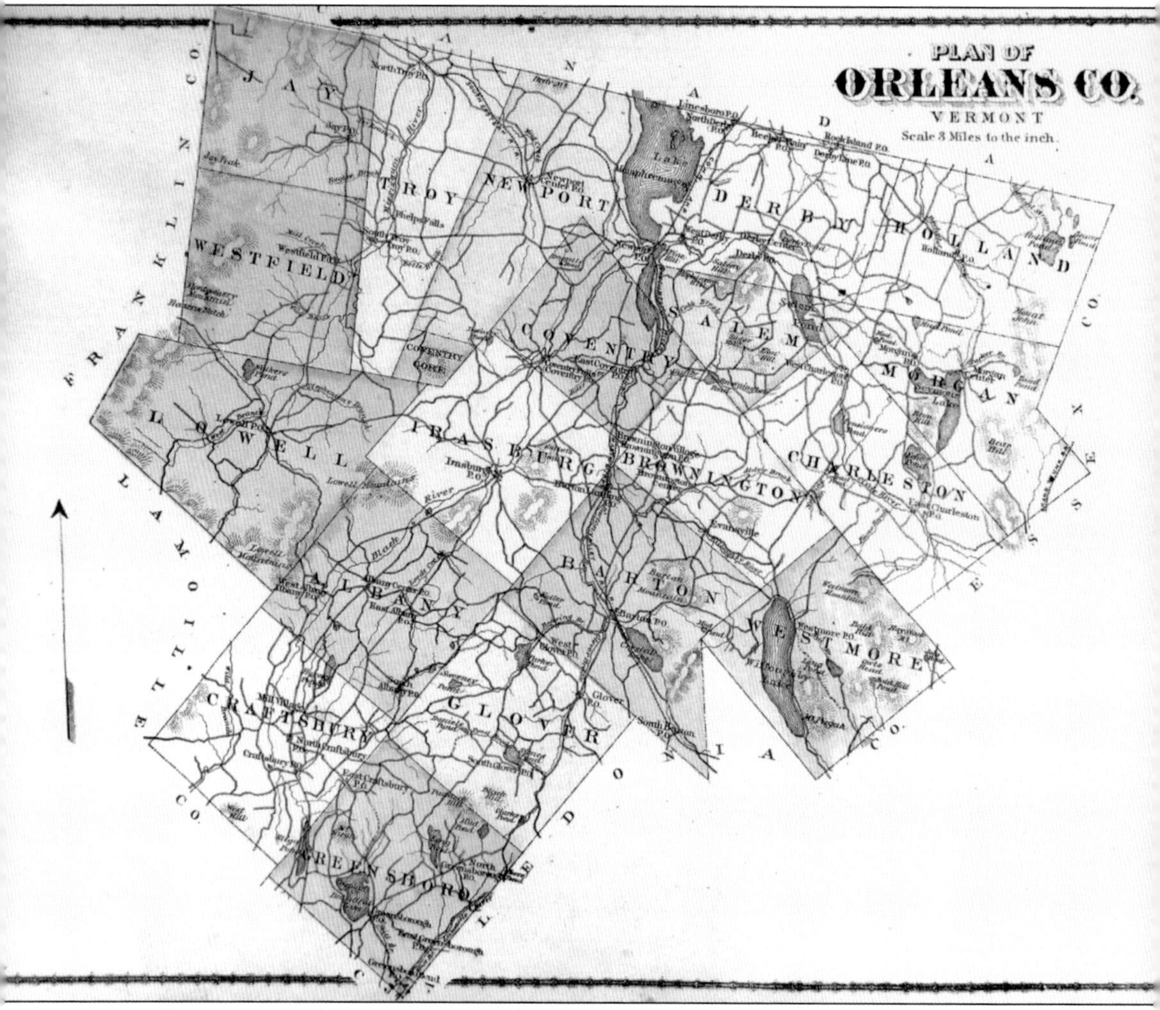

In 1878, the Beers Atlas was published with maps of the towns of Orleans County and their villages. On this map, Salem and Coventry Gore no longer exist. Newport City and Derby incorporated parts of Salem, and Newport Town incorporated Coventry Gore. (Orleans County Historical Society Archives.)

On the Cover: A few miles east of Lake Willoughby is Long Pond, a large pond with an island at one end. This hunting party camped out at the pond and brought their dogs to help them catch their bounty. (Orleans County Historical Society Archives.)

IMAGES
of America

ORLEANS COUNTY

Sarah A. Dumas and the
Old Stone House Museum

ARCADIA
PUBLISHING

ISBN 978-0-7385-7412-7

Published by Arcadia Publishing
Charleston, South Carolina

Printed in the United States of America

Library of Congress Control Number: 2010932934

For all general information, please contact Arcadia Publishing:
Telephone 843-853-2070
Fax 843-853-0044
E-mail sales@arcadiapublishing.com
For customer service and orders:
Toll-Free 1-888-313-2665

Visit us on the Internet at www.arcadiapublishing.com

Dedicated to the Vermonters who came before us

Contents

Acknowledgments

In the research of this book, I received help from many individuals and various historical societies in Orleans County. A great thank you to Scott Wheeler, Janice Lamoureux, Dave Drew, and Chuck Dumas of Tivoly, Inc.; Doris Monette; Allen Yale; Joan Alexander; Earl and Penny Tice; Rod Ames; Kimball Johnson; Richard Petit; Tonya Gunn; Yves Daigle; Richard Colburn; Emeline Harmon; Carolyn Arel; Daphne (Dolan) Christiansen; Dave Linck; Linda Pelletier; Shirley Pion; Thomas Bradley; Cathie Wilkinson; Beverly May; Fred Webster; John Miller; Eva Dannenberg; Jim Oliver; Paul Daniels; Raymond Gardner; Bruce Shields; the staff of the Old Stone House Museum for allowing me to do my research during a busy time of the year; and Elizabeth Nelson for all the help with the draft of this book. To Hilary Zusman, my Arcadia editor, thank you for being quick and helpful when answering all my questions.

Thank you to the authors of histories of the various towns in Orleans County, which I used frequently, and to the Vermont Folklife Center for great information about the cultures in Orleans County we used in our introduction.

Thank you to Roger Cartee for generously granting us permission to use the Richardson-Cartee Collection, a collection of Harry Richardson's photographs.

Unless otherwise noted, the images in this volume are from the Richardson-Cartee Collection (RCC), the Alexander Postcard Collection (APC), or the Orleans County Historical Society Archives (OCHS).

Introduction

Abenaki creation stories are rooted in America. They believe that their ancient ancestors originated on this continent. The Abenaki of the 1600s were part of a larger Wabanaki group that extended throughout Vermont into Quebec, Canada; New Hampshire; and Maine. These are the settlements in the lake and river valleys that the Europeans met when they first came to Vermont's Green Mountains. The Abenaki migrated seasonally to various locations within the family or band's territory for hunting, trading, and recreation. At the time the Europeans arrived, the Abenaki had developed new farming methods and had less violence in their lives than the Europeans did. The arrival of Europeans was the beginning of rapid and drastic changes to their way of life.

The flow of explorers, hunters, and trappers; land speculators; and settlers from Southern New England started around 1775. The already distinct Yankee culture in America had been created by the first European settlers, including African slaves and freemen. Yankees typically lived in villages rather than separate farms, which fostered local democracy in town meetings and communal moral behavior and civic duty. The first areas settled were the highlands, thought to be healthier than the river valleys, as well as offering a wider vantage point of the surrounding land. In 1780, Gen. Moses Hazen constructed the Bayley-Hazen Military Road from Newbury, Vermont, through Greensboro north to Lowell. From 1791 to 1793, Timothy Hinman built the Hinman Settler Road linking Greensboro to Derby and Canada. The Hinman Settler Road and the Bayley-Hazen Military Road cut through untracked forests and gave settlers access to the interiors of Orleans County.

During the War of 1812, the growth of Orleans County stalled. The newly settled residents of Orleans County reacted to the rumors of British invasion from Canada with fear for their lives. Soldiers were drafted and blockades were built. However, when the war began, most people gathered their things and left the new land for a safer home farther south. The only action seen in the county was a raid on an unguarded barracks in Derby in 1813 by British soldiers stationed in Stanstead, Quebec, Canada. Until the invasion, local inhabitants opposed the war, and some had smuggled supplies to the British. After the invasion, their enthusiasm for their neighbors diminished substantially.

Many returned when the threat of war was over. Unfortunately, they were met with another extreme situation. The year of 1816 began normally, with the planting of crops followed by ordinary growth in the spring. On June 9, a killing frost covered the ground, followed by a foot of snow. Thus began the year without a summer. The early growth of crops was destroyed. People survived on immature wheat and exorbitantly priced foods imported from abroad. The one crop the settlers could easily trade with was tree ashes, also known as potash. They were able to sell the potash to merchants who used it to create lye to resell in the cities. This became a cash crop for early Vermonters. Despite the terrible conditions, no one in Orleans County died that year from starvation.

French Canadians have been coming south to this county for over 150 years. The Patriotes Rebellion of 1837 against the British because of discrimination, worn-out soil, and crop failures caused many French Canadians to move into Franklin and Orleans Counties to farm. Today, French Canadian descendants are the largest minority group, as a whole, in Vermont.

During 35 years of immigration, from 1821 to 1856, some 60 families from one area of Scotland came to form a community in East Hill—the triangle where Greensboro, Craftsbury, and Glover meet. Because they were not the original settlers in the area, the Scots usually bought existing farmsteads from Yankees who had begun to migrate west. Today, few remain on farms that have been in the family since the 1830s.

Along with the Yankees, the Irish were among Vermont's pioneer settlers. The potato famine from 1844 to 1849 in Ireland forced many to leave home or face starvation, resulting in immigration to East Albany and other towns in Orleans County. Some Irish immigrants came with money, and some came as indentured laborers to work on farms and then later buy them.

When the railroad arrived in Orleans County in the mid-18th century, the stations were built along the valleys, encouraging growth of industry. The railways provided faster travel and easier transportation of products. Places like Newport and Orleans, where the railroad stations were, began to grow in population, while others on the hills, such as Brownington, began to decrease.

The Great Vermont Flood of 1927 would change Vermont forever as communities turned to the state, and the state turned to the federal government, for assistance. Vermont was devastated. The state flooded from Newport to Bennington. Eighty-five people died, and 9,000 were left homeless. Many of Vermont's roads and over 1,200 bridges were washed away.

Starting in the early 1960s, the so-called Back-to-the-Landers began moving to Vermont. These mostly young people were searching for an alternative to the materialistic consumer society in the urban and suburban areas where they had grown up. This influx of people into the quiet towns of Orleans County elicited many different reactions from those who had lived here for generations. Some were hostile and closed their doors and minds to people who had different ways of organizing their lives. Some were intrigued and enthusiastically welcomed the newcomers' energy and ideas. Usually it was a mix of both responses. It took about 20 years for the blending. Some left for new opportunities or were defeated by the climate; the rest stayed and flourished as vigorous transplants.

The agriculture has continually changed in Orleans County. At first, settlers cleared the forests for lumber and land to grow crops, and then logging became a viable industry. In the early to mid-1800s, thousands of sheep grazed on the hillsides of Vermont, and the land was 85 percent deforested. Sheep farmers began to migrate west, and dairy cows became the predominant domestic animal. Trains carried butter and cheese to the cities of New England. Gradually, fluid milk became an important market for dairy farmers as refrigerated train cars were invented in 1910. In the 1950s, public health regulations required more of dairy farmers. This caused many small farms to cease dairying. In the last 30 years in Orleans County, small family farms of 10 to 50 dairy cows grew to larger farms of 200 to 1,000 cows. This change has allowed the farmer to have a similar lifestyle as his neighbors employed in business, health, or education. To compete in the commodity markets, the cows have had to become producers of greater quantities of milk at lower production costs.

Today, Orleans County's population is about 27,000, with the highest poverty rate in Vermont and the fifth lowest average household spending in the United States. Although education is important to the community, with 78 percent having at least a high school education, only 16.1 percent have an undergraduate degree. Orleans County's revenue industries are tourism, agriculture, wood products, and small manufacturing.

One

Newport, Newport Town, and Derby

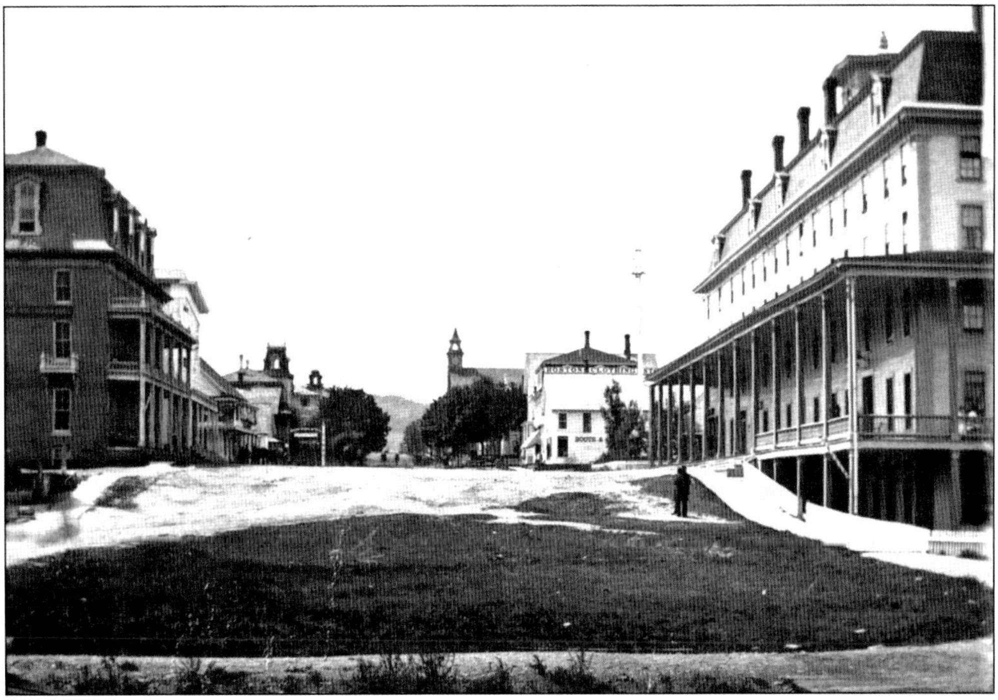

This is Main Street in Newport around 1885. The Memphremagog House, the large hotel on the right, burned on May 15, 1907. Originally, Newport included the town and the village of Newport. When Newport Village decided to incorporate with the neighboring villages of West Derby and Salem, this became Newport City. (RCC.)

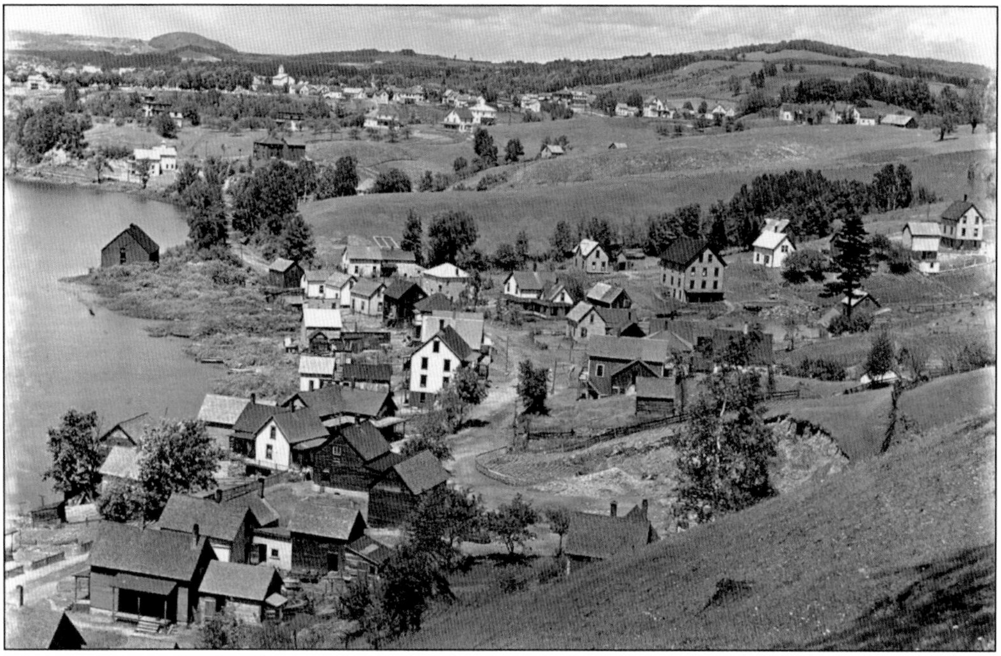

The land along the South Bay of Lake Memphremagog in Newport, now Glen Road, was once called Glen Side and was a part of Salem, Vermont. There were no settlements in 1816, when it was annexed to Newport. When the railroad came to Newport, houses began to pop up around the lake. (RCC.)

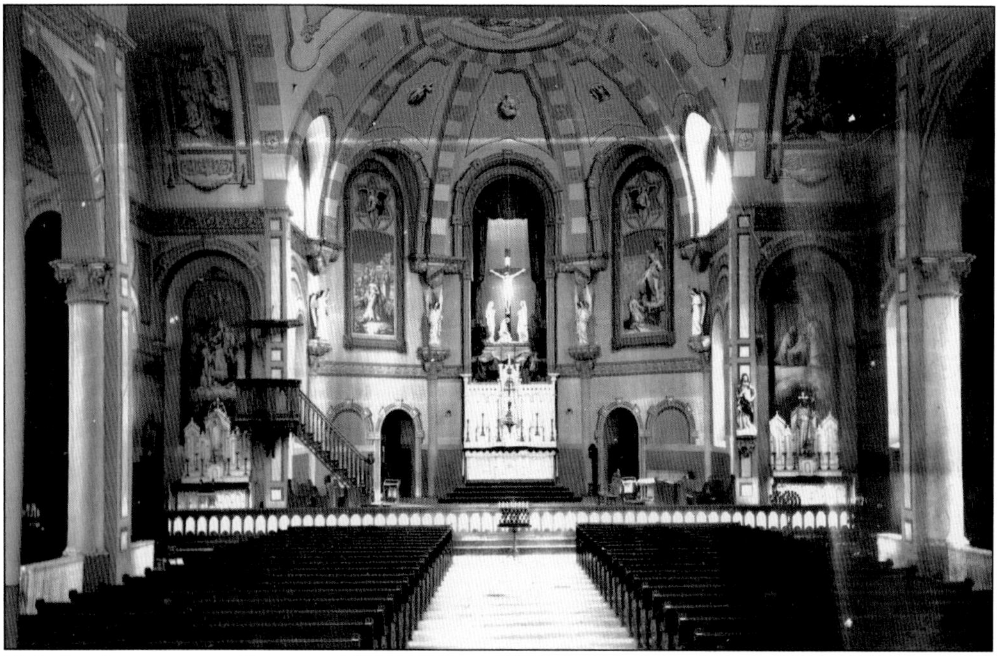

N.O. Rochon, an artist living in Newport, painted St. Mary's Star of the Sea, a Catholic church in Newport that was formally dedicated in 1909. He was a student of Napoléon Bourassa, a famous painter, sculptor, and architect in Quebec, and the artwork was modeled after original artwork by the artist Tissaud. (RCC.)

Seymour Lane's daughter Ruth and her husband, Dean Dwinell, owned this building on Main Street in Newport. It is seen here all decked out in patriotic and Masonic regalia. The Masonic lodge used the second floor above the Lane and Dwinell department store from 1888 until 1925, when the Masons moved to their Second Street building. (APC.)

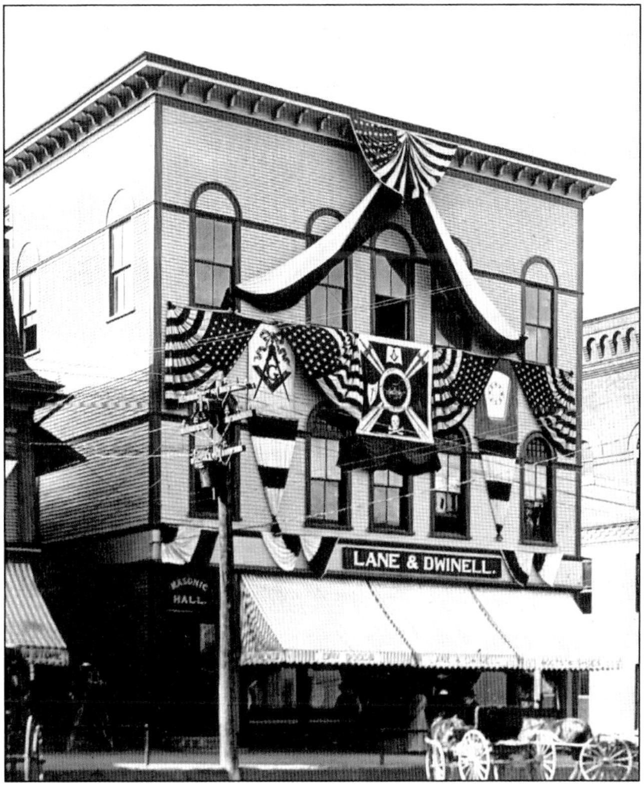

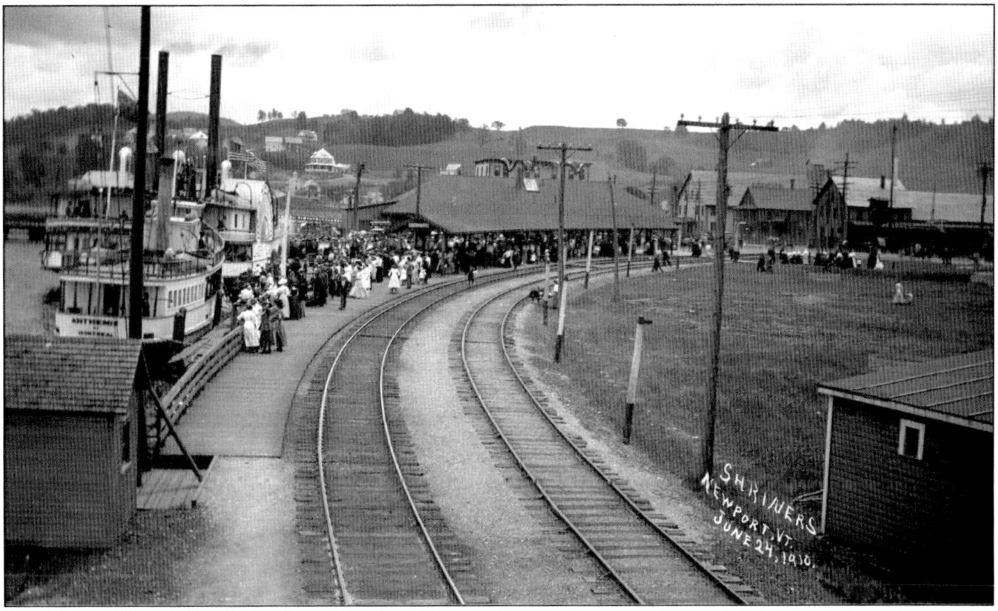

On June 24, 1910, seven hundred Shriners from Vermont came to Newport to celebrate the annual Masonic meeting. That morning, the Shriners marched in a parade up Main Street. When they returned to the lakeshore, the steamship *Lady of the Lake* was there to pick them up. After their meeting on Owl's Head Mountain, they returned for a banquet meal at the high school. (RCC.)

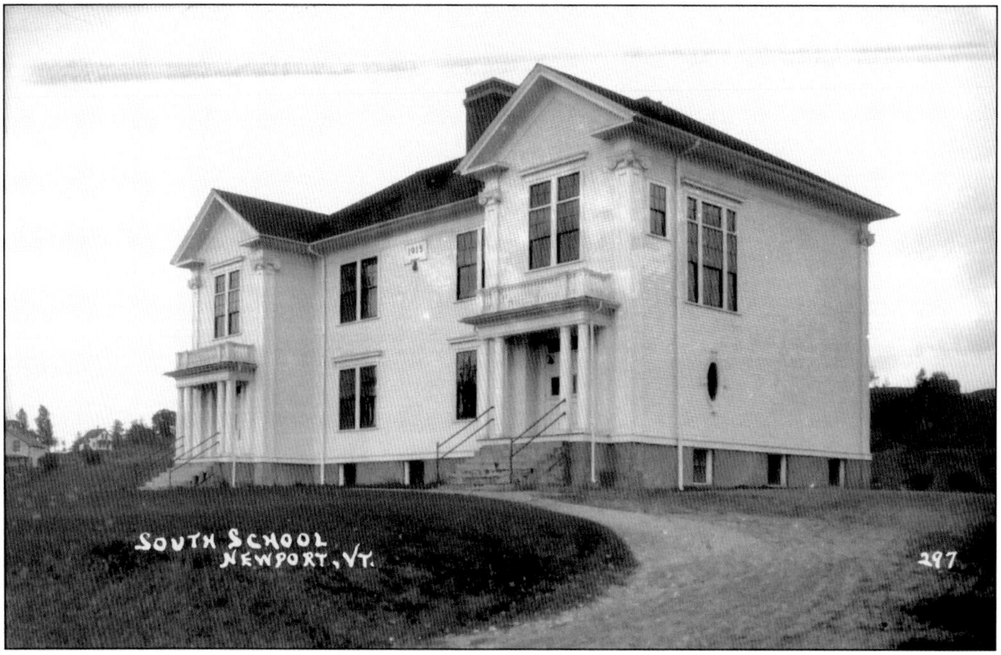

This Newport City school was called the South School, one of three elementary schools in Newport in the mid-1900s. Overlooking Glen Road and the lake, it was used until the Hillside School was built on the east side of town. It was then sold to Sel-Bar Weaving in 1963, and then, in 2009, to Life in Christ Fellowship, a local church. (RCC.)

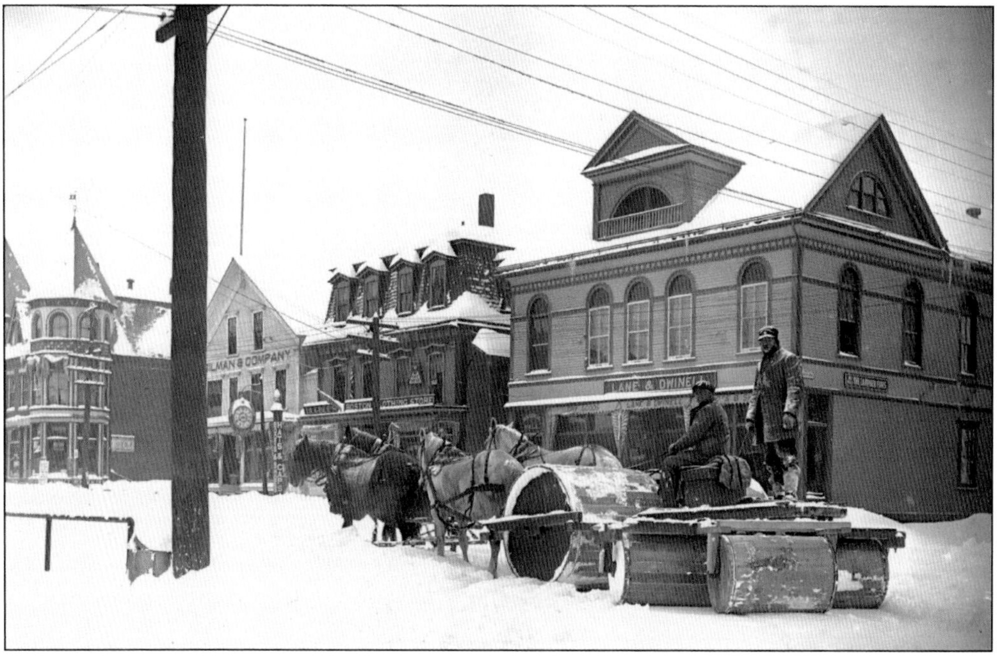

Before there were snowplows, the towns had to use snow rollers to pack the snow on the roads for horses and carriages. These two men are packing down snow on Main Street in Newport. Behind them is the Lane Block, with the Lane and Dwinell department store and Bugbee's Jewelry Store. (RCC.)

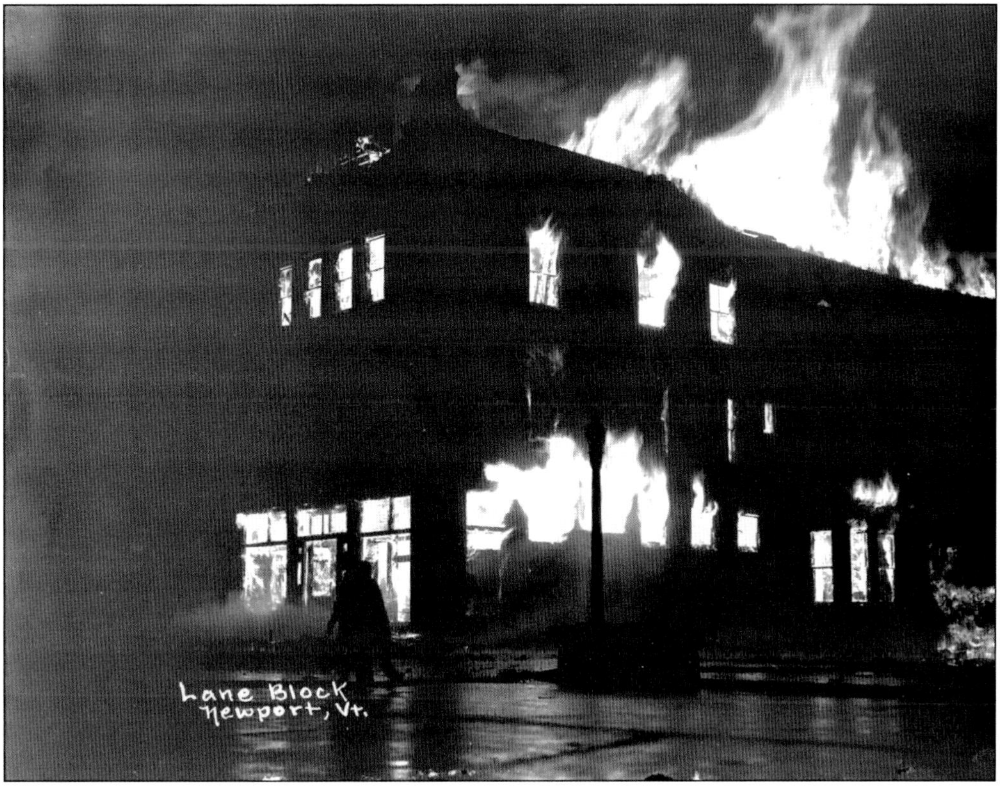

A three-story building called the Lane Block on Main Street in Newport went up in flames early on the morning of December 6, 1923. The fire started at 12:40 a.m. on the second floor of the building, which was serving as an opera house. More than 10 hoses were used to try to put out the fire, but it was impossible to save the building, so the firefighters focused on containing the fire. No other building was lost, but nearly 10 businesses—including a department store, a dentist office, a seamstress, a barber, and a life insurance office—lost everything. (Both, RCC.)

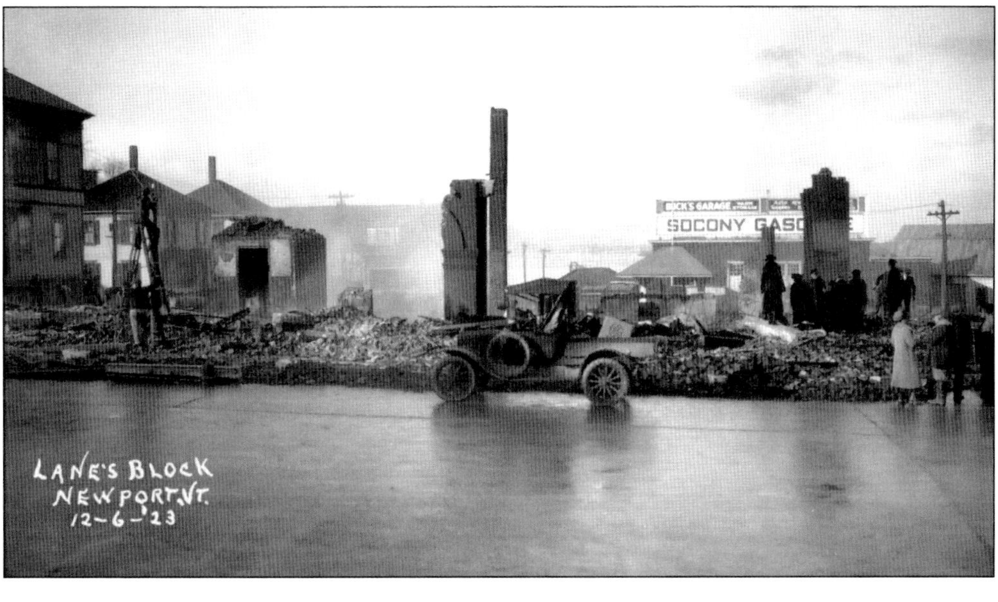

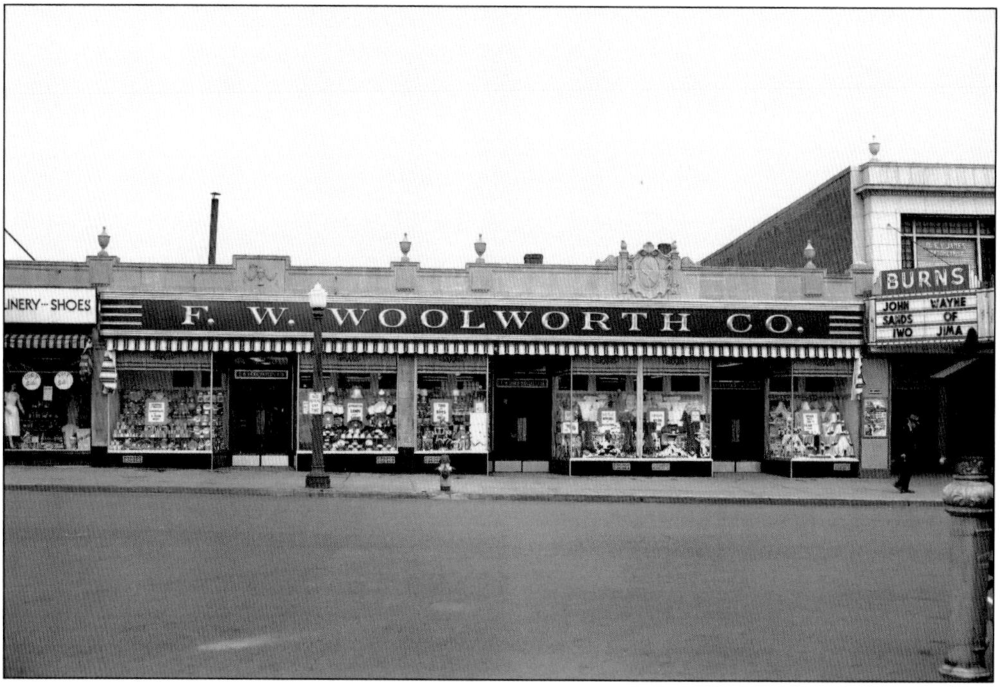

F.W. Woolworth's five-and-dime department store, whose headquarters were in New York City, came to Newport in 1924. Woolworth's was one of the first stores in America to put merchandise out on tables instead of behind a counter. (Both, RCC.)

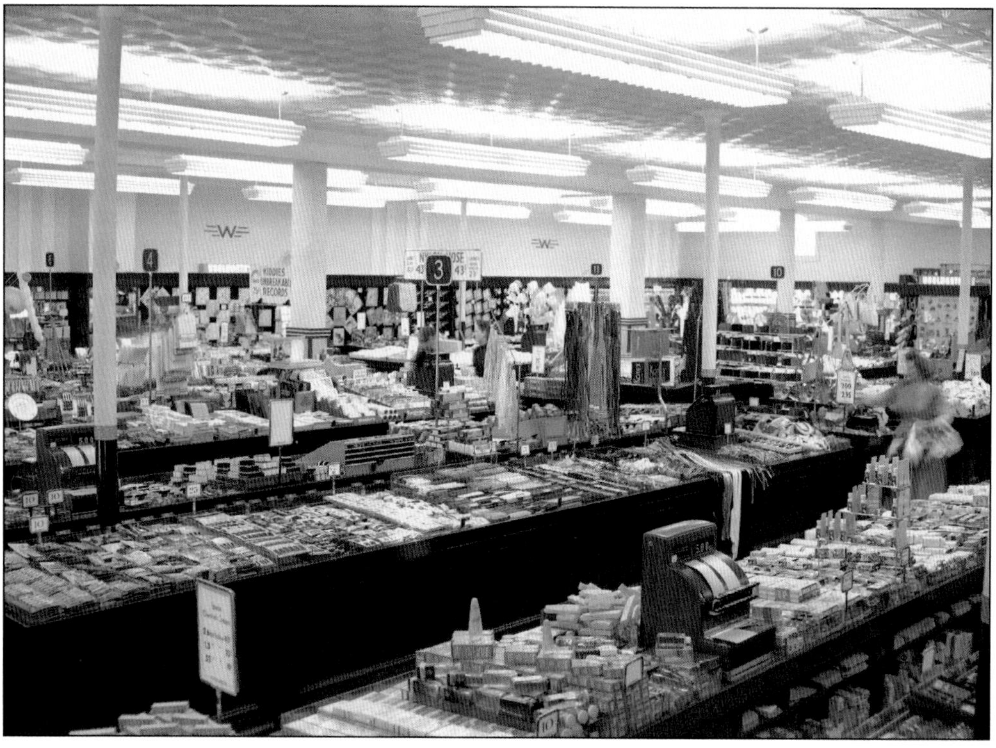

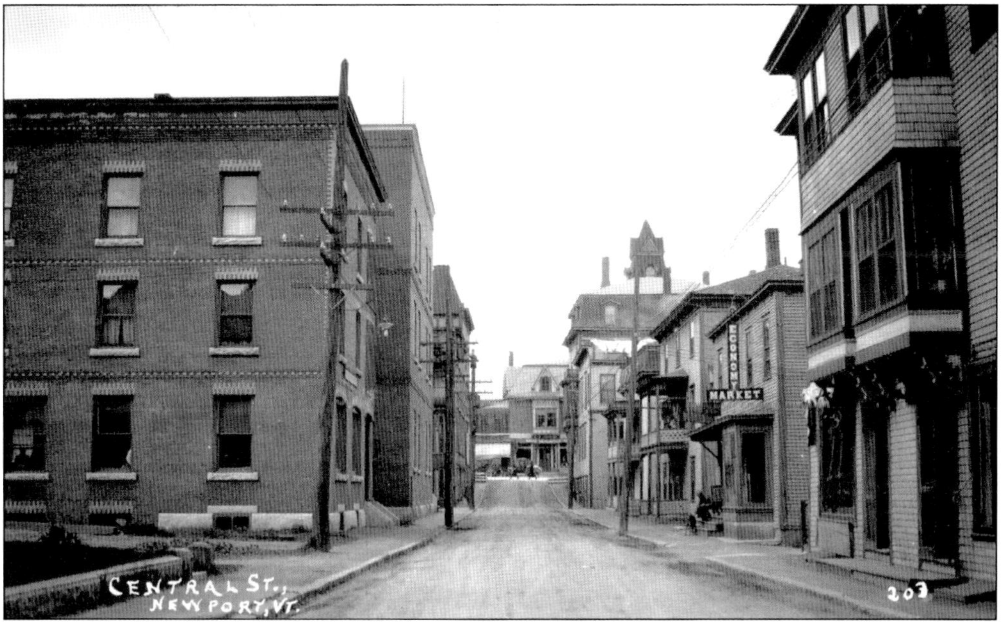

There were many businesses on Coventry Street facing Main Street in Newport. The first building on the left was the Express and Standard's printing house, built in 1913. The taller building next to the printing house was the meeting place of the International Order of Odd Fellows, which burned in 1961. Also on Central Street were a cabinet shop, a butcher shop, a cobbler, and a baker. (RCC.)

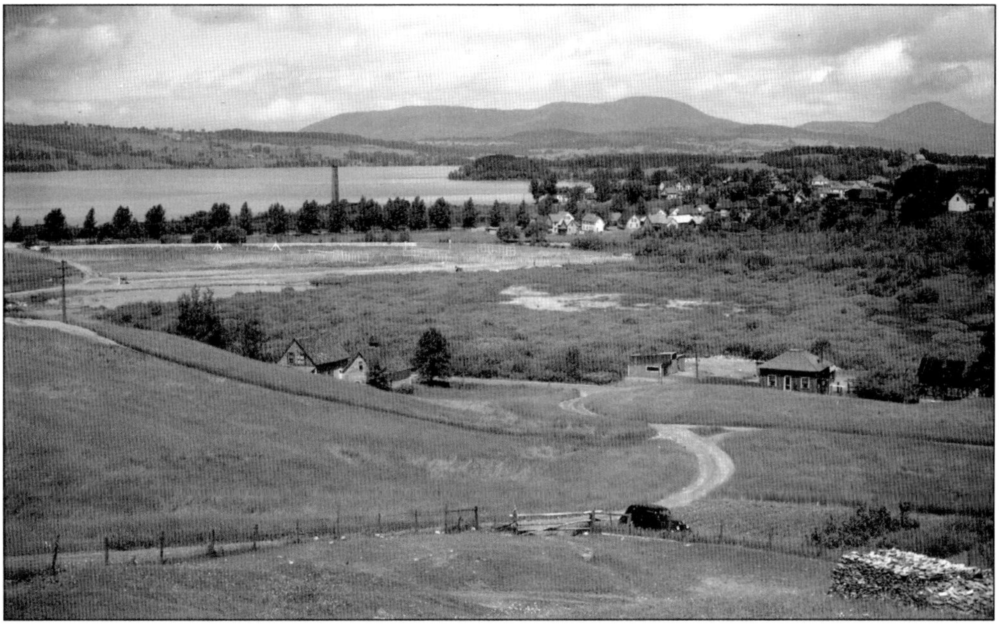

The area of land in Newport where Gardner Park is now was once swampland. Named after Newport City's first alderman, James T. Gardner, the park began as a Works Progress Administration project in 1935 to give employment to those who lost their jobs in the Depression. Truckloads of filler were needed to create a solid ground base. In 1936, the playground was built. The grandstand was built in 1939. (RCC.)

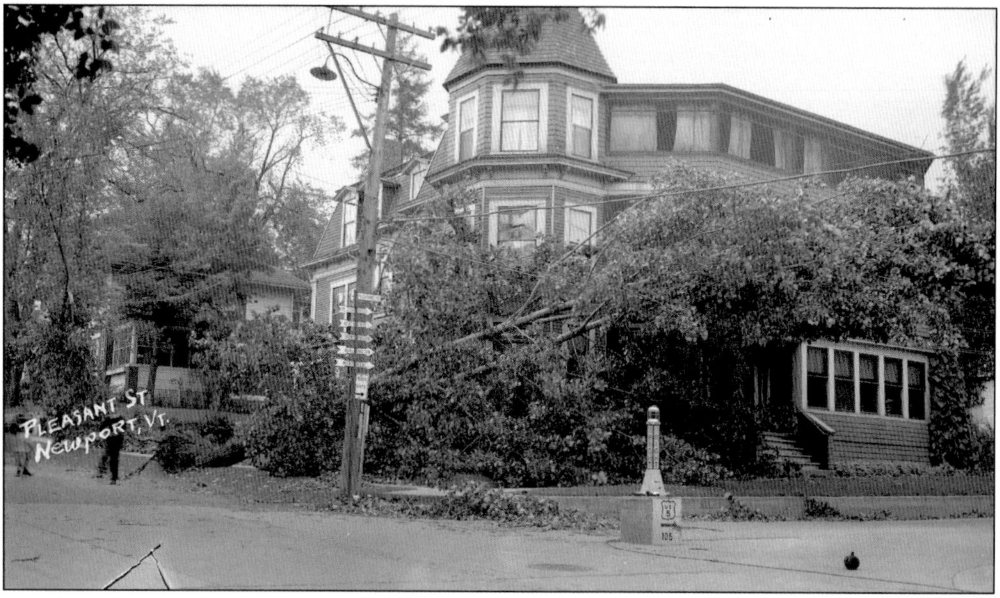

On September 21, 1938, a Category 5 hurricane made landfall in Long Island, New York, and continued a track of destruction north. When it reached Vermont, it was a tropical storm. It hit Newport at 8 p.m. with 80- to 100-mile-per-hour winds, battering the city for four hours. It did great damage in a short period of time. Electricity was out for two days, telephone lines were down, the wire service was out, and trains were not running due to rail damage. The *Newport Daily Express* printed a single-sheet issue the next morning using a gasoline engine handpress. The physical damage was extensive, with trees down all over Orleans County, including the streets of Newport City. The town clock narrowly escaped destruction, surviving with severe cracks in its facade. (Both, RCC.)

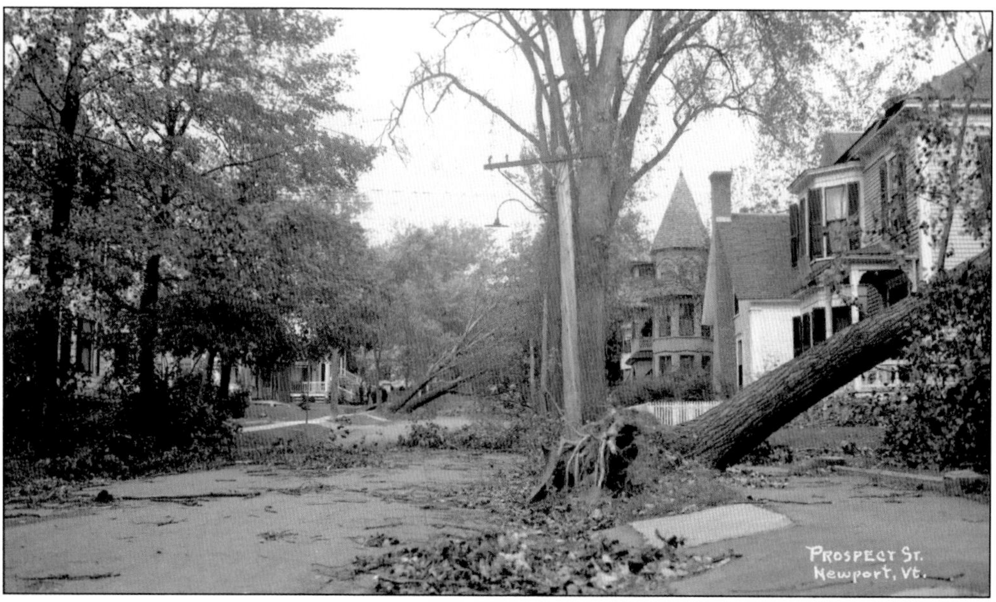

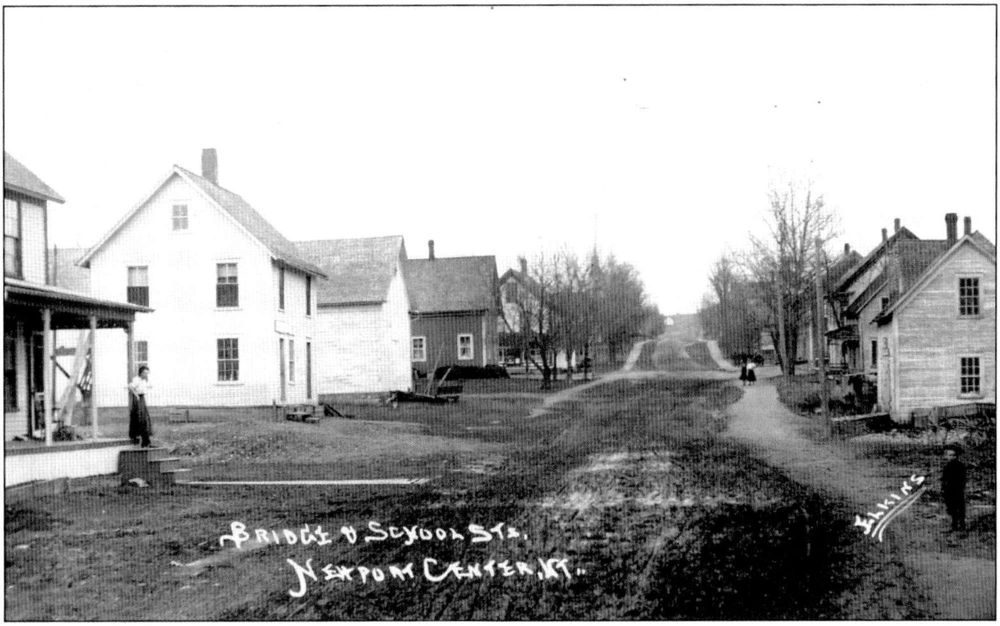

Also known as Newport Center, the small town of Newport is located to the west of Newport City. Newport Center was separated from Newport City in 1917. In the late 1800s, the South Eastern Counties Railroad went through the middle of Newport Center. The South Eastern Railroad was bought by the Canadian Pacific Railroad in the 1880s. (Above, APC; below, RCC.)

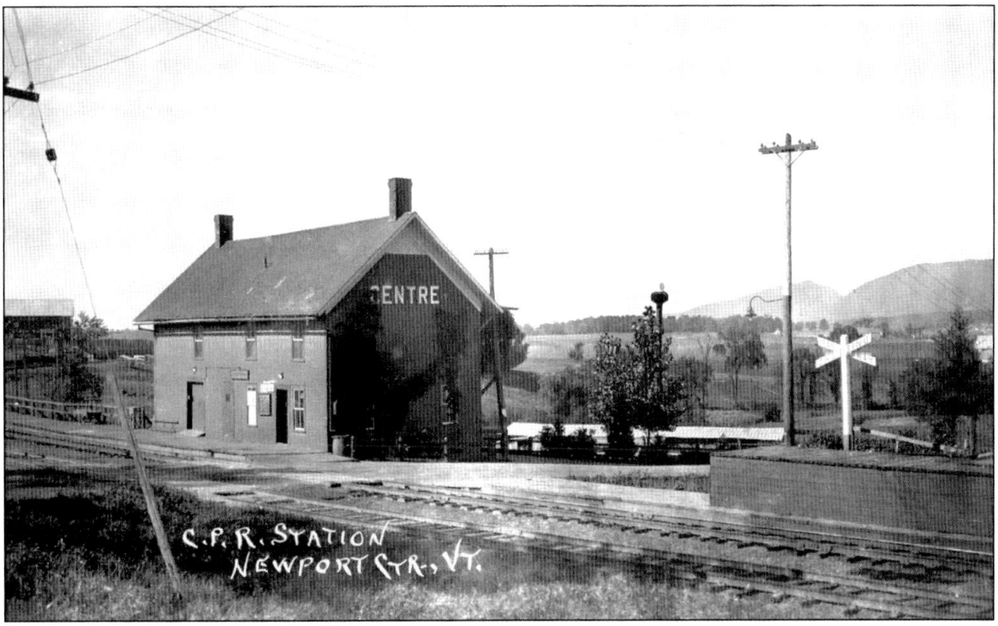

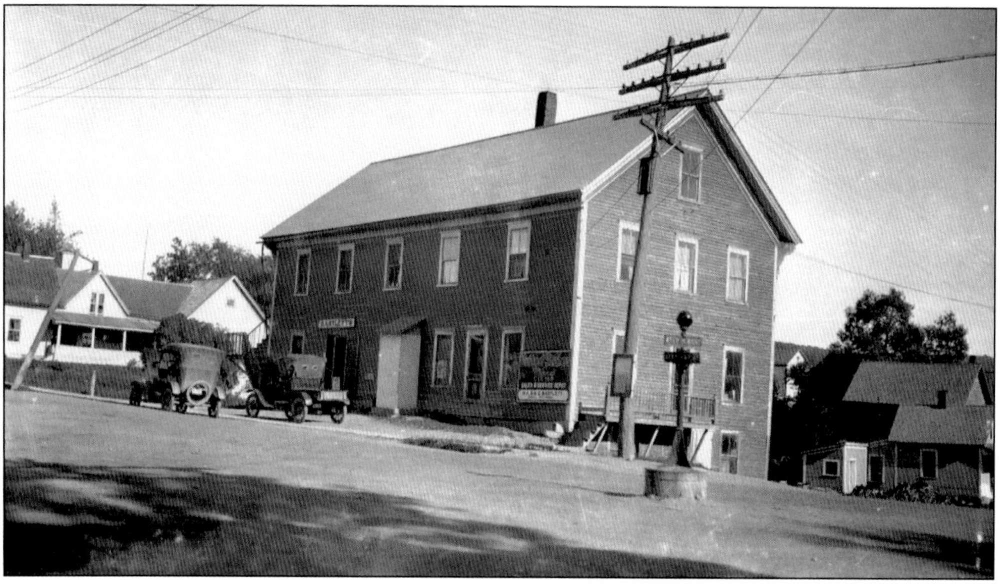

This building still stands at the corner of Vance Hill Road and Vermont Route 105 in Newport Center. In the 1920s, a tire business owned by H.A. Bartlett operated here. (RCC.)

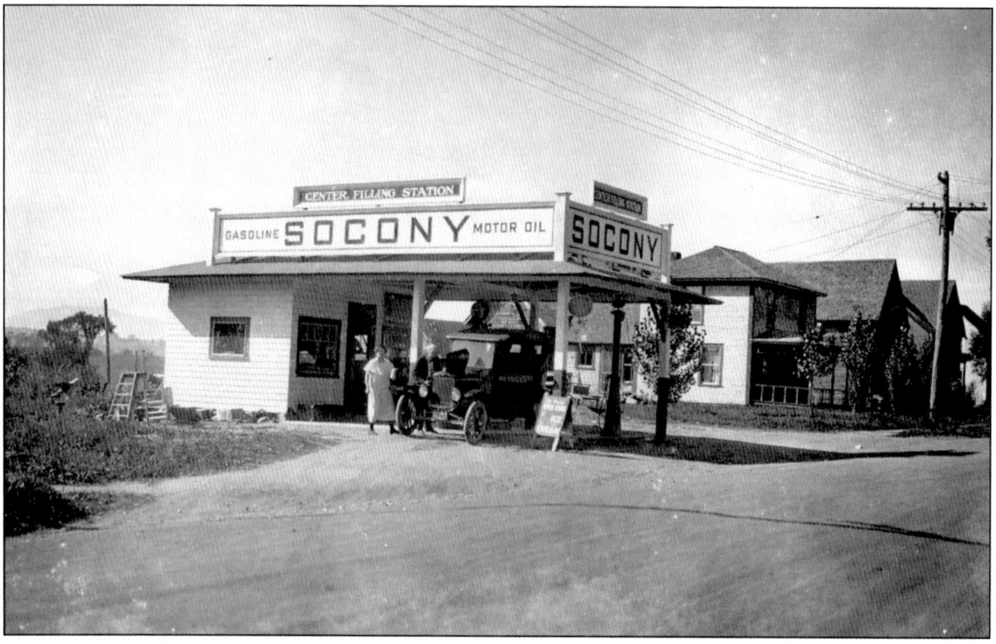

Newport Town had an early gas station on the road through town, which is now Vermont Route 105. (RCC.)

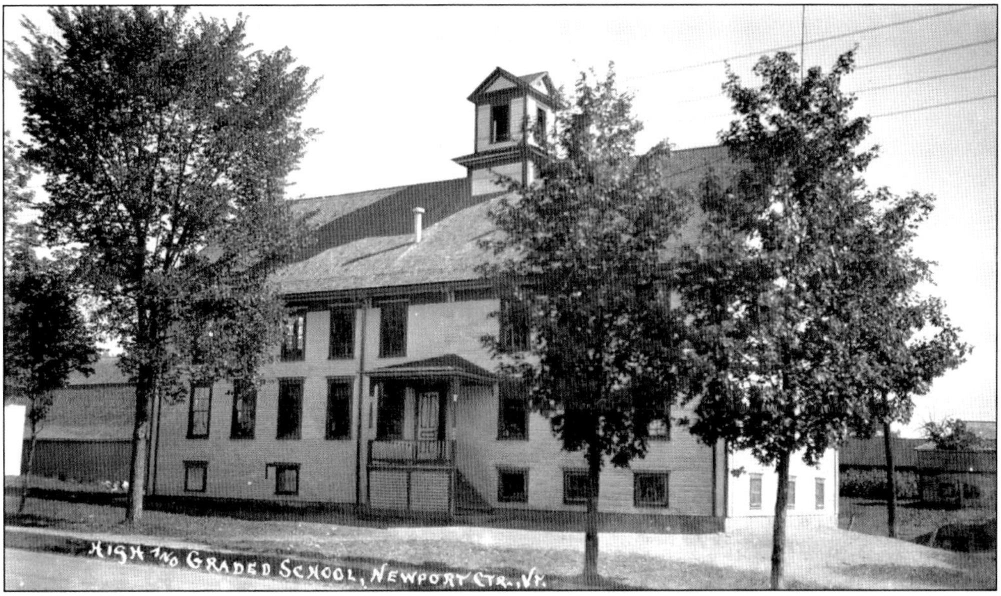

The Newport Center School was built in 1901 to serve as the high school and elementary school. When North Country Union High School opened in 1967, Newport Town began sending its high school students to Newport City, and elementary and middle school students remained in the town. (RCC.)

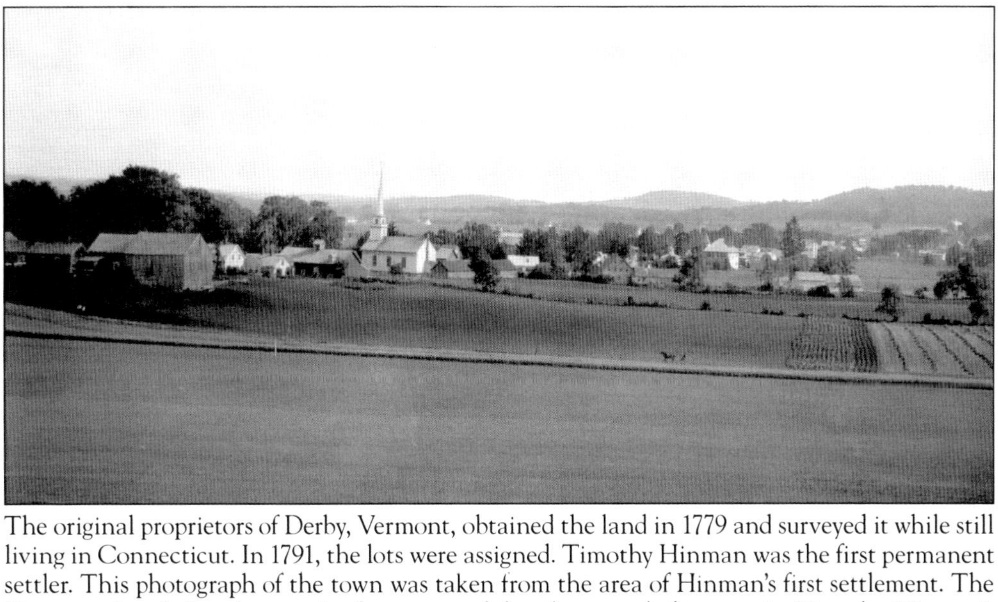

The original proprietors of Derby, Vermont, obtained the land in 1779 and surveyed it while still living in Connecticut. In 1791, the lots were assigned. Timothy Hinman was the first permanent settler. This photograph of the town was taken from the area of Hinman's first settlement. The Congregational church, seen in the center of the photograph first met in Timothy Hinman's home, as the first church building was not finished until 1820. (RCC.)

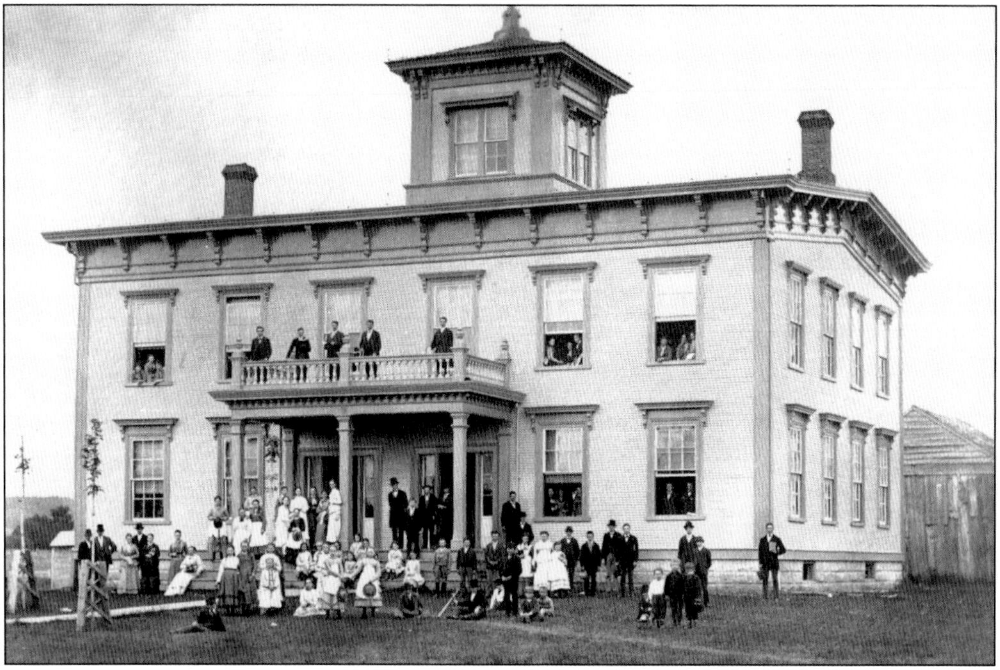

The Derby Academy began as the Derby Literary and Theological Seminary in 1840 with three school buildings on the campus. The school became Derby Academy five years later. In 1918, the academy became a public high school. In 1957, the original Derby Academy was torn down and a new school was built. In 1967, the new school became the junior high school for that district. (RCC.)

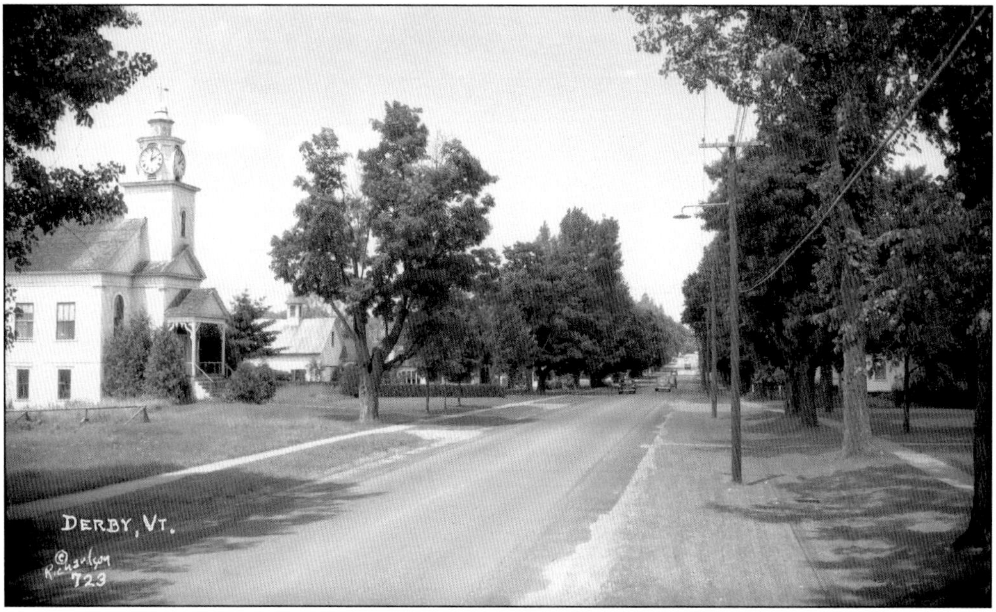

This is Main Street, Derby, across from Derby Academy in the 1950s. The church building on the left was built in 1836 for the Baptist community, with land, material, labor, and funds donated by Chester Carpenter. In 1905, the building in the picture was raised, and another level was built underneath. (RCC.)

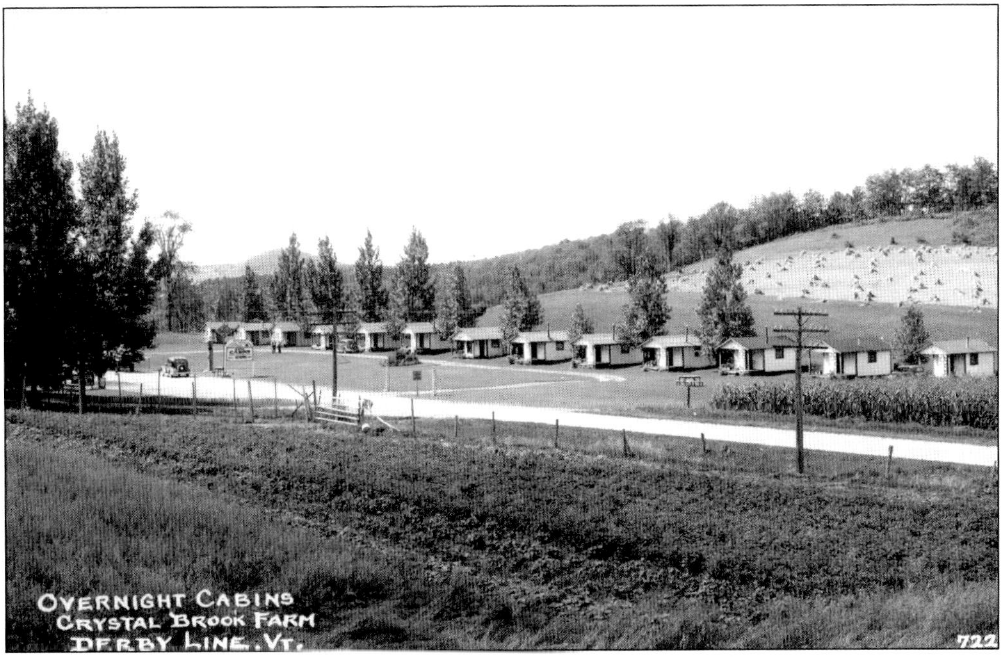

The Kelley's Crystal Brook Farm on Route 5 between Derby and Derby Line was an impressive establishment for the Northeast Kingdom. Not only did it have a central building for visitors, it also had overnight cottages, a gas station, and a restaurant. It served its own vegetables and dairy and maple products. The establishment rented cars, gave horse and pony rides, and had a collection of wild animals for show, including a black bear, young deer, coyotes, raccoons, and monkeys. (Above, APC; below, RCC.)

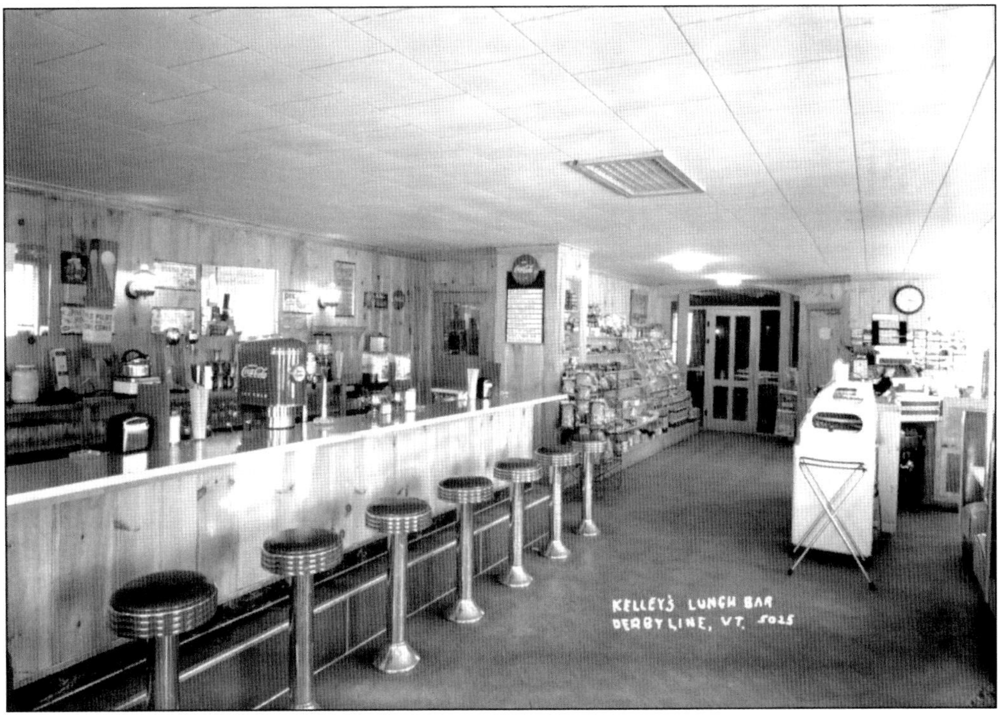

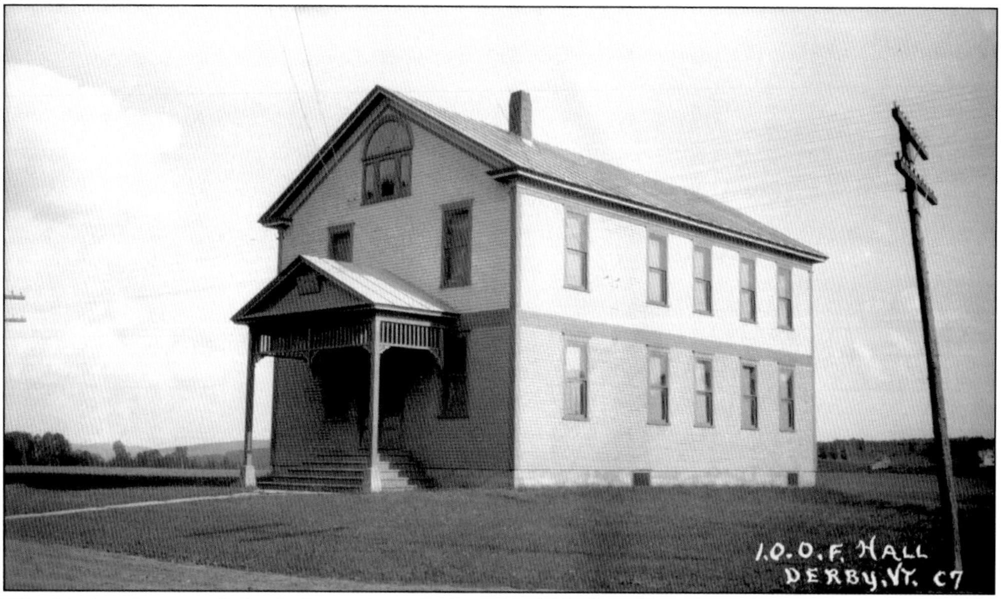

The Derby chapter of the Independent Order of Odd Fellows began in the 1880s as a fraternity group. The members would visit the sick and shut-in on a regular basis and would give sick pay to members who were ill. This building was completed in 1910 at the cost of $2,500. (RCC.)

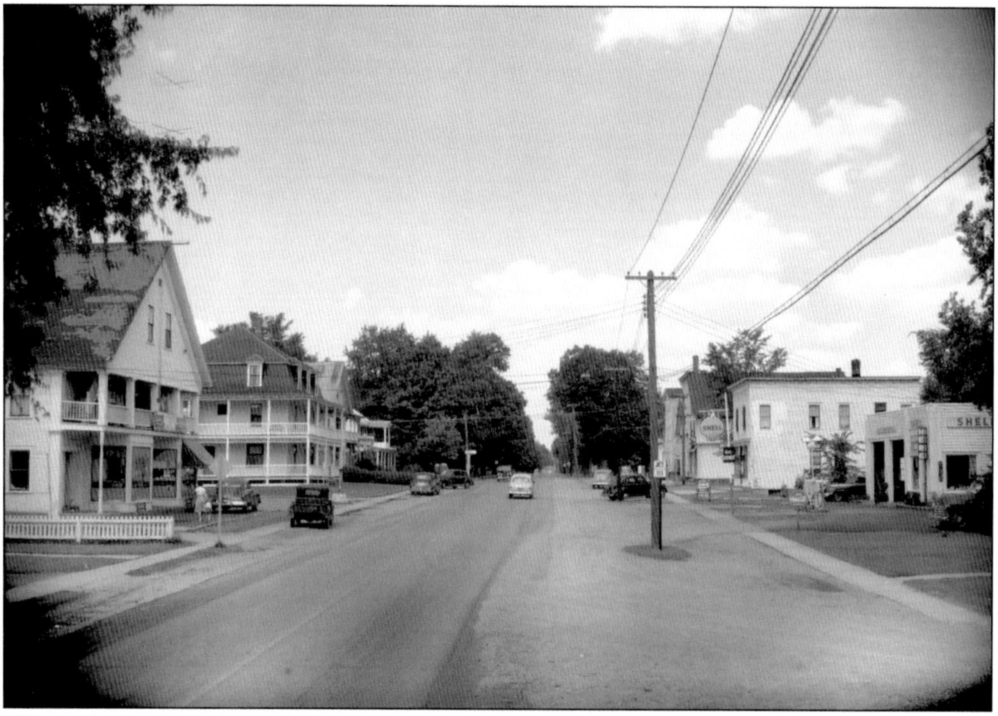

This is the south end of Main Street in Derby. On the left, the front building is the Gage and Rice General Store; behind it is the old Derby House hotel, and just beyond that is the Robbins Drug Store. Behind the Shell station is the post office and W.M. Taylor's General Store. The store is still a viable business, though it has changed hands several times through the years. (RCC.)

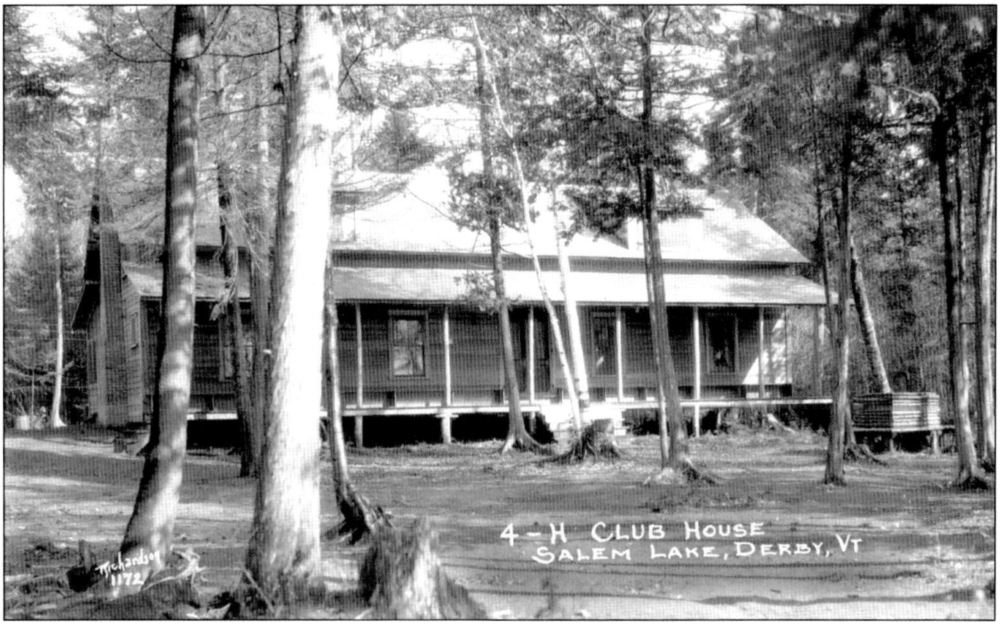

The Orleans County 4-H Club was renamed Coutts-Moriarty 4-H Camp after the two women who worked tirelessly on the project. Flora Coutts, the first 4-H extension agent for Orleans County, wanted to create a summer camp for children in the area. Lake Salem became that place in 1931. In 1962, Marion Moriarty worked hard to get a bunk building finished for the campers, and her name was added. (RCC.)

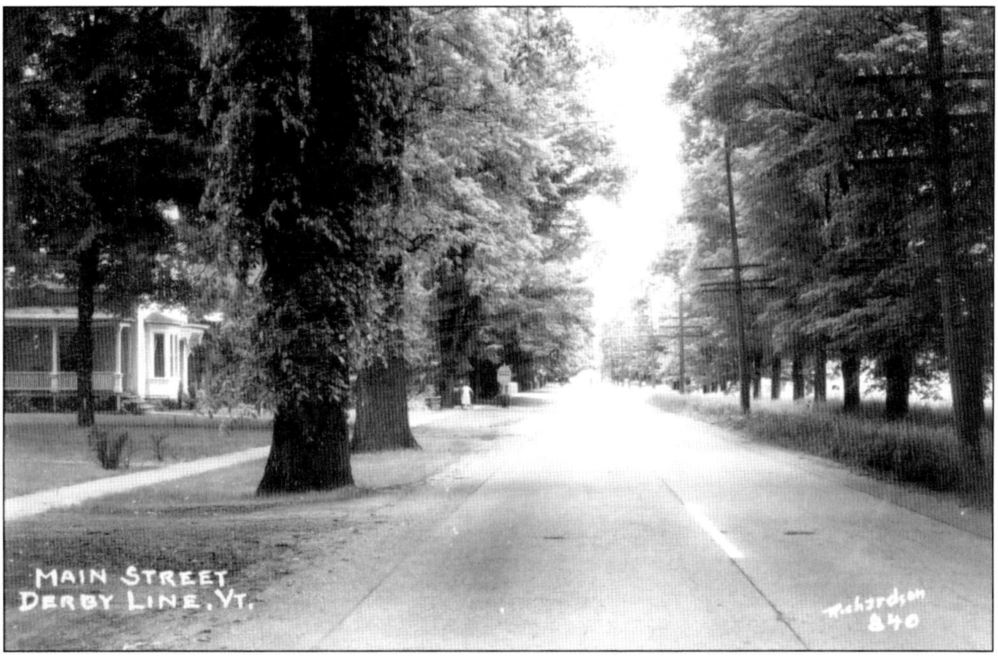

Main Street, Derby Line, was once densely lined with elm and maple trees. The village became a hub of trade with Canada. When the border was drawn, it was farther north than the original 45th parallel, due to a mistake by the surveyors. The border question was answered in 1842 with the Webster-Ashburton Treaty, which settled the boundary at its present location. (APC.)

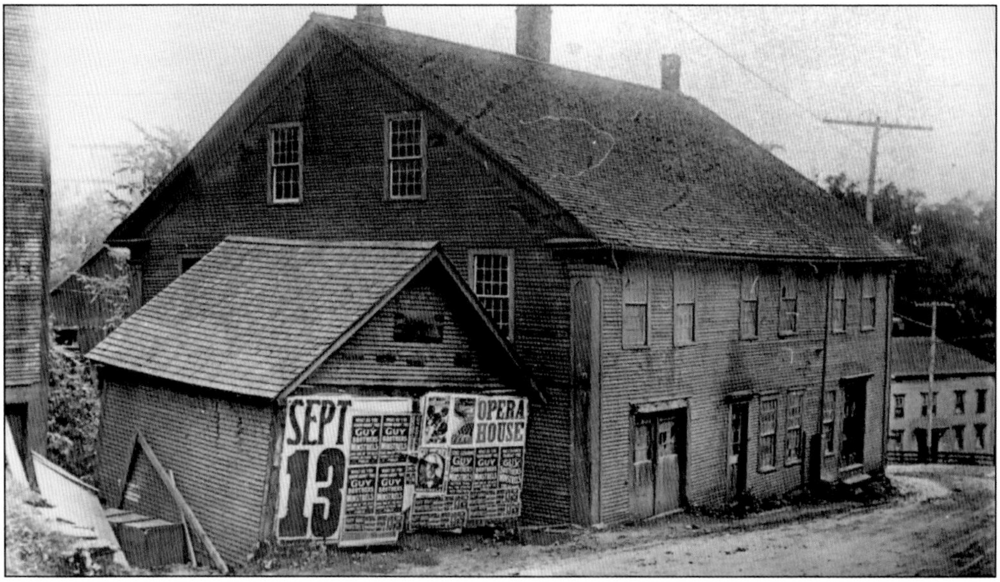

Union Butterfield, a cutting tools factory in Derby Line now owned by Tivoly, Inc., began in 1880 in Rock Island, Quebec, Canada. This was its original structure, a small two-story building half a mile away from its present location. The creator of the business, Lewis Young, had traveled throughout Quebec and New England selling his axle cutter. When demand became too high to sell by wagon, he went into business with Col. F.D. Butterfield and moved into the building above. They employed John Hay and George Reece, who invented the Reece Screw Plate, a tool sold at Butterfield for many years. Butterfield employees pictured below are, from left to right, (sitting) Lewis Young, John Hay, and George Reece; (standing) F. Gagnon, C. Eastman, H. Collins, and C. Lorimer. (Both, Tivoly, Inc.)

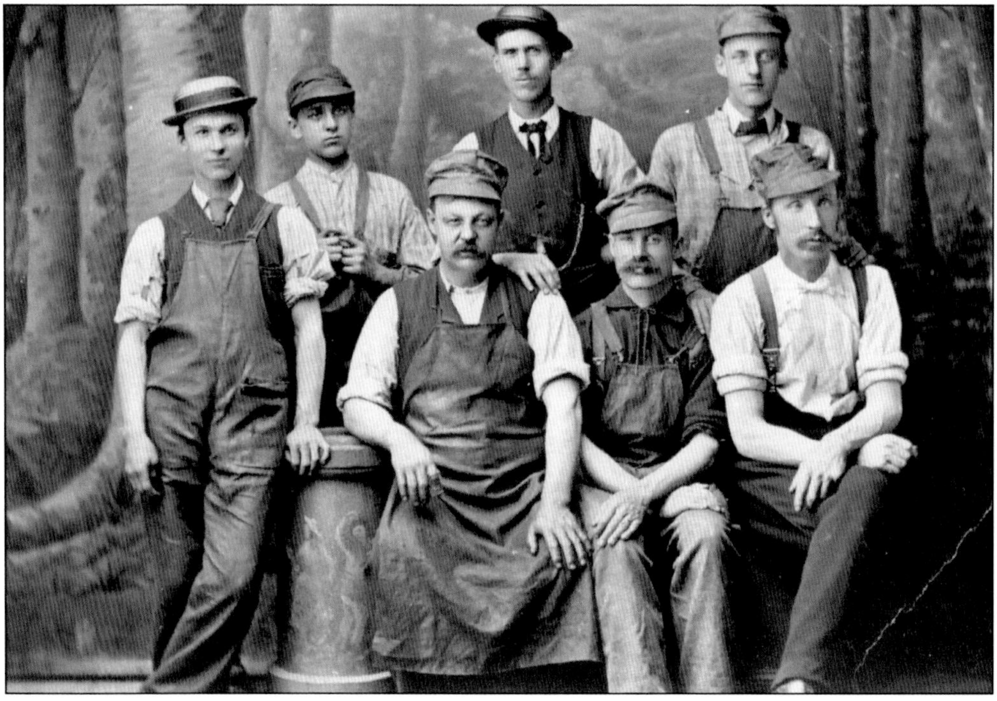

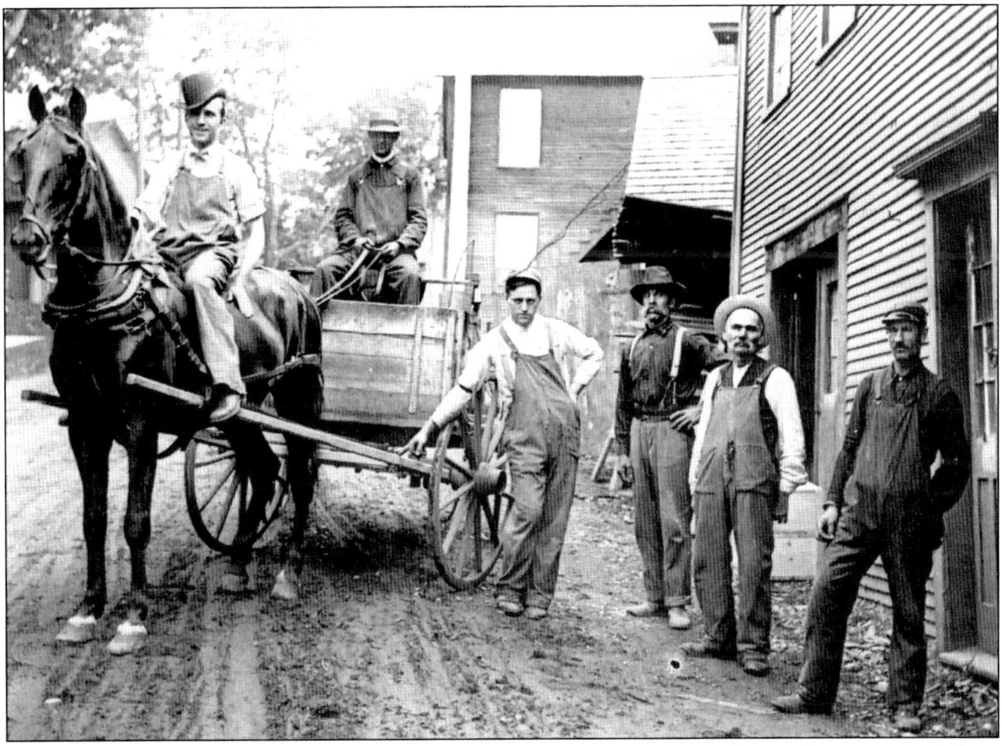

This photograph, taken June 25, 1910, shows a few of Butterfield's early employees. From left to right are F. Villeneuve, Freeman Haskell, Fred Perkins, Eugene Gagné, Joe Roy, and Joe Ritchie. (Tivoly, Inc.)

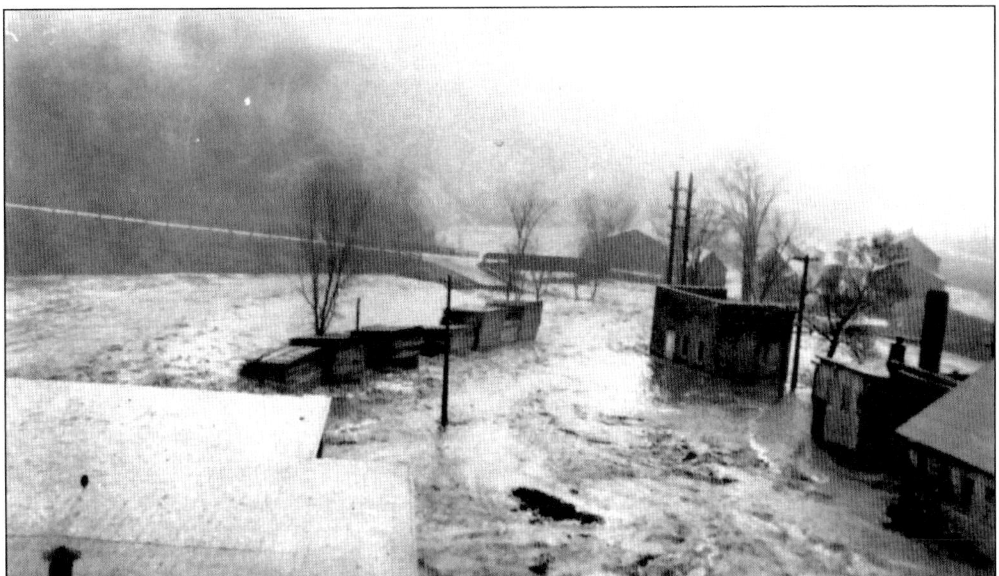

During the November 1927 flood, Butterfield was under water for days. Basements filled with water, and 450 tons of coal and piles of lumber were carried down river. When the waters receded, townspeople were able to salvage coal and lumber from the banks of the river. (Tivoly, Inc.)

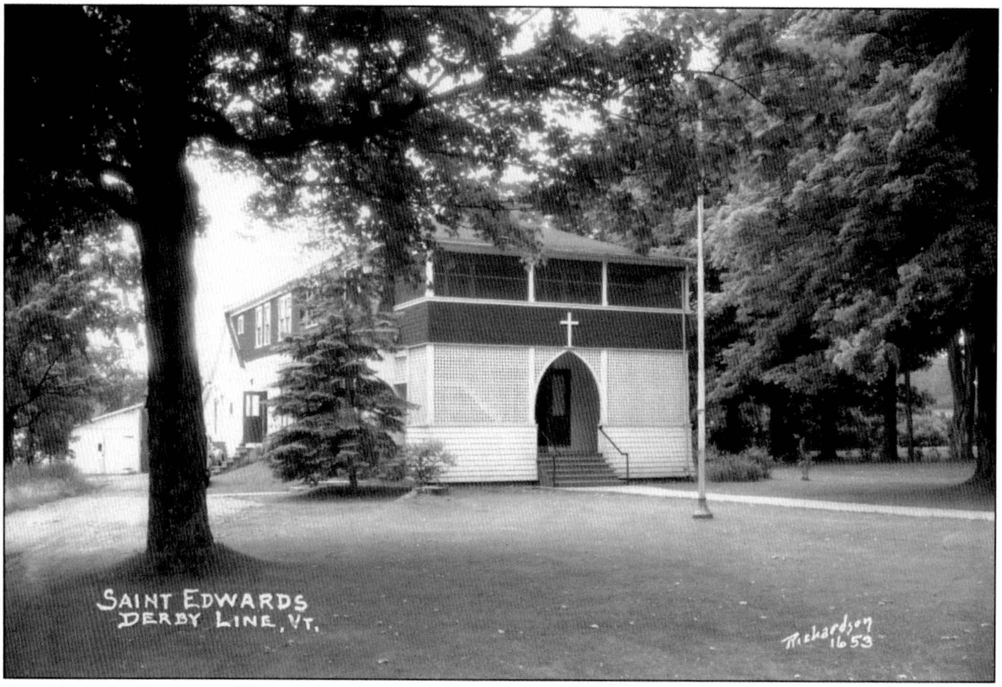

St. Edward's Catholic Church began in 1947 in a remodeled home on Elm Street in Derby Line. In 1964, Roland Whittaker rebuilt the church with a more modern design. The church blessing took place on April 12, 1964. Rev. Armand Fortin was the first priest of the church. (RCC.)

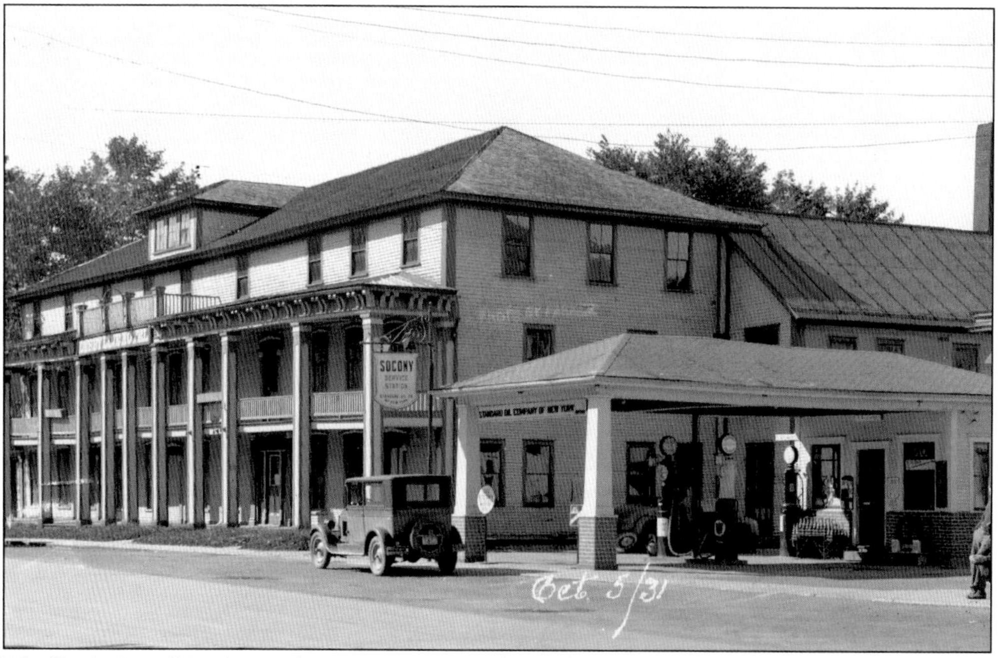

The Derby Line Hotel served many international travelers for 100 years between 1830 and 1930. The actual date of construction is unknown, but there was a tavern on this spot since 1830. In 1931, the building was sold to the US government and torn down to make space for the US Customs and Immigration building. (RCC.)

Two

Charleston, Holland, and Morgan

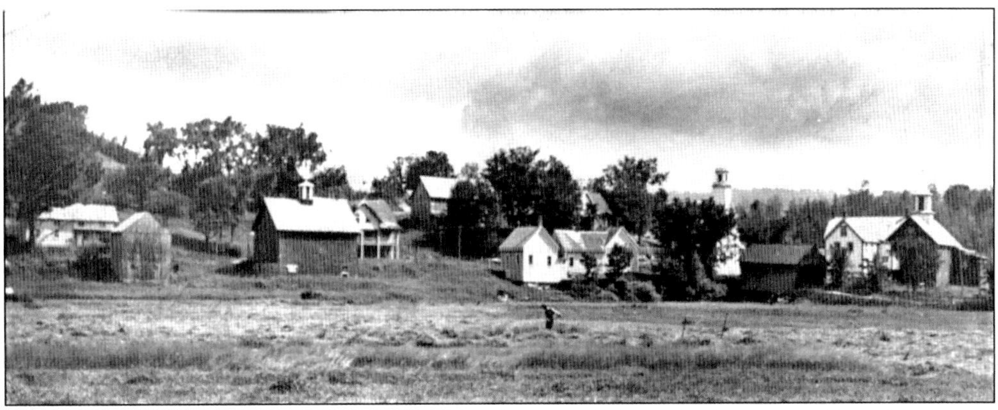

The town of Charleston has two villages six miles apart: West Charleston and East Charleston. When the town was chartered, it was to be called Navy. However, the town was renamed Charleston. The west village was settled first, in 1802, and the east village was settled in 1820. This early picture of East Charleston shows a man in the front mowing his field with a scythe. (OCHS.)

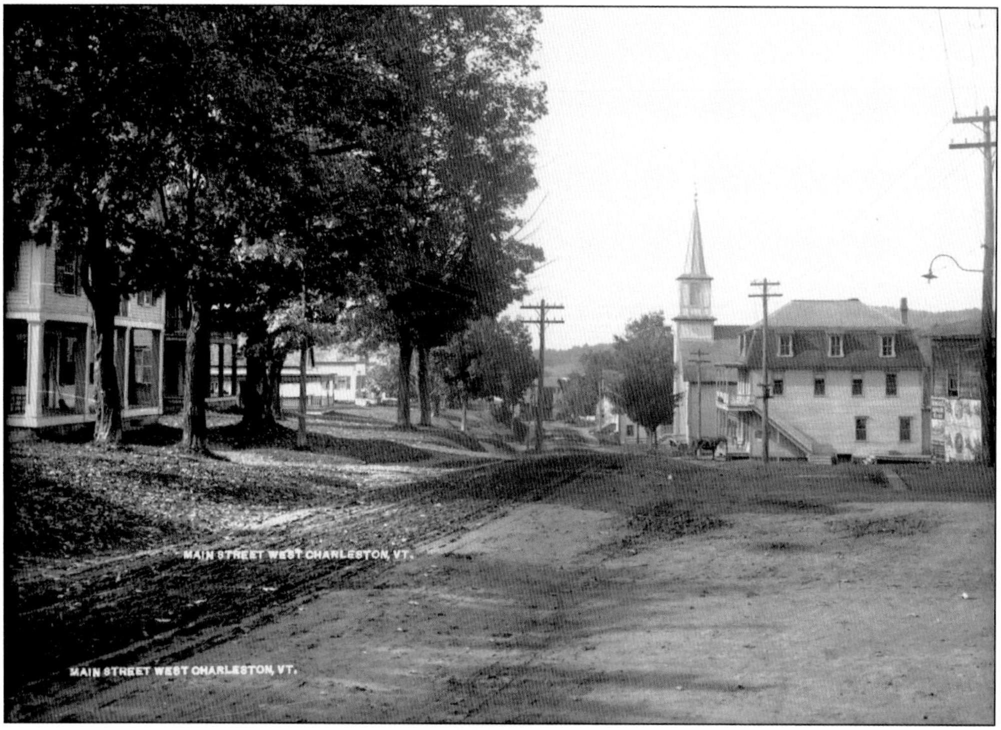

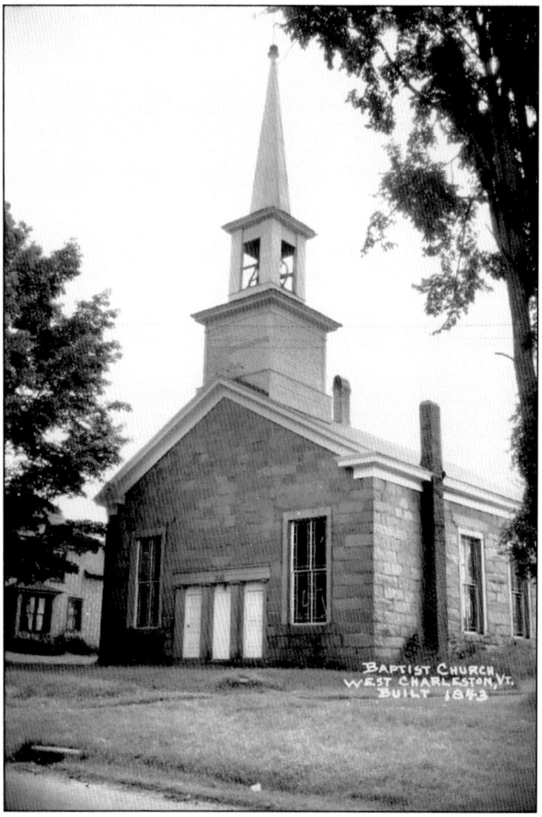

On Main Street, West Charleston, there was a hotel, the Congregational church, and residential homes. The buildings along the street on the right were destroyed in 1924 by a terrible fire. The Congregational church in the picture had served the community since 1859. After the fire, the members began attending the Baptist church. (RCC.)

In June 1843, this granite church was built and dedicated in West Charleston. The granite came from a local field, with most of it part of a single boulder. It served as a Union church, with Methodists, Congregationalists, Universalists, and Baptists sharing the building until the denominations built their own churches, leaving the Baptists here. The bell was added in 1902, and in 1904, the church was wired for electricity. (RCC.)

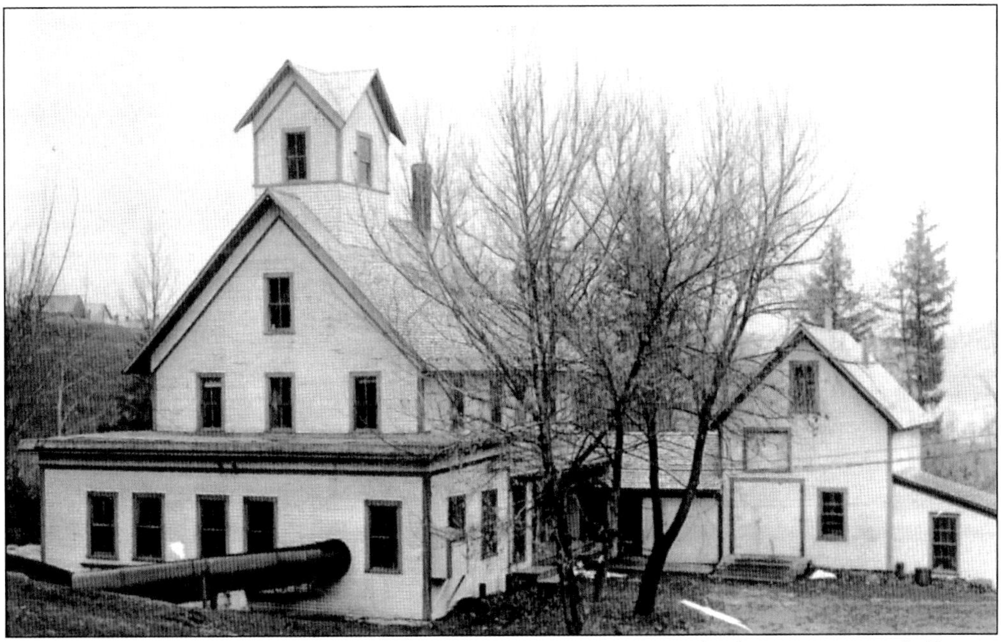

Built in 1895, the hydroelectric plant on the Clyde River in West Charleston, commonly known as the Barton Power House, was owned by Barton Village, Inc. Even though Barton is about 15 miles away, to this day, the town uses the hydropower as an additional source of electricity for its grid. (Charleston Historical Society.)

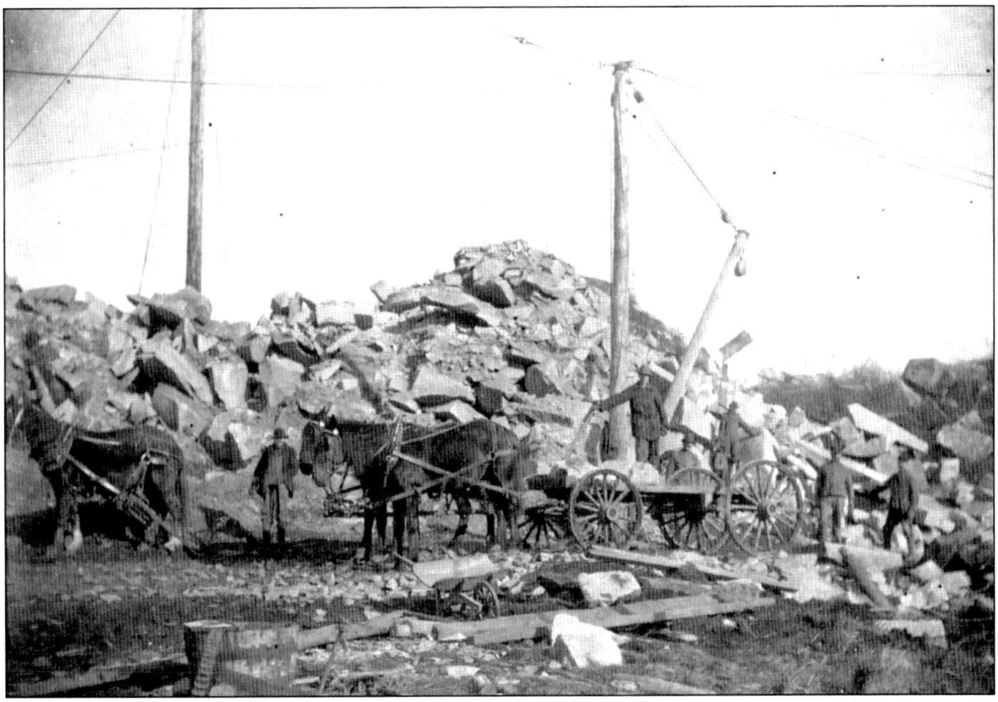

These men in Charleston were loading stone from a local quarry for lower electric light dam, known today as the Echo Lake Dam and owned by Citizens Utilities, around the year 1900. (OCHS.)

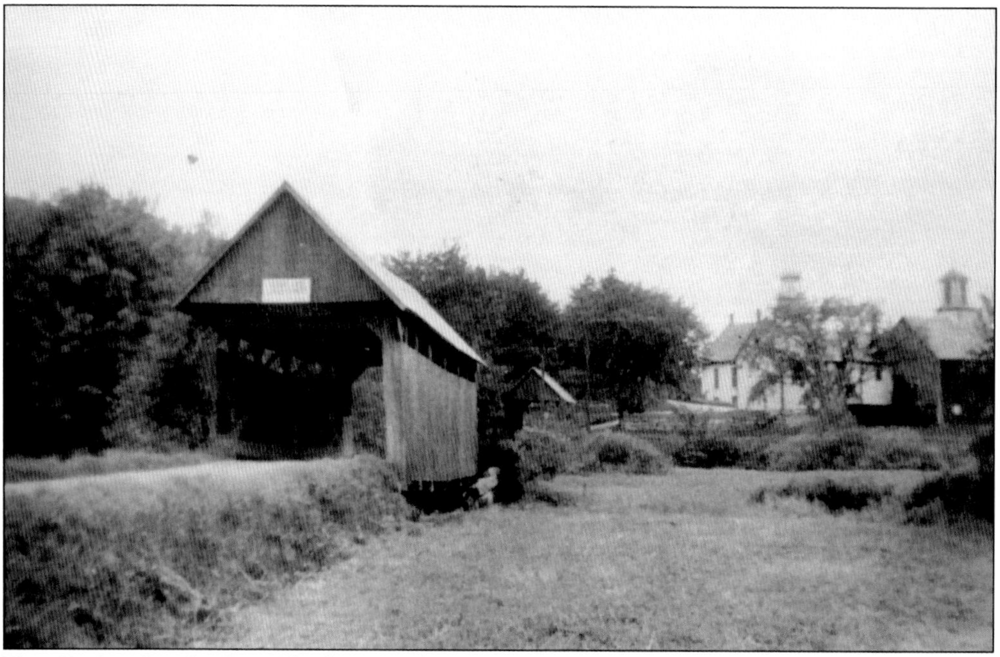

Twin Bridges Road in East Charleston is shown with the Plymouth Congregational Church in the background. This covered bridge was one of two over the Clyde River on this road, with the second one behind it, hence the road name Twin Bridges Road. M.C. Davis once owned the barn. The barn sat next to the East Charleston general store until 2007, when it was torn down. (RCC.)

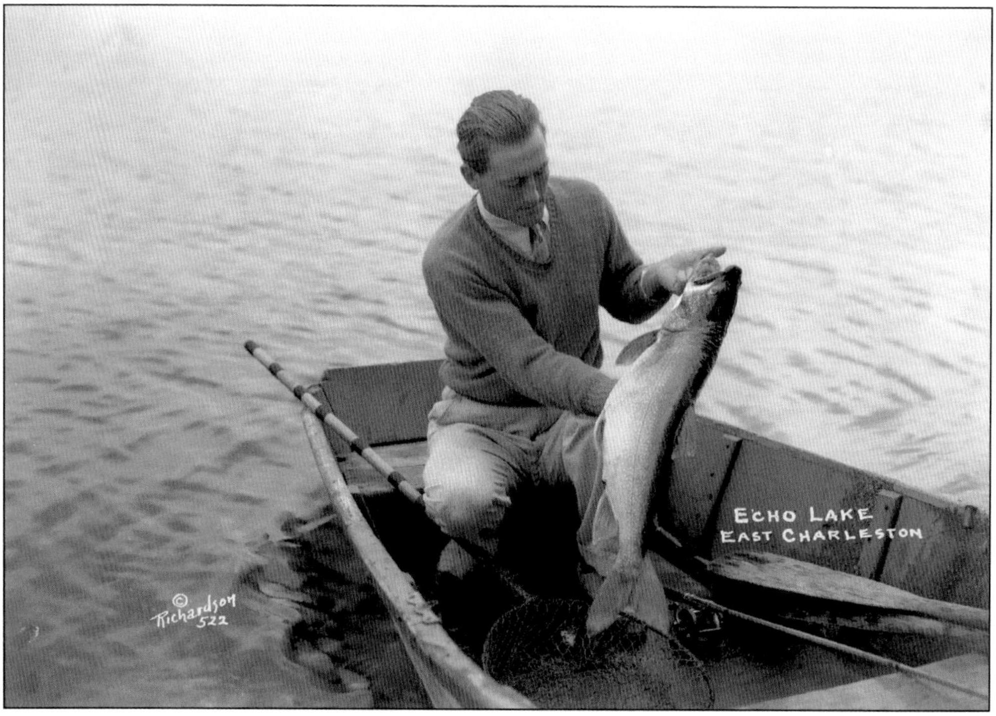

This gentleman cast his line in Echo Lake in East Charleston and came up with a good-size lake trout. Lake trout thrive in deep, cold water, making Echo Lake a perfect habitat. (RCC.)

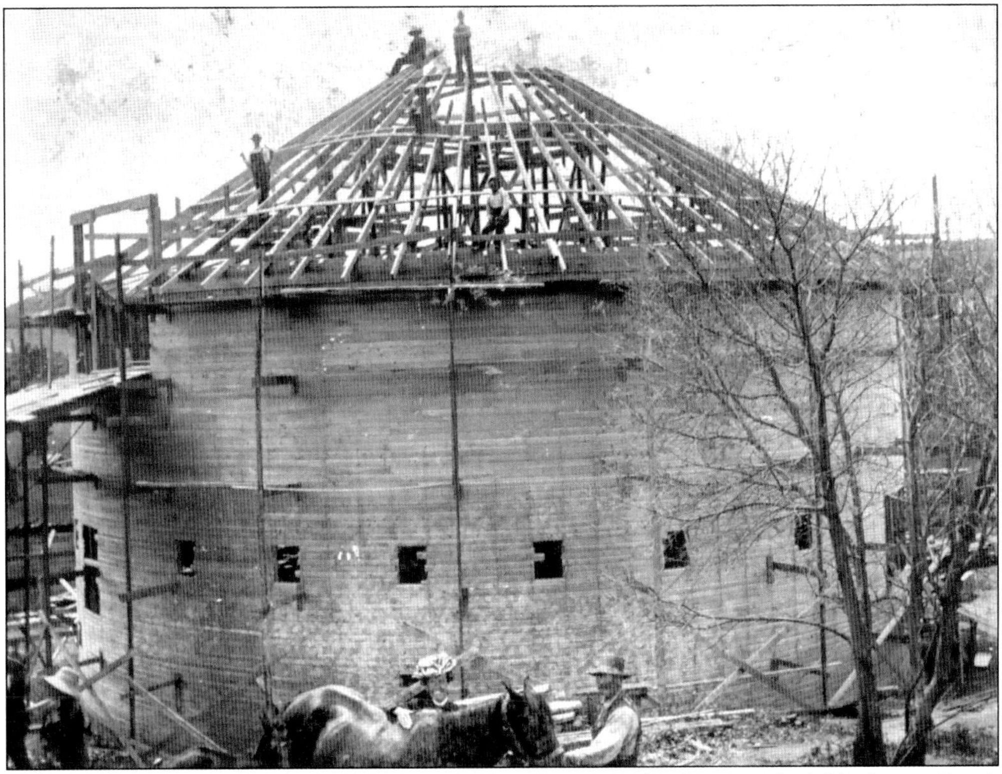

Bert Lang of East Charleston built this round barn in 1908 on his farm on Ten Mile Square Road. He sold it to another farmer, and in 1919, the barn burned to the ground. A postcard published before 1919 called it the "largest round barn in New England." (Above, Charleston Historical Society; below, Raymond Gardner.)

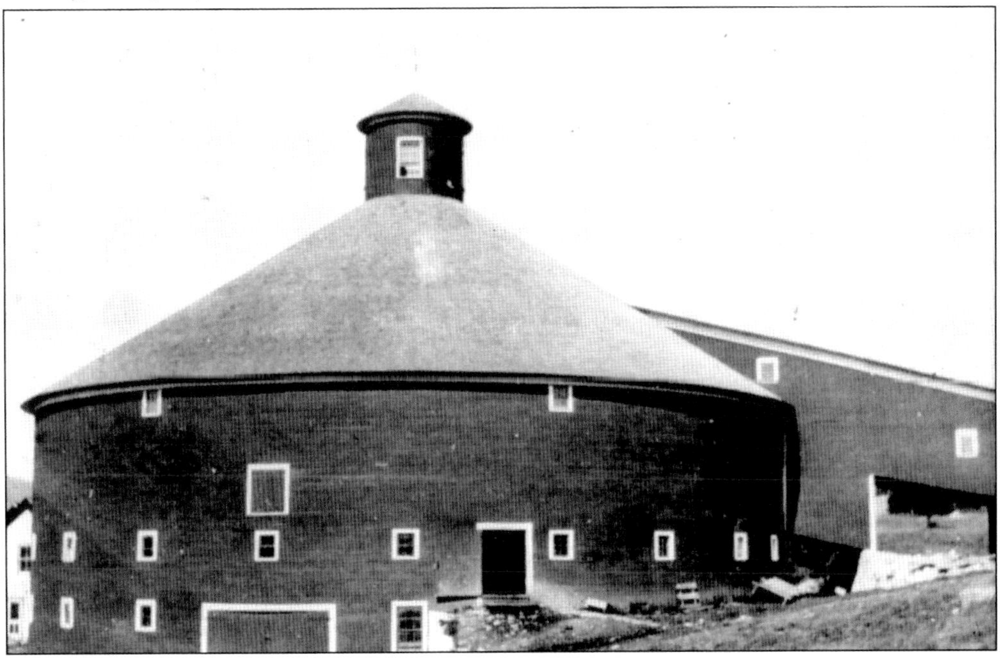

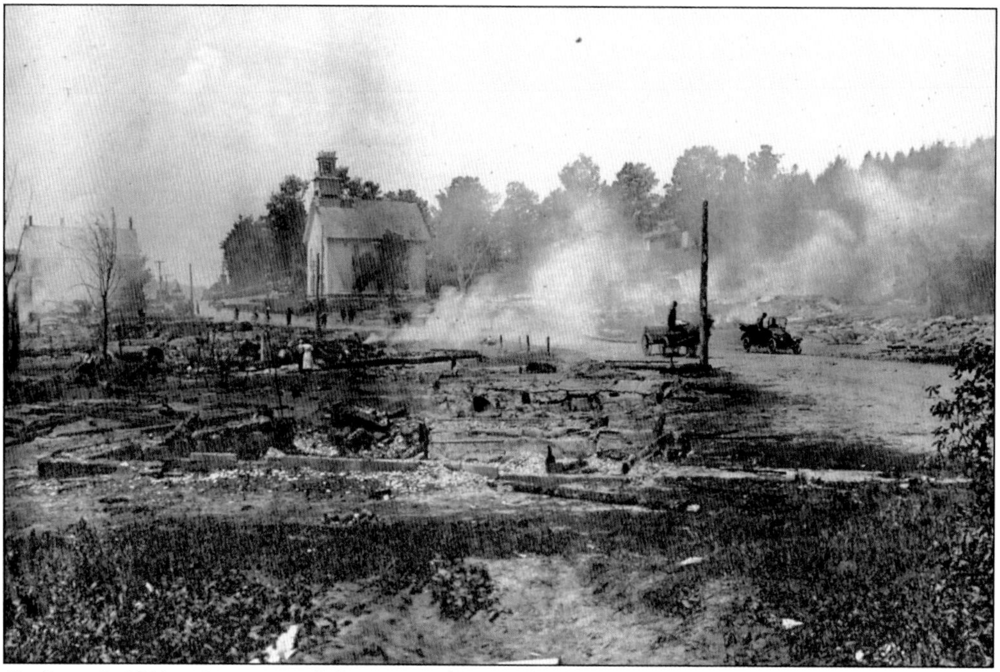

On June 8, 1921, a fire ravaged the town of East Charleston. Pictured above are the smoldering remnants of the town. Twenty-six buildings burned in three hours' time. Almost three years later, East Charleston suffered another fire on Sunday morning, May 18, 1924. The Charleston Lumber Company, which had been owned by W.C. Hinton and H.C. Canning for seven years, burned to the ground. It was a complete loss, since an insurance policy had just lapsed. The lumber company was the biggest employer in town. After the fire, 22 men were unemployed. That morning, Hinton had checked on the mill on his way to Island Pond, only an hour and a half before the fire began. (Above, Charleston Historical Society; below, RCC.)

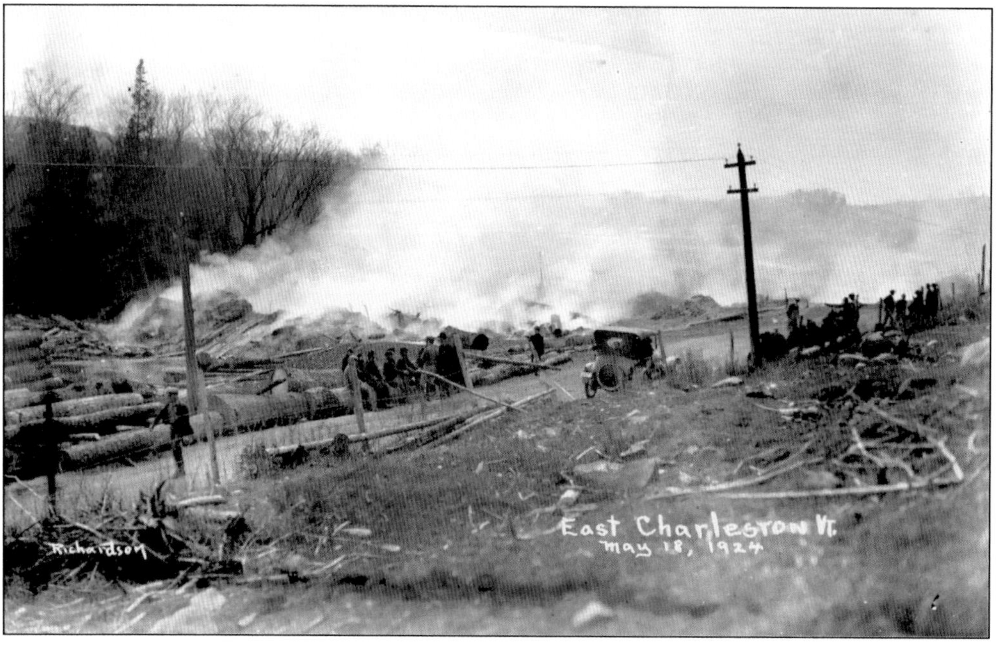

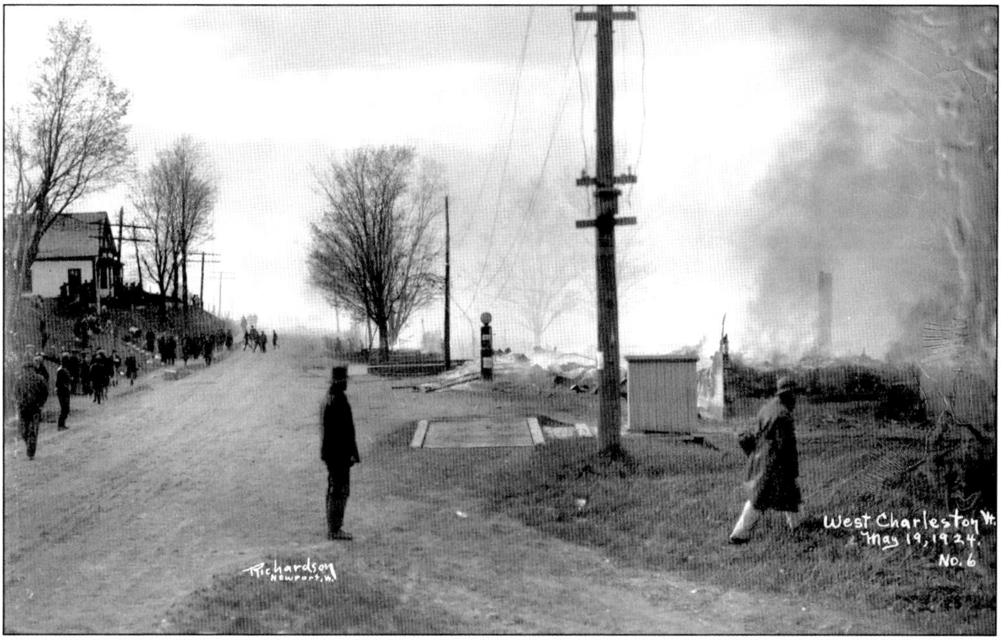

On May 19, 1924, less than 24 hours after East Charleston's devastating lumber fire, Charleston once again was battling a fire. This time it was in the village of West Charleston. A fire broke out in the Davis shoe repair shop on Main Street, and it quickly spread to the Clyde River Hotel and continued north along the street where all the businesses were located. Firemen from Charleston, Derby, Derby Line, and Island Pond fought the fire for four hours. A fireman from Derby almost lost his life when he found himself trapped in a burning livery—fortunately, one of his friends saved him. Not only were nearly all the businesses in town destroyed, six families were also left homeless. (Both, RCC.)

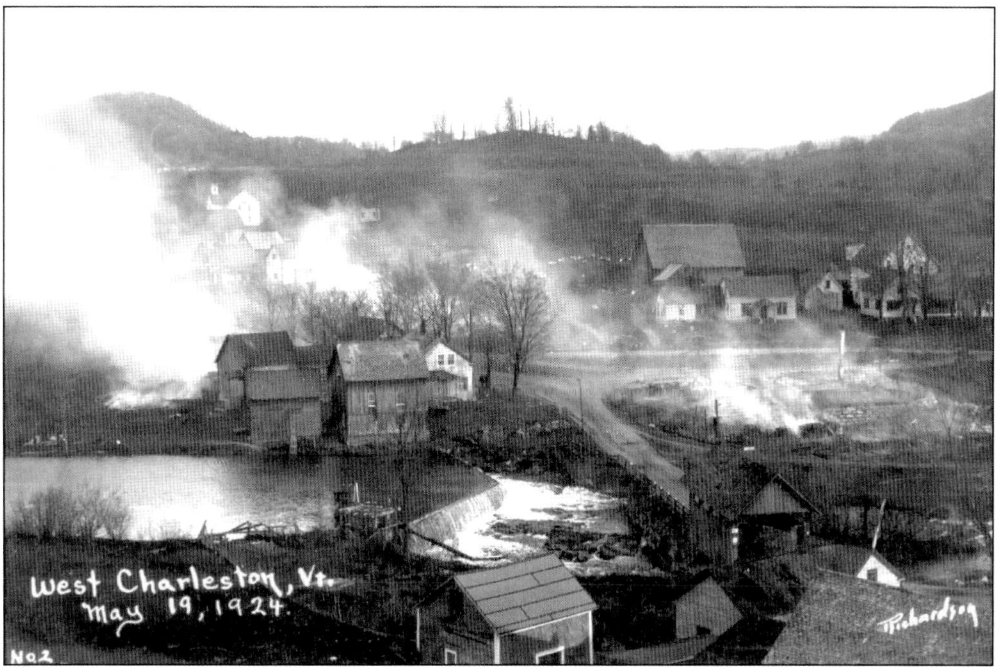

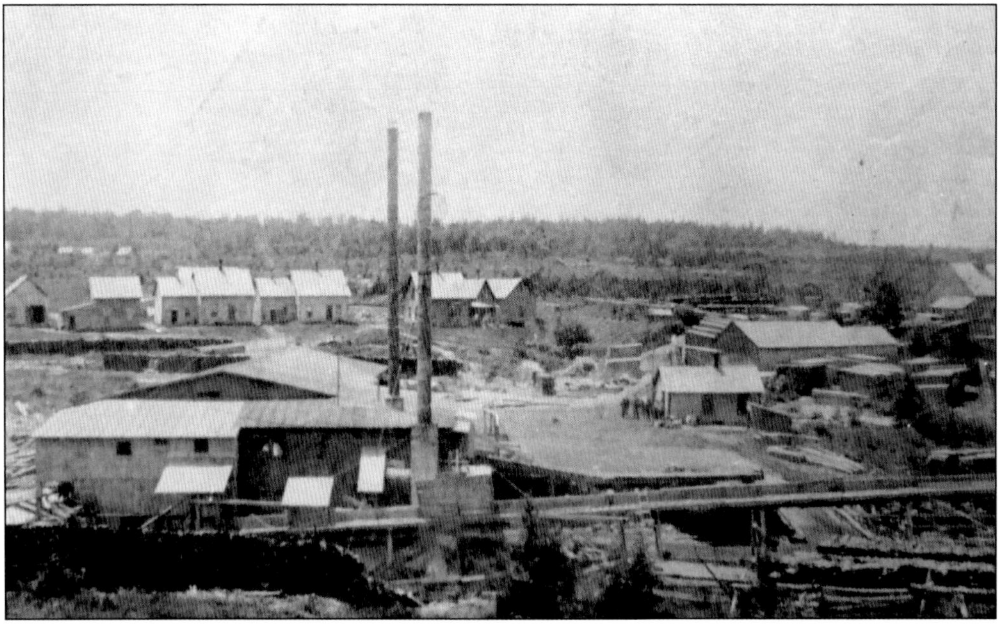

Holland was settled in 1800, with hundreds of acres of untouched forests. It later became a big mill town. This is a photograph of Caswell's Mill, which was built up around Holland Pond by George Caswell in 1867. The mill employed 25 men and cut millions of feet of lumber every year. They used a sluiceway from Holland Pond to float the lumber into the mill. The mill closed in 1914. (Holland Historical Society.)

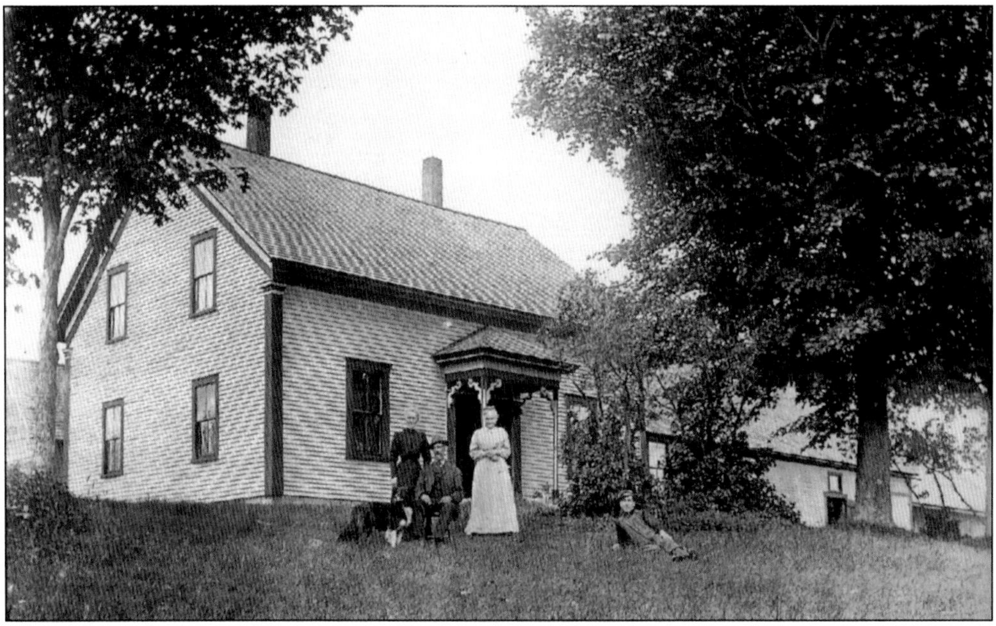

In the southwest corner of Holland, this house was built on the stagecoach road prior to 1878. George Hinman, a lecturer at the Orleans County Grammar School in 1841 and the Natural and Civil History Society's secretary for five years beginning in 1853, resided in the house in 1878. In this picture is the Bradford family, who lived in the house in the early 1900s. (Holland Historical Society.)

The Rossiers powered their household in southwestern Holland with electricity from this windmill. They had a collection of car batteries that they charged through wind power, which ran the electricity in their home. Mrs. Rossier, a very likeable woman, was well known in town for her demonstrations on how to make homemade soap. (Holland Historical Society.)

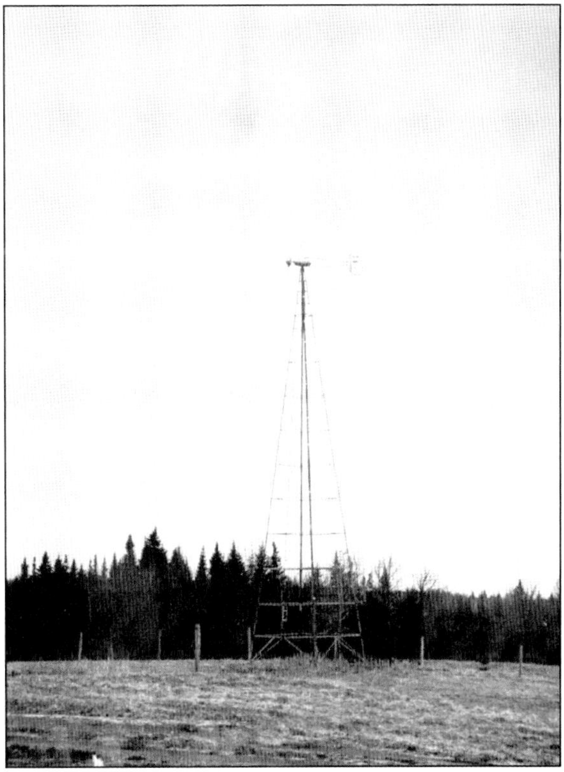

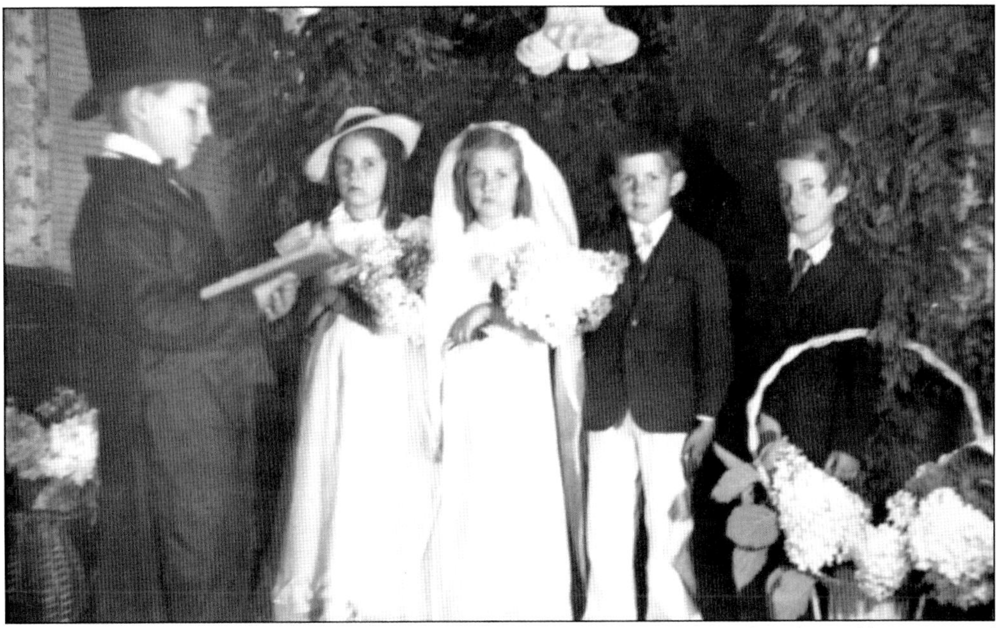

The bridal shower of Edith (Smith) Selby of Holland featured a Tom Thumb Wedding. Named after Gen. Tom Thumb (born Charles Stratton), who was three feet tall at his wedding, these mock wedding ceremonies presented children as the wedding party. Everson Laythe was the minister, Iris Green the bridesmaid, Joyce Selby the bride, Rodney Gray the groom, and Irene Laythe the groomsman. (Holland Historical Society.)

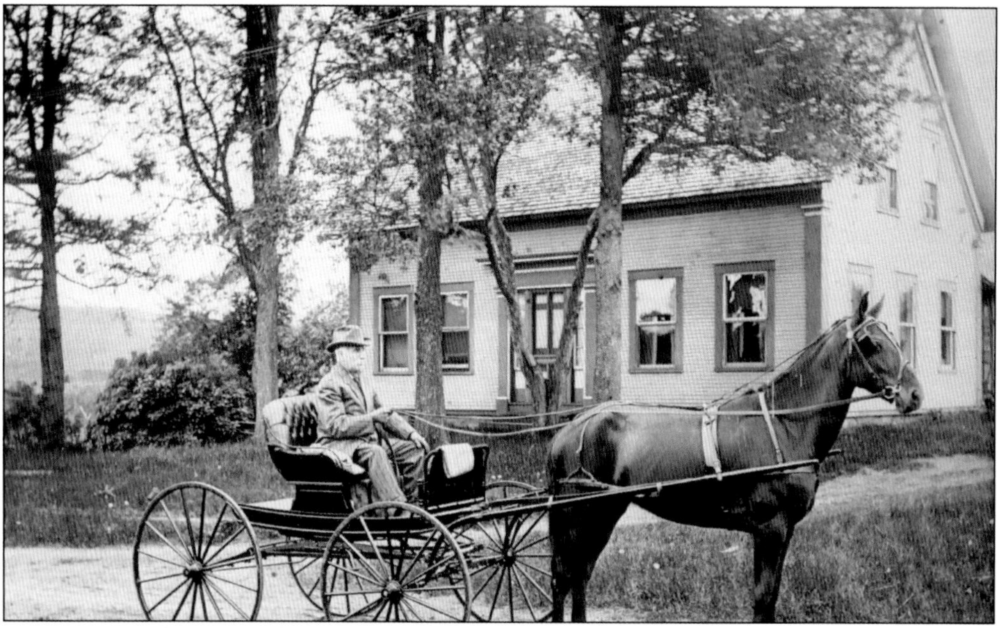

George Tice of West Holland sits in his buggy in front of Ernest Moulton's house in town. George, a Civil War veteran, was injured at the Cedar Creek battlefield. Fought in 1864, Cedar Creek was one of the two largest battles in the Shenandoah Valley of Virginia. George owned 800 acres of timber woods, his own sawmill, and 50 acres of farmland in the late 1800s. (Holland Historical Society.)

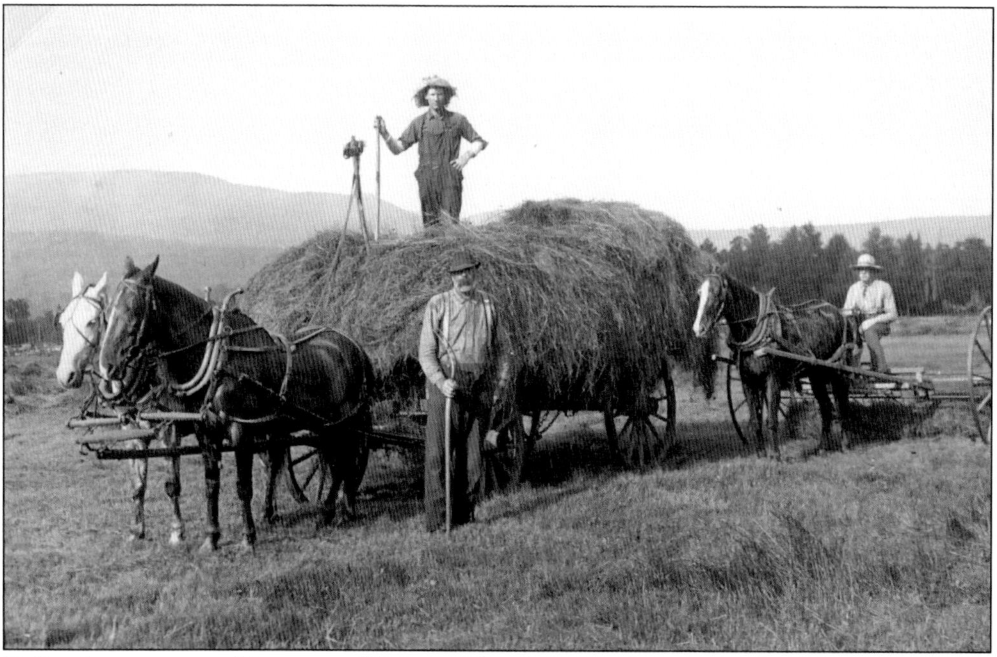

Holland was a town of farmers and loggers. This farmer, Nelson Lahue, is taking in his hay in late summer, and Charles Sanborn is working with the rake. Haying usually began in July and continued through August. These gentlemen were using horses, rather than oxen, to collect the hay. (Holland Historical Society.)

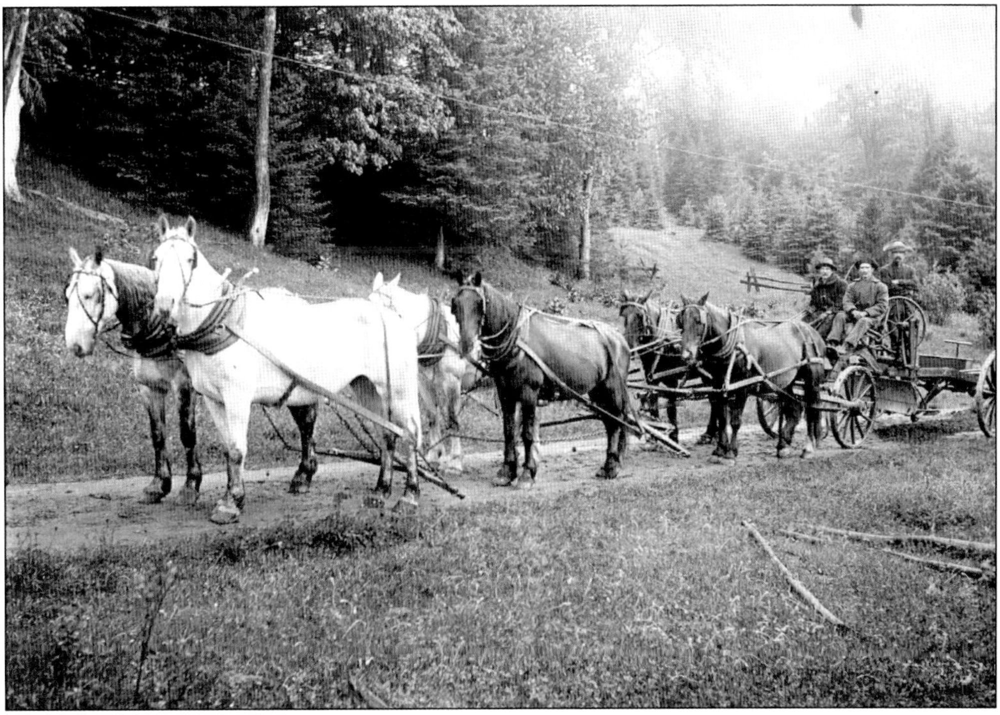

A grading machine was used to smooth out the road in Holland. The roads were a rutty mess in the spring and very hard to clear out during winter snowfalls. In 1888, Holland voted to buy its first snow roller to pack down the roads during the winter months. The first automobile in town was purchased in 1907 by George Ames, beginning a new era of transportation and a need for smooth roads. (Holland Historical Society.)

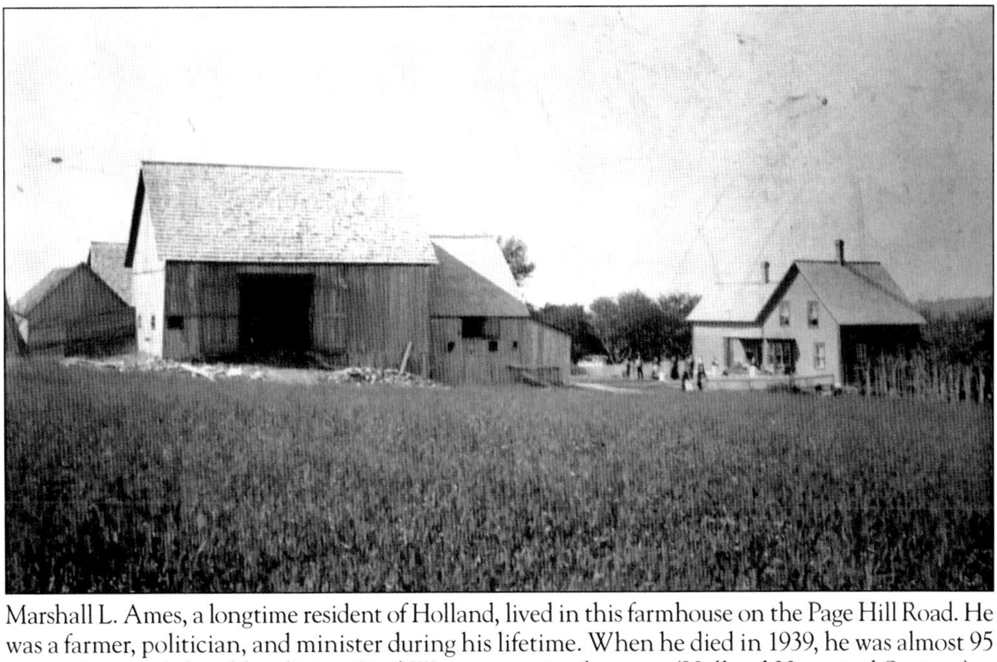

Marshall L. Ames, a longtime resident of Holland, lived in this farmhouse on the Page Hill Road. He was a farmer, politician, and minister during his lifetime. When he died in 1939, he was almost 95 years of age and the oldest living Civil War veteran in the area. (Holland Historical Society.)

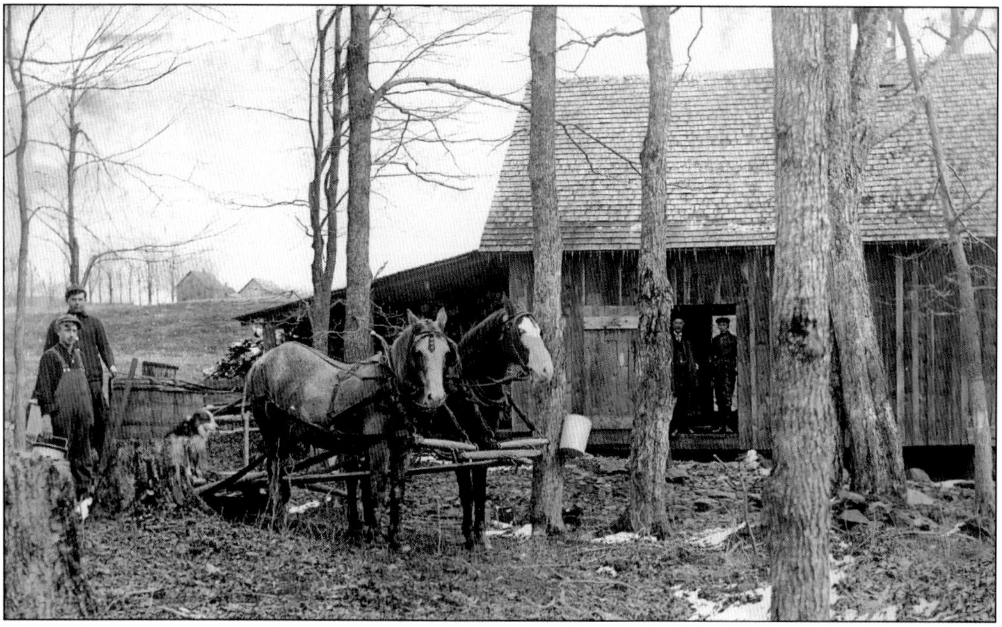

With all the forests in Holland, the townspeople were able to make a surplus of maple syrup and maple sugar. Usually starting in the month of March, much time was spent in the sugarhouse boiling the sap. This sugarhouse on Bates Hill near the Holland/Derby border belonged to Hollis Ames, who is standing in the doorway with the knee-high boots. His son Roy is at the front left. (Rod Ames.)

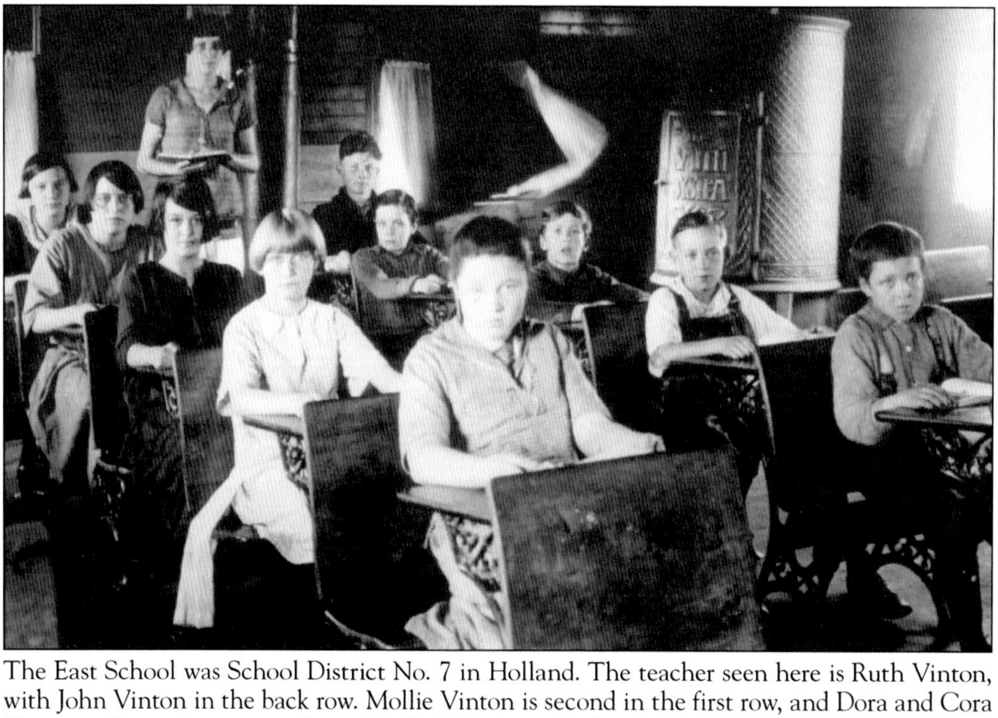

The East School was School District No. 7 in Holland. The teacher seen here is Ruth Vinton, with John Vinton in the back row. Mollie Vinton is second in the first row, and Dora and Cora Trucotte, Cassie Jenness, and possibly Earl Mosher are also pictured. This photograph is dated from around 1925. (Holland Historical Society.)

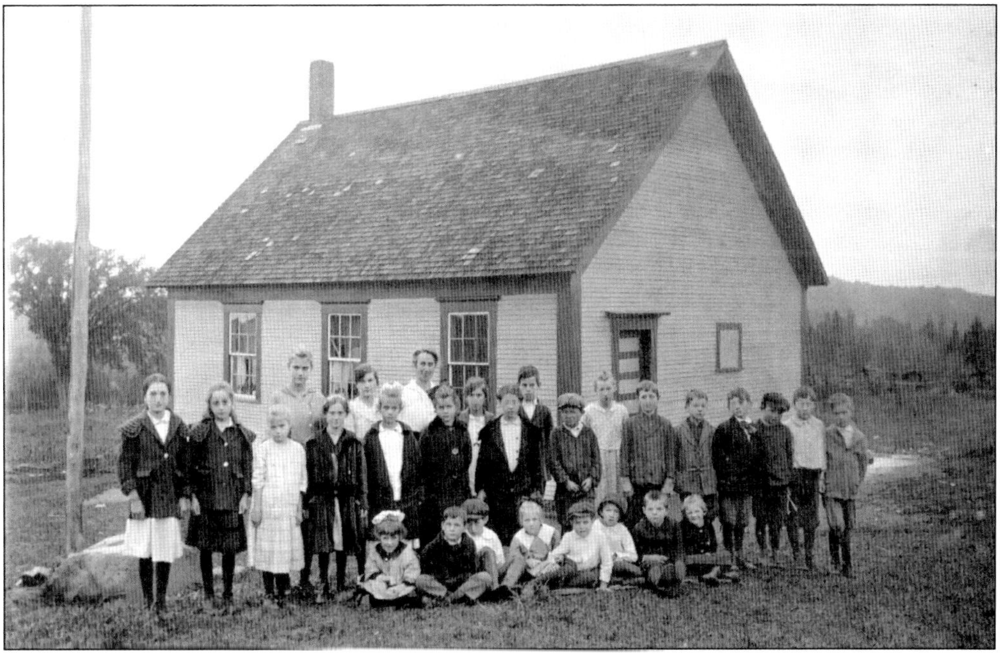

The Musgrove School, also called the South school, was School District No. 1 in Holland. The teacher is Jenney Lackey. From left to right are (first row) Verna Trucotte, Warren Lackey, Ernest Musgrove, Helen Rice, Elmer Currier, Lance Currier, Grover Batchelder, and Dot McDonald; (second row) Ellie Musgrove, Ethel Musgrove, ? Langmaid, Eva Trucotte, Ruth Currier, Gertrude (Kidder) Daggett, unidentified, and Perly Batchelder; (third row) Lena Langmaid, Allison Lackey, Jenney (Huntoon) Lackey, Madeline (Musgrove) Gray, Warren Rye, Irene McDonald, Charles Musgrove, Merle McDonald, Stanley Rice, Clifton Batchelder, Bernard Daggett, and Harold Rye. (Holland Historical Society.)

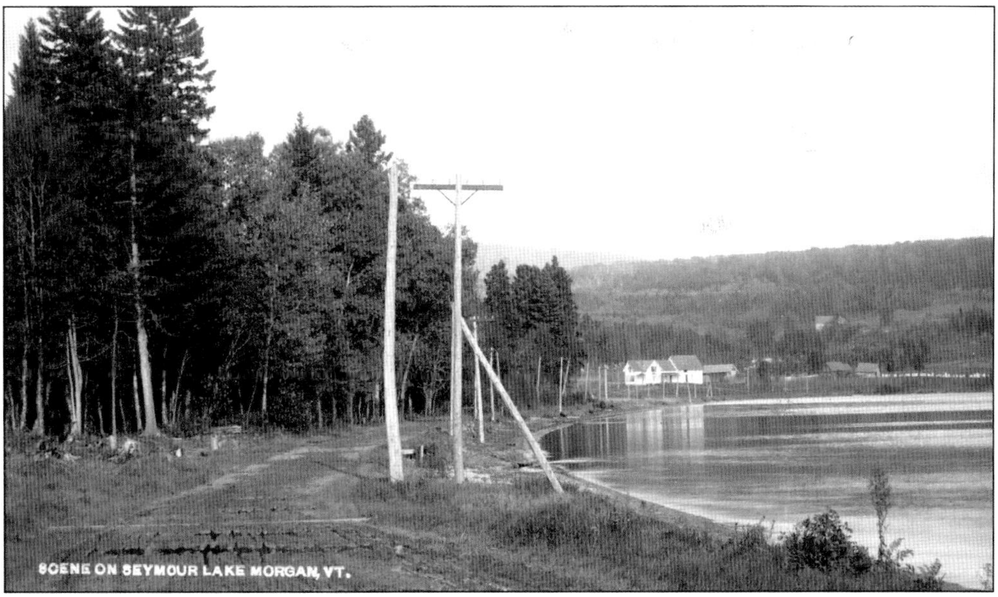

This is an early picture of Morgan Center's beach on Lake Seymour when there was only forest and no cottages. Morgan's first settler, Nathan Wilcox, arrived in 1802. (APC.)

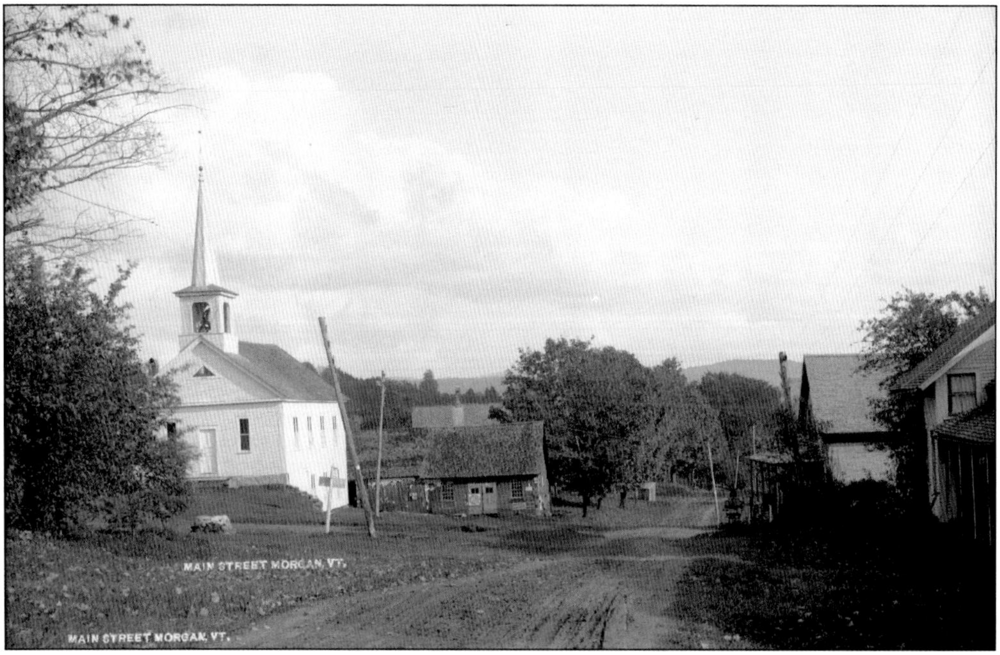

This picture shows the Morgan Four Corners in the 1920s. The Corner Methodist Church and Society built this church in 1843, and it became a member of the Methodist Derby Circuit, which included Derby, Holland, Morgan, Salem, Charleston, and Newport. Across from the church was the corner Morgan Store. (RCC.)

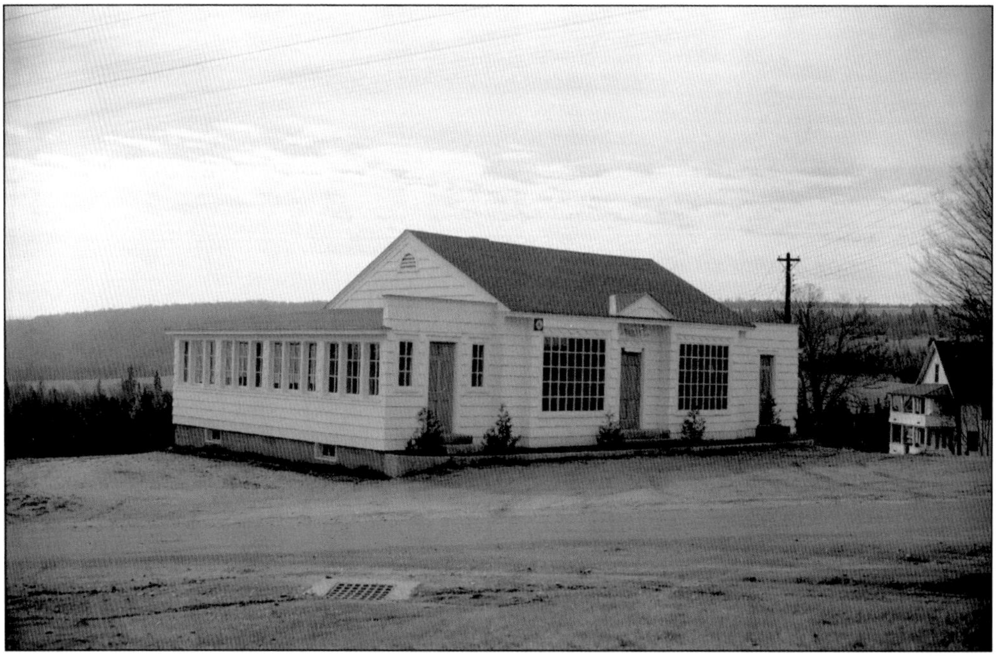

This Morgan Store at the four corners in Morgan, which contains the post office, was a replacement building for one that burned in April 1950. The previous building was constructed in the early 1800s and at one time housed B.F. Moore's overall business, which later became Slalom Skiwear in Newport. The general store sold clothing, stationery, groceries, medicine, and wallpaper. (RCC.)

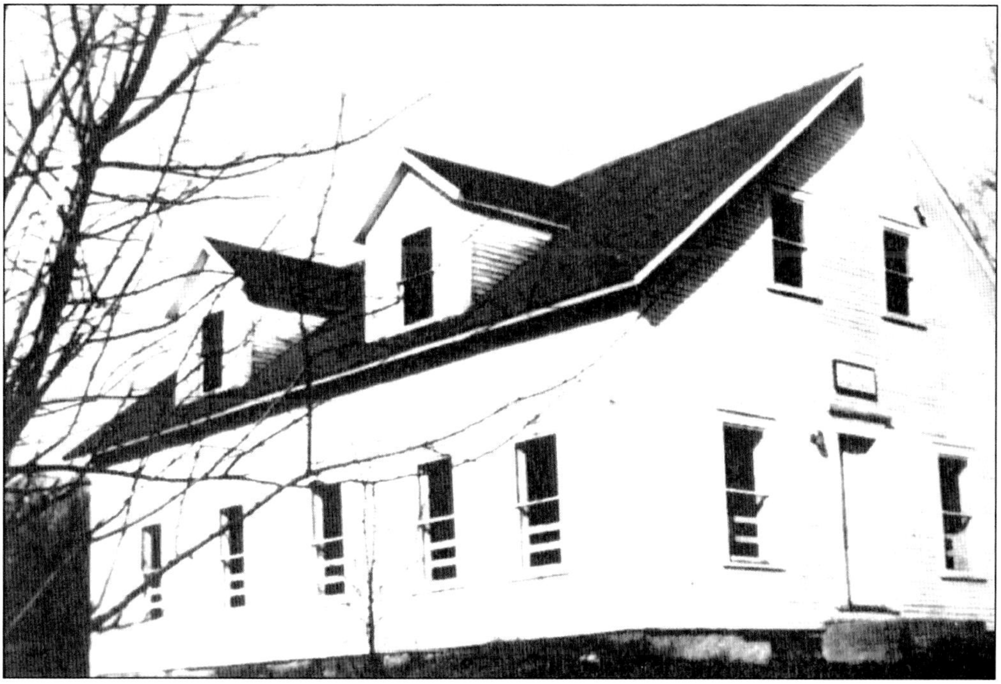

In 1942, the former home of Addie Lord in Morgan became the Community House, complete with its own committee. Additions to the building were done in the late 1940s, and it was used for community events, such as dances, plays, and town meetings. (Morgan Historical Society.)

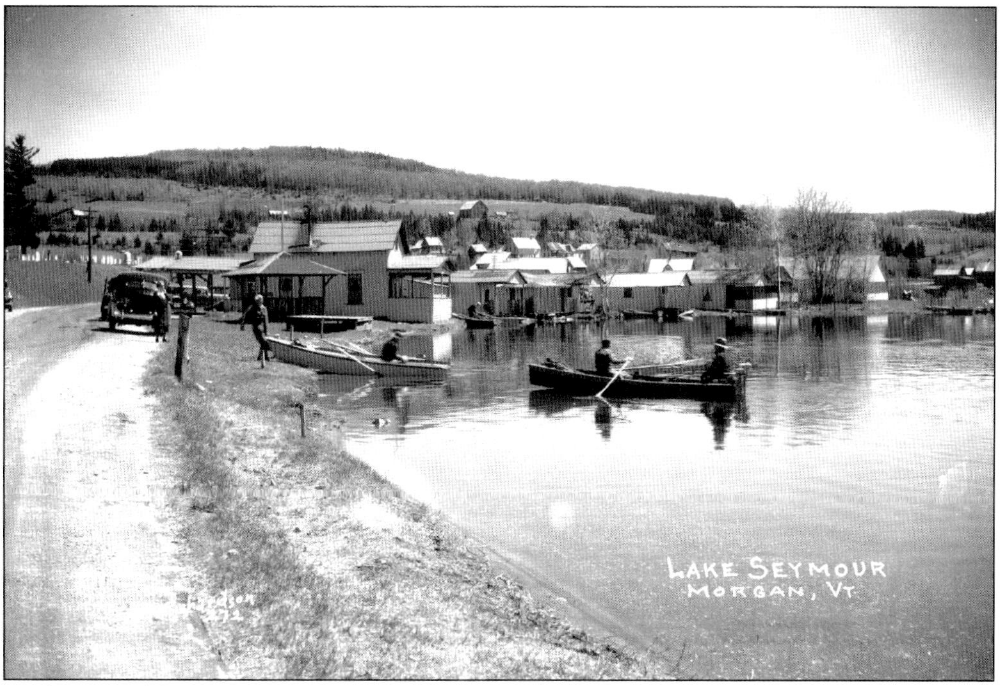

As the second largest lake entirely in the state of Vermont, Seymour Lake in Morgan has always been attractive to fishers, both in winter and summer. There is now a public beach, public parking, general store, and fishing access available for visitors. (RCC.)

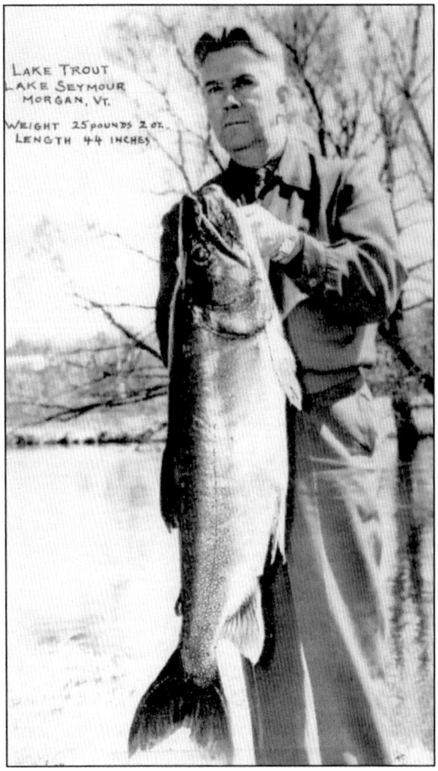

This fish was pulled out of Seymour Lake in Morgan by Curt Cobb, a fisherman and guide in the 1950s. (Morgan Historical Society.)

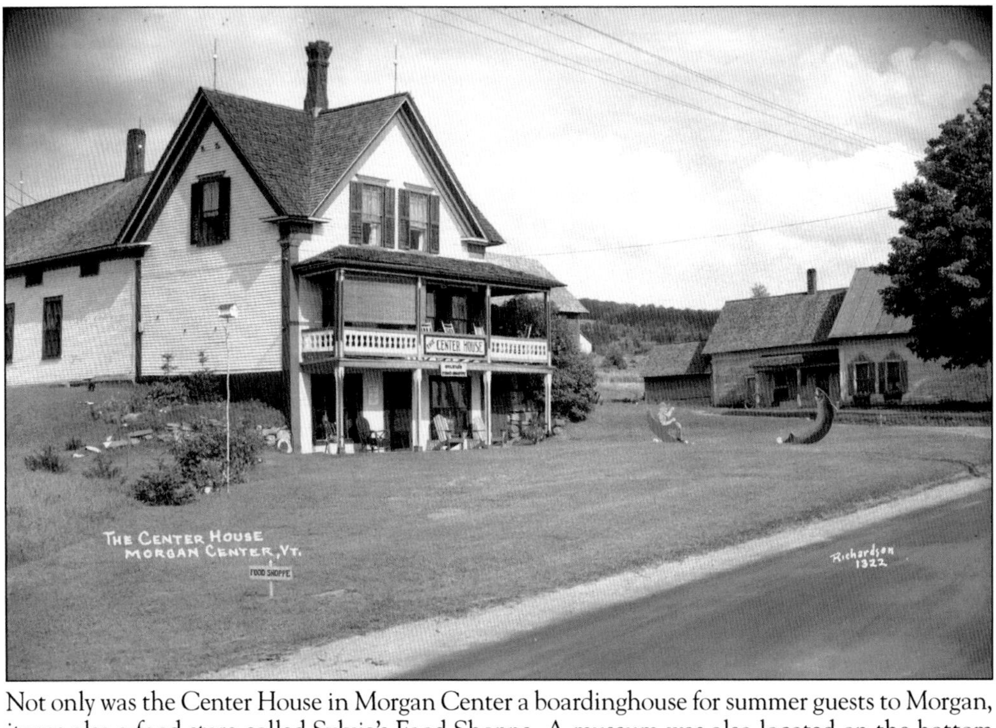

Not only was the Center House in Morgan Center a boardinghouse for summer guests to Morgan, it was also a food store called Sylvia's Food Shoppe. A museum was also located on the bottom floor. Within walking distance of the public beach, this was a great place to visit. (RCC.)

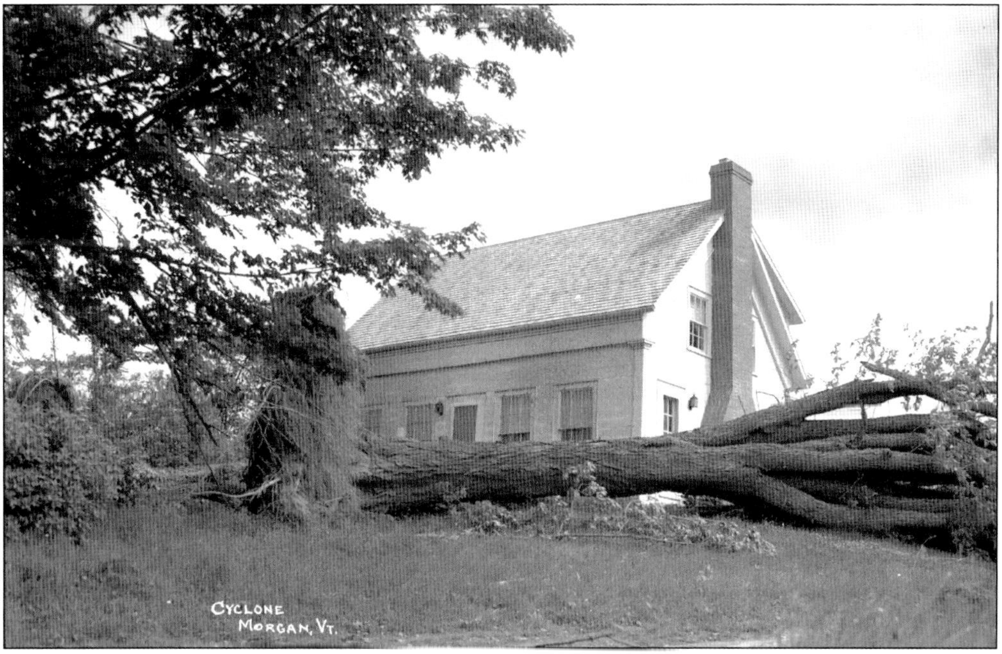

On June 19, 1940, a tornado tore through Morgan, destroying Herbert Flynn's farm and damaging his house. It happened in the middle of the day, when Flynn was out in his barn. His family hid inside the house while the twister went through his property, and in the end, no one was harmed. Items from the house were found all over the area; a bedspread was found three miles away in the woods. (Both, RCC.)

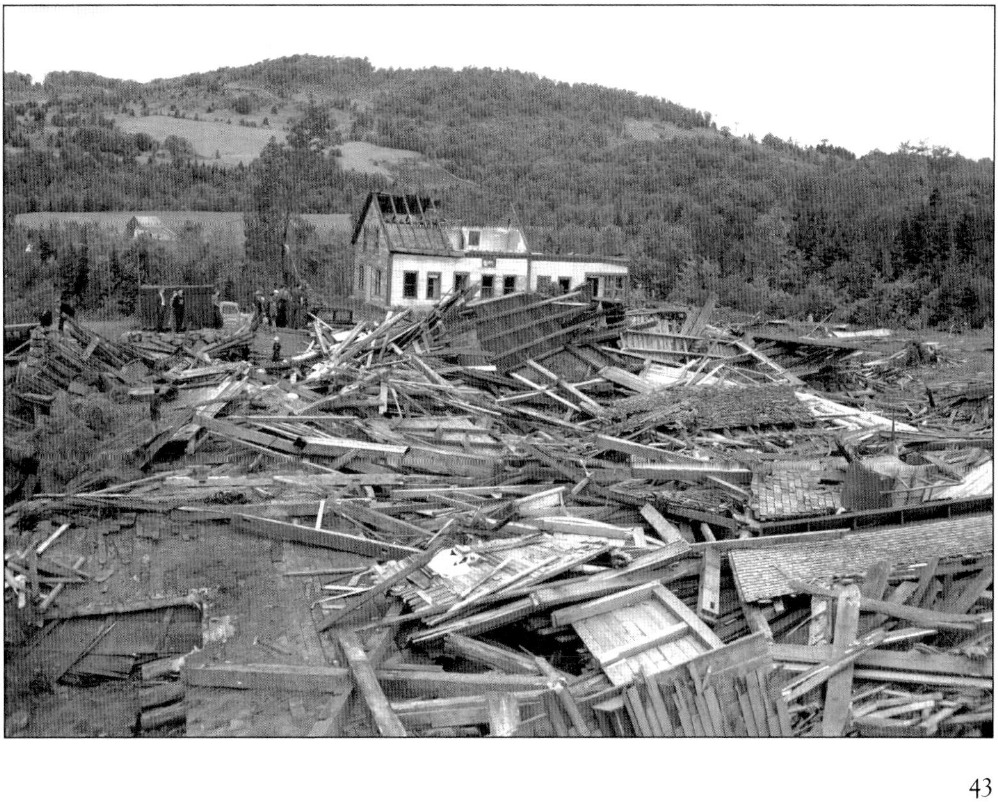

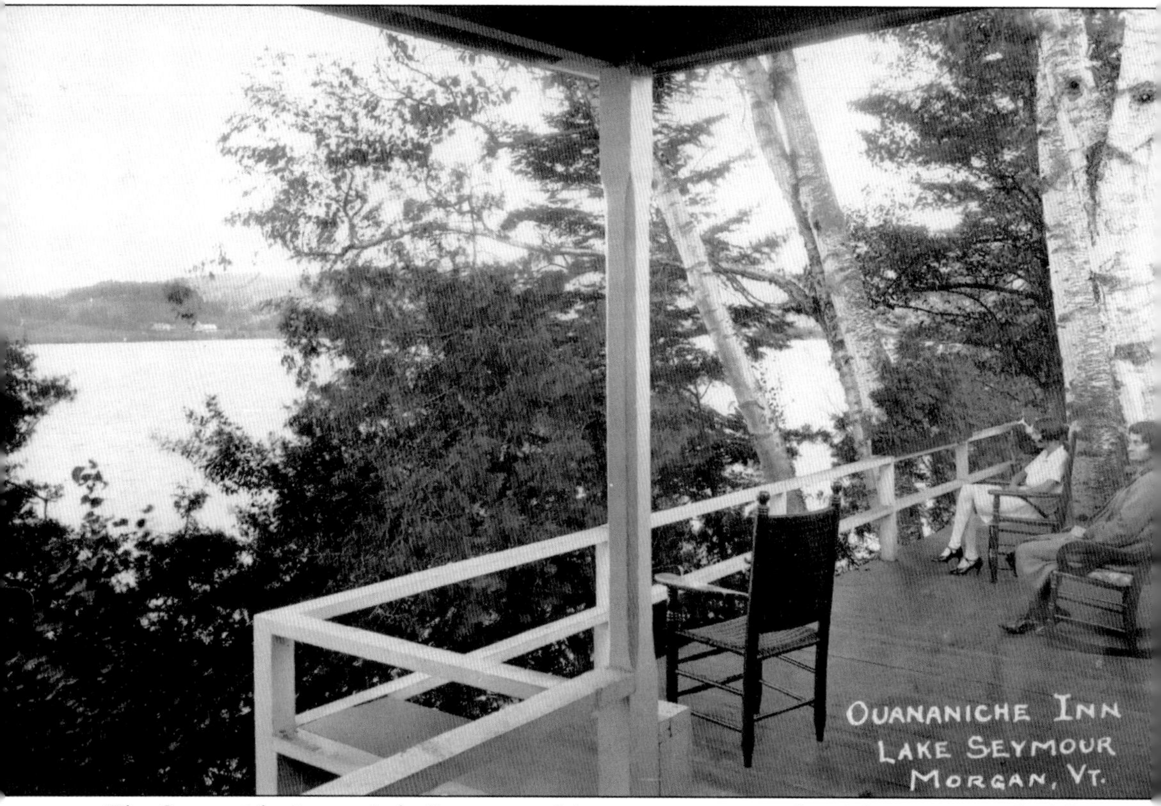

The Ouananiche Inn on Lake Seymour in Morgan was a summer hotel for visitors on the lake. The name Ouananiche comes from a type of Atlantic salmon that visit northern lakes to spawn in the spring. (APC.)

Three

Brownington, Coventry, and Westmore

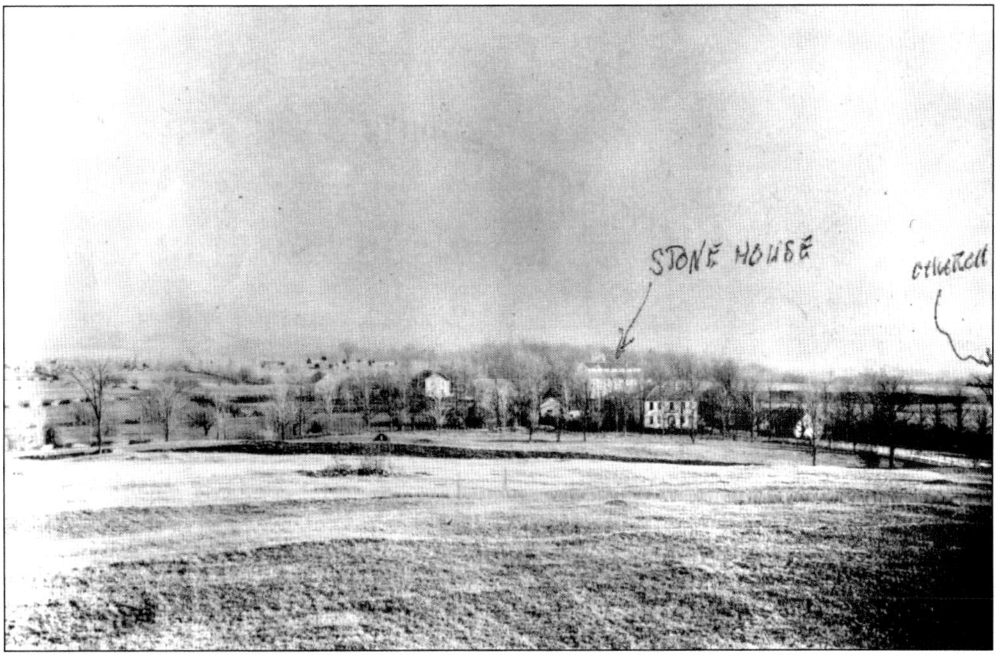

Brownington was chartered to Timothy and Daniel Brown in October 1790. The first settlement was by a potter named Peter Clark at the beginning of Old Stone House Road on the grounds of the Old Stone House Museum. Brownington's growth was aided by the construction of the Orleans County Grammar School, the county's only upper school for almost 10 years. (OCHS.)

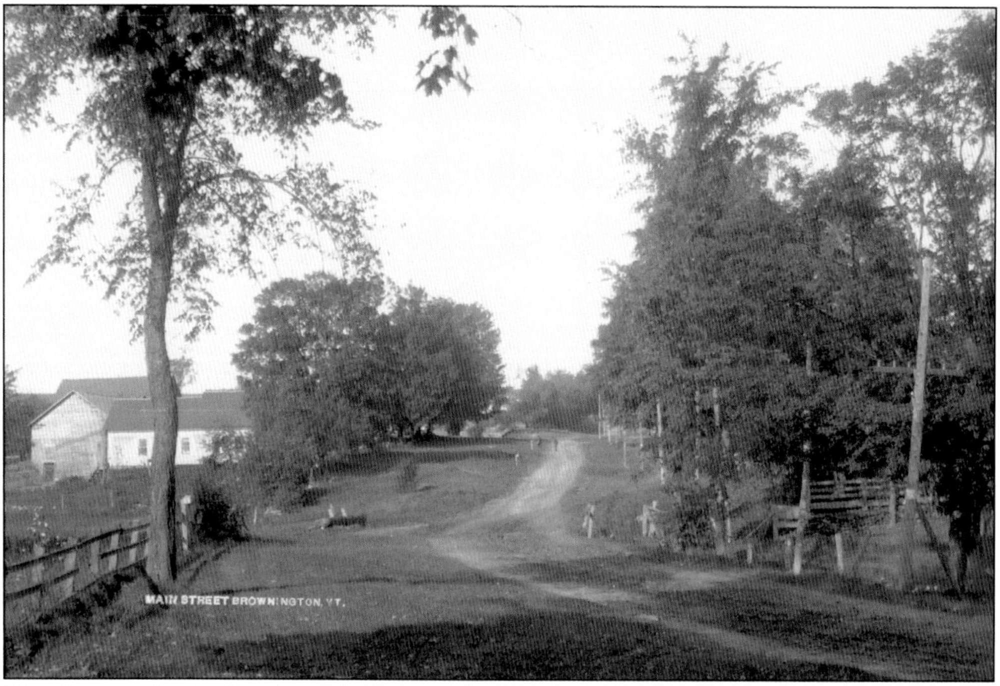

The Hinman Settler Road was the first road running south to north through Orleans County. Brownington Village, where this picture was taken, was an important place in the northern part of the county in the early 1800s because it had the first county-wide grammar school (today's high school). Brownington was also a half-shire town. (RCC.)

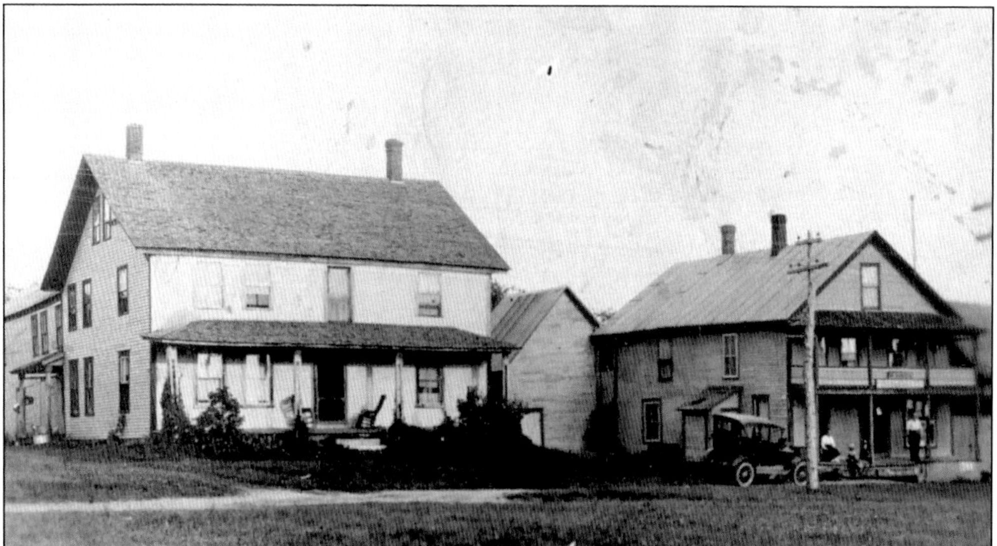

In Brownington Village, there were two large inns. The building on the left, built in 1815, was called the Rice and Going Hotel, and it served many visitors who came through on the stagecoach. The road in front of the hotel was a part of the route from Boston to Montreal. The building next door was the Brownington Village general store, and William Davies owned it in the early 1900s. (OCHS.)

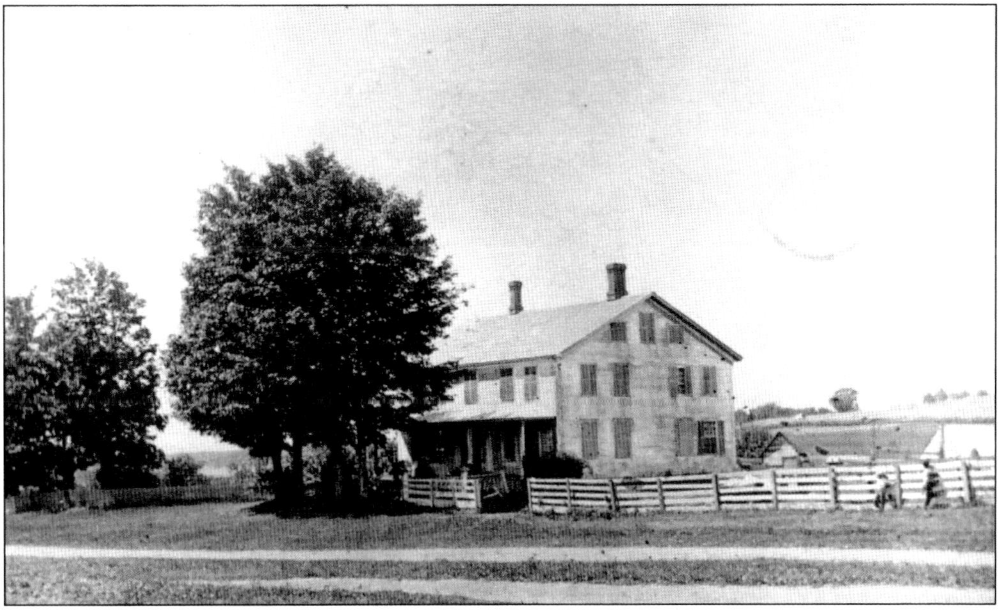

This was the second inn in the village of Brownington. Run by the Strong family, it was a dry tavern for the town. William Barstow Strong, born at this inn in 1837, grew up to be the president of the Atchison, Topeka, and Sante Fe Railroad. The inn was destroyed by fire. (OCHS.)

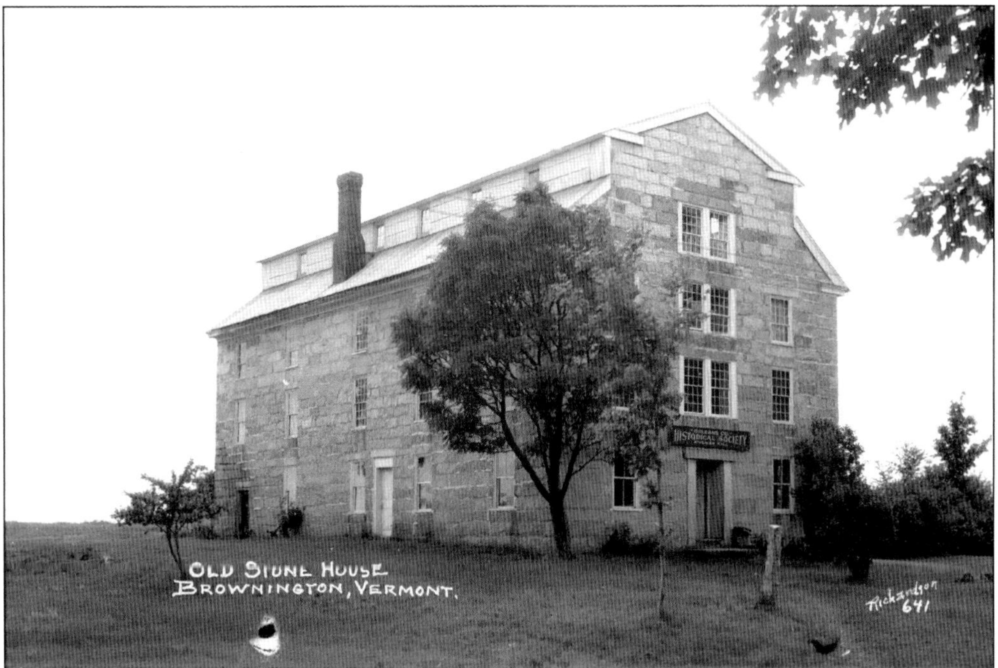

The granite dormitory, called Athenian Hall, was built by Alexander Twilight in 1836. He was the first African American to graduate from an American university. He was the preceptor, or principal, of the Orleans County Grammar School as well as the first black state legislator in the United States. Twilight taught in Brownington from 1829 until two years before his death in 1857 (OCHS.)

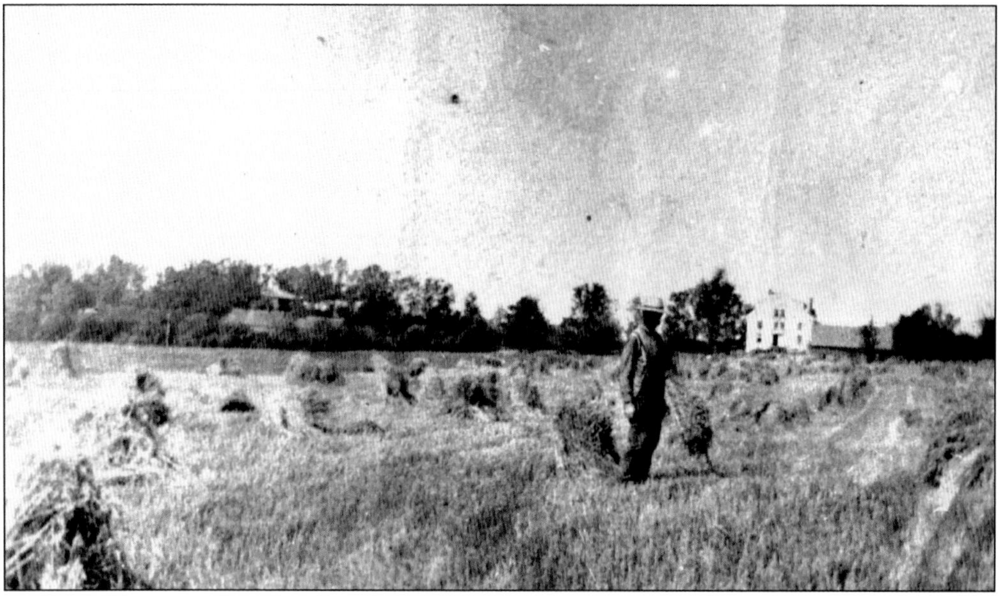

Erwin Kelley owned and farmed the land behind the Old Stone House and lived in the former Rice and Going Hotel. He traveled with his farm products throughout Orleans County and even to the White Mountains of New Hampshire in the summer. Here he is working in the field, where the grass is drying in hayricks. (OCHS.)

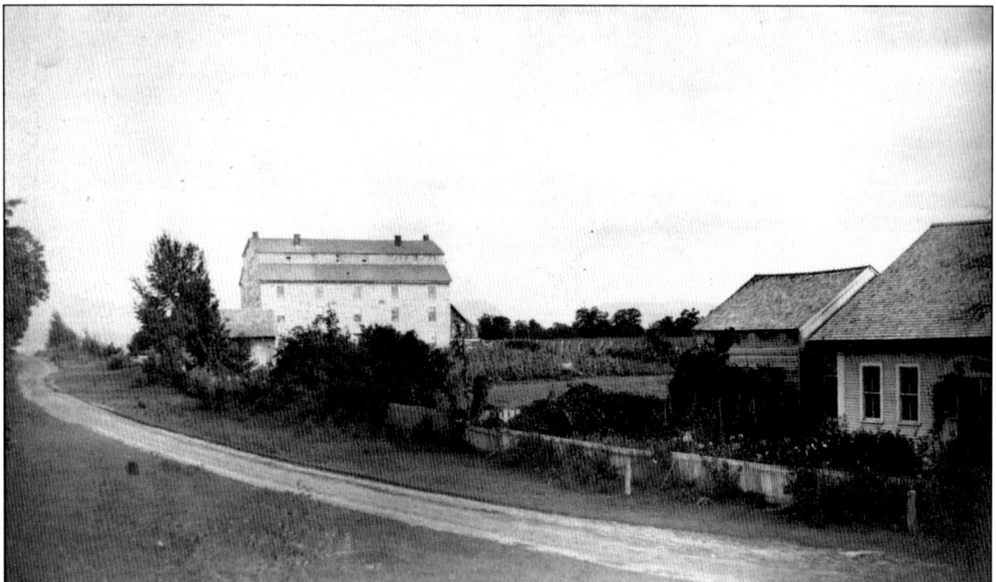

In 1916, the Orleans County Historical Society bought the building known as the Old Stone Boarding House to use as a museum of the history of Orleans County. Today the Old Stone House Museum is a part of the Brownington National Historic District. The society has grown to include six buildings, a blacksmith shop, an observatory, and 55 acres of farmland. (OCHS.)

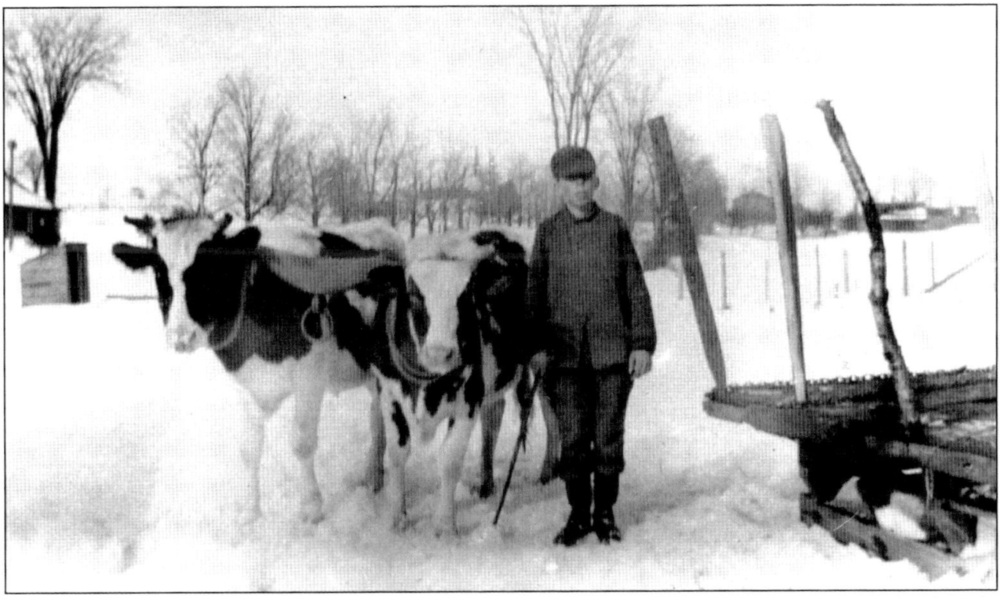

Laurence Kelley, Erwin's son, poses with his steer. The Brownington Congregational Church, Samuel Hall house, and Cyrus Eaton House are seen in the background. (OCHS.)

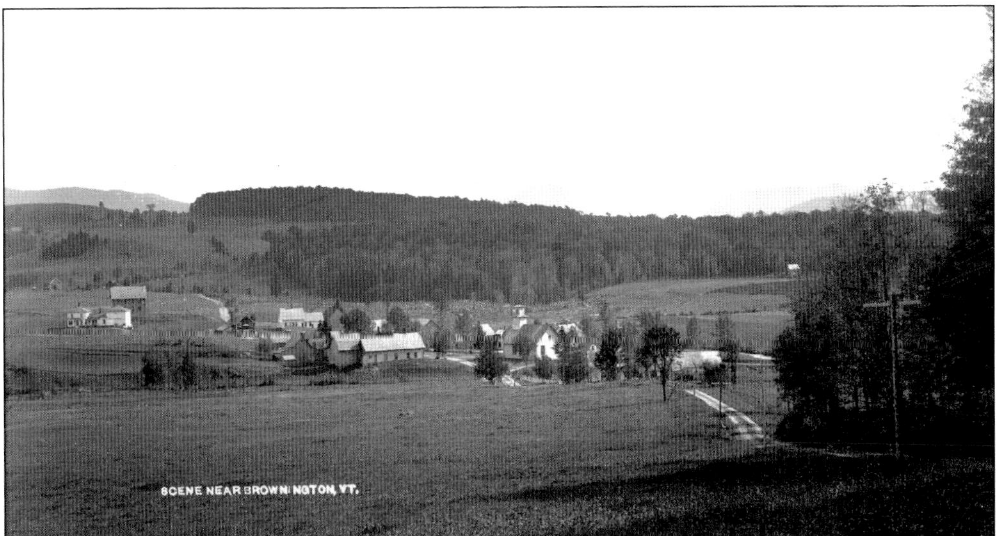

Brownington Center had its own school, church, and general store. A few miles east of Brownington Village, it was settled a few years later. (RCC.)

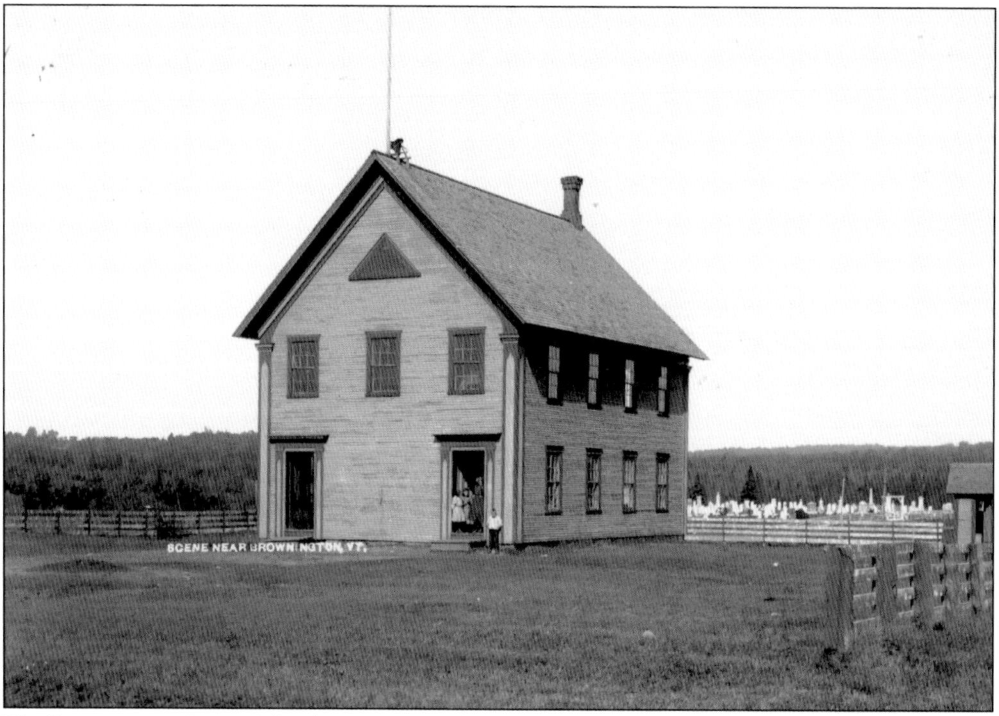

The Brownington Center School was in use until the 1960s, when the new unified elementary school was built just up the road. It was one of many schools that served the town of Brownington. (APC.)

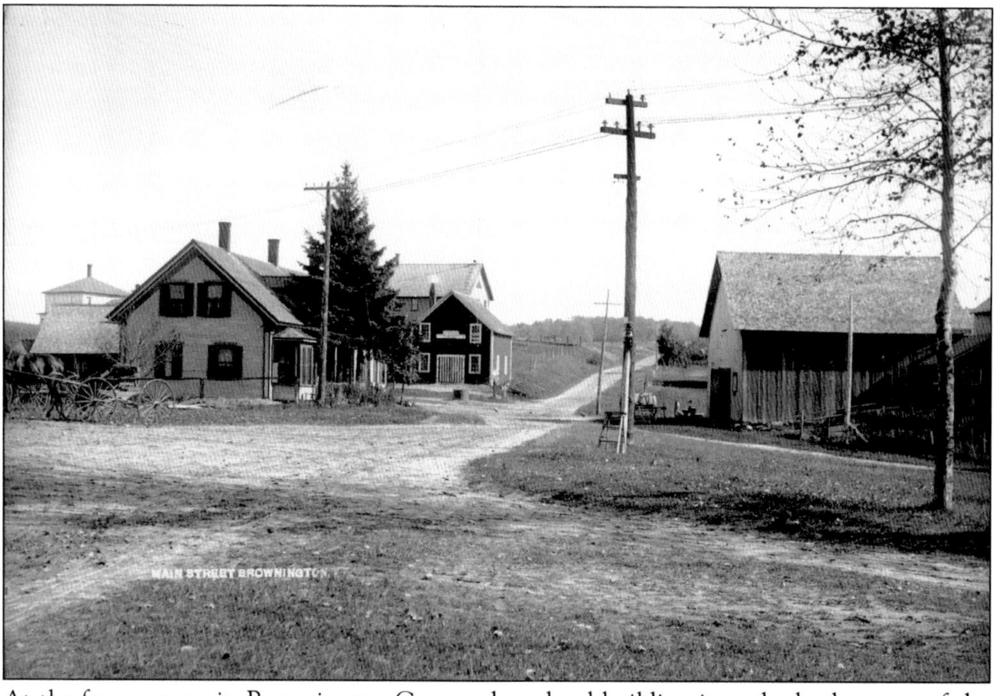

At the four corners in Brownington Center, the school building is at the back center of the photograph. There was once a general store and blacksmith shop located here. The land surrounding Brownington Center was owned mainly by one-family dairy farms. (APC.)

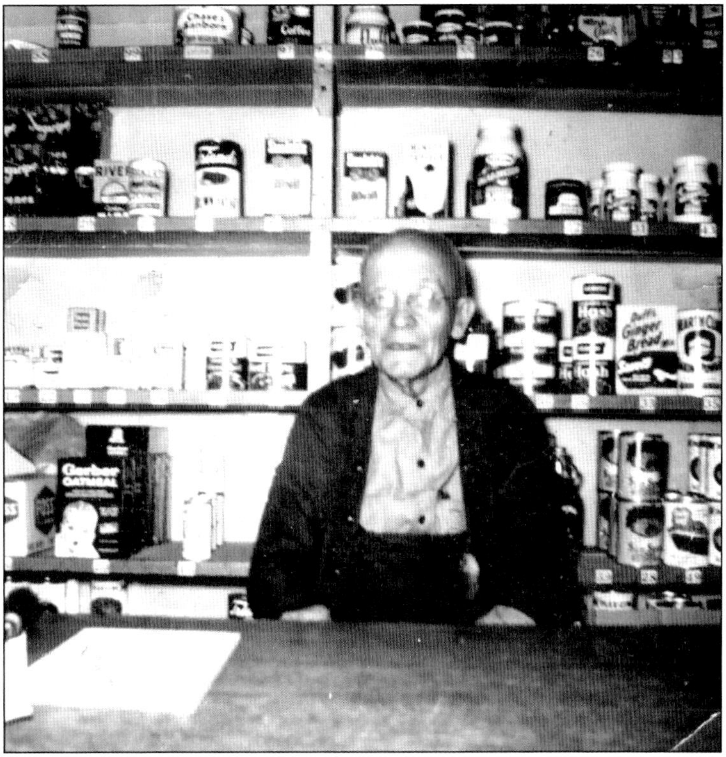

Myron P. Willard, the owner of the Brownington Center General Store, ran his business from the 1930s until the 1970s. The store sold a little bit of everything, including food and home and garden supplies. It was a gathering place to hear the local gossip. (Shirley Perry.)

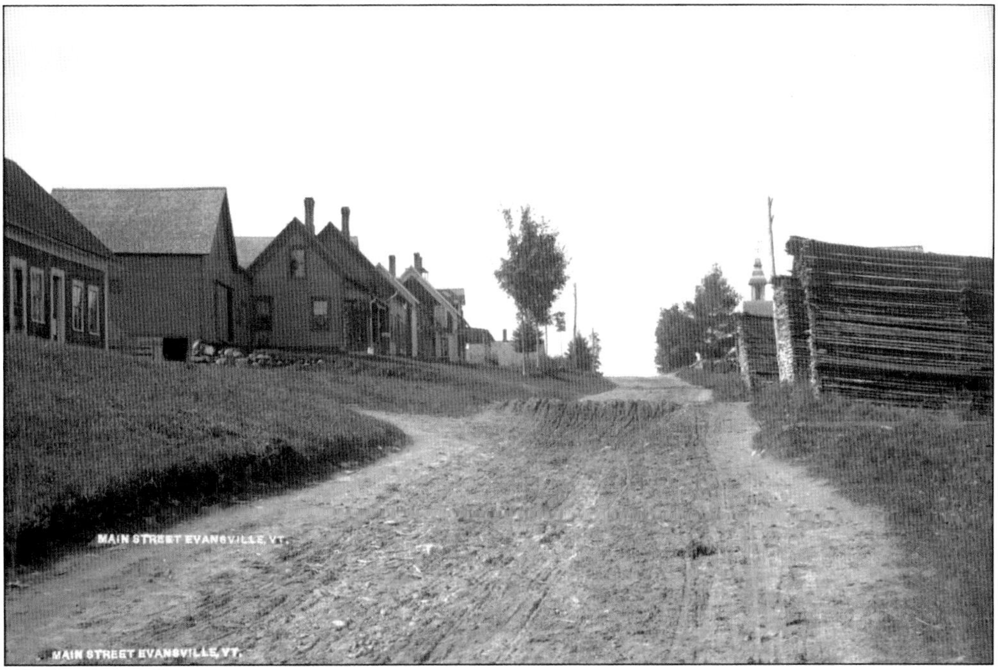

Before 1870, Evansville was called Skunk Hollow. The residents decided to change the name, but they did not know what to name it. The two earliest settlers, Joseph Evans and John Marshall, had a contest. They got on either side of a large pine tree, and whoever could chop it down on their side won and had the town named after him. Joseph Evans was the winner. (APC.)

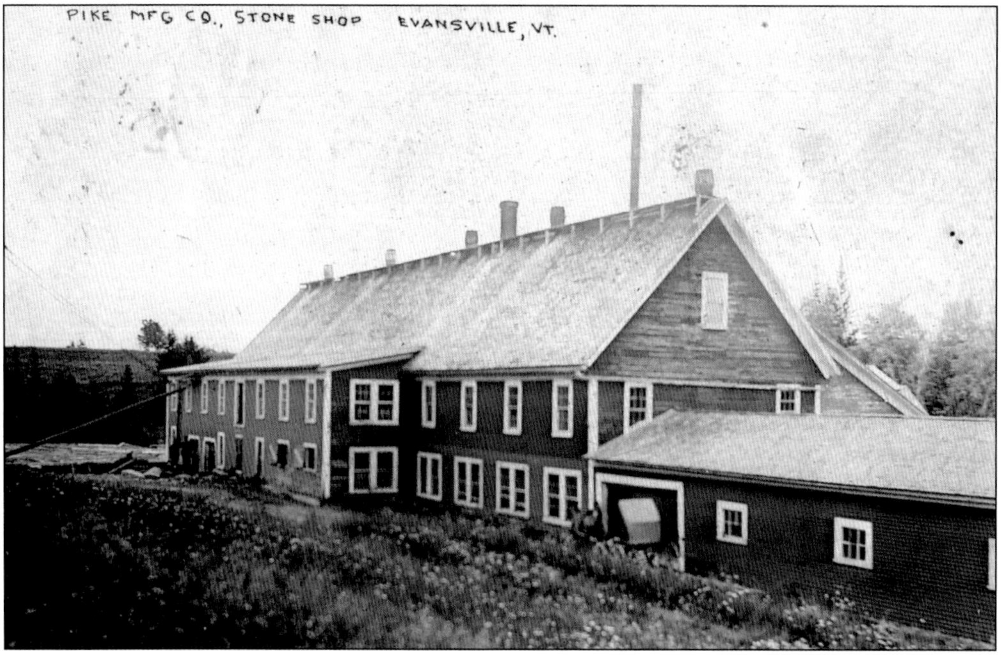

The A.F. Pike Manufacturing Company, on the border of Evansville and Westmore, ran this whetstone factory from 1881 to 1932. The whetstone quarry had been in use since 1875, but it closed in 1936. (APC.)

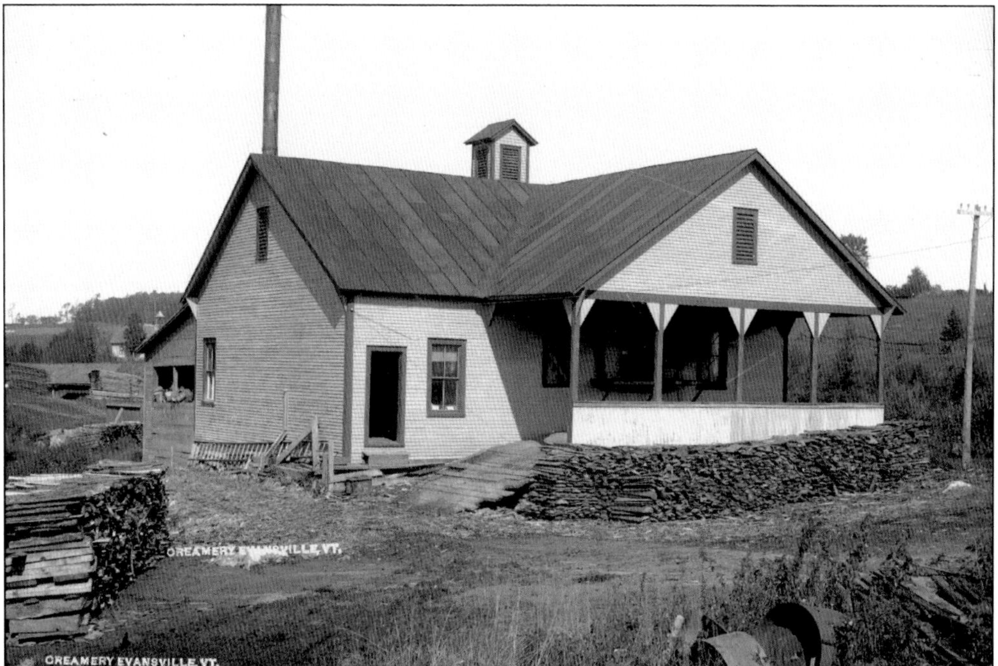

J.G. Turnbull, who had creameries in 13 other northern Vermont locations in 1912, owned this creamery in Evansville. Turnbull came from Canada to Orleans, known then as Barton Landing, and opened his first creamery in 1891. He served as the president of the Central Savings Bank and Trust Company of Orleans as well as a state representative and mason. (APC.)

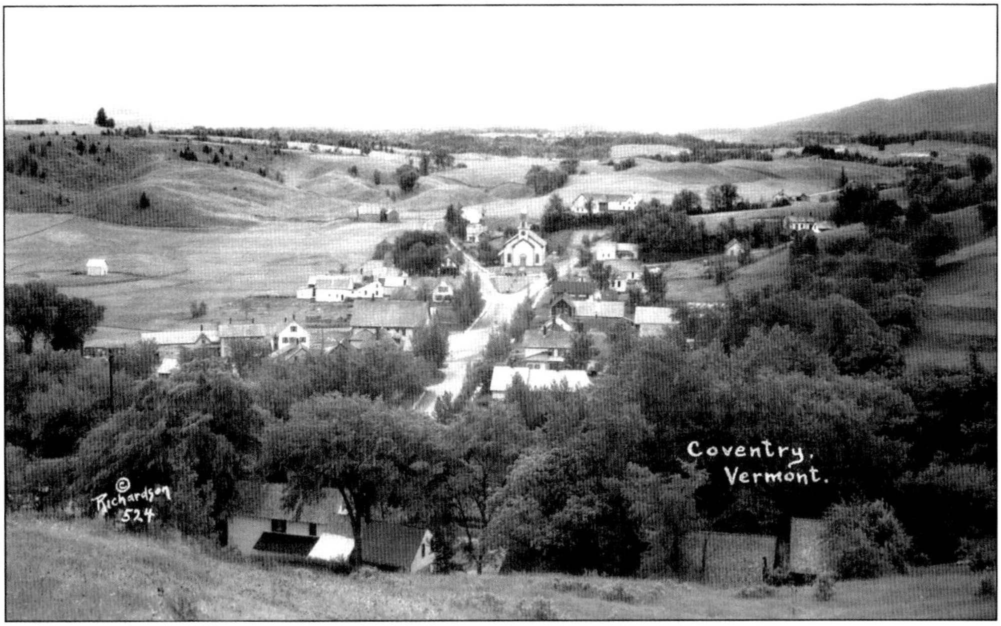

Coventry, named after the town in Connecticut, was chartered in 1780 to Maj. Elias Buel and 59 others but was not settled until 1800. The area in the picture is now Coventry Village but was originally called Coventry Falls. The first settlement in town, named Coventry Center, was four miles east. The general population began moving to the village, where waterpower from the Black River could be utilized. (RCC.)

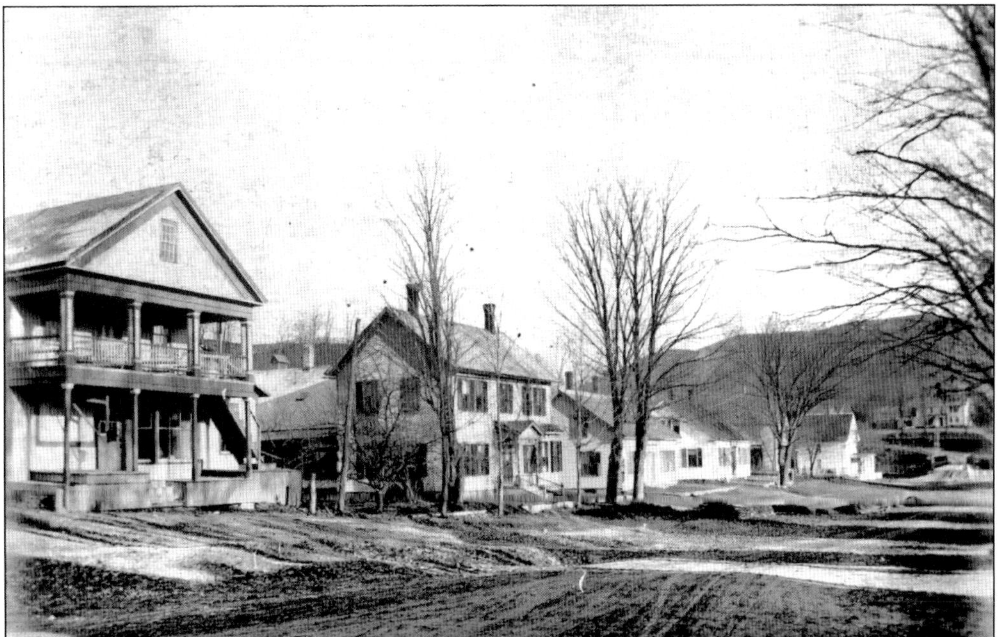

In 1803, the few residents of Coventry were required to spend four days in June and two days in September to maintain or improve the roads. In October 1805, the first public roads were laid out. Previously, the roads were more like paths, barely wide enough for a team of oxen. The first road from Coventry Falls to Coventry Center, or west to east, was built in June 1806. (APC.)

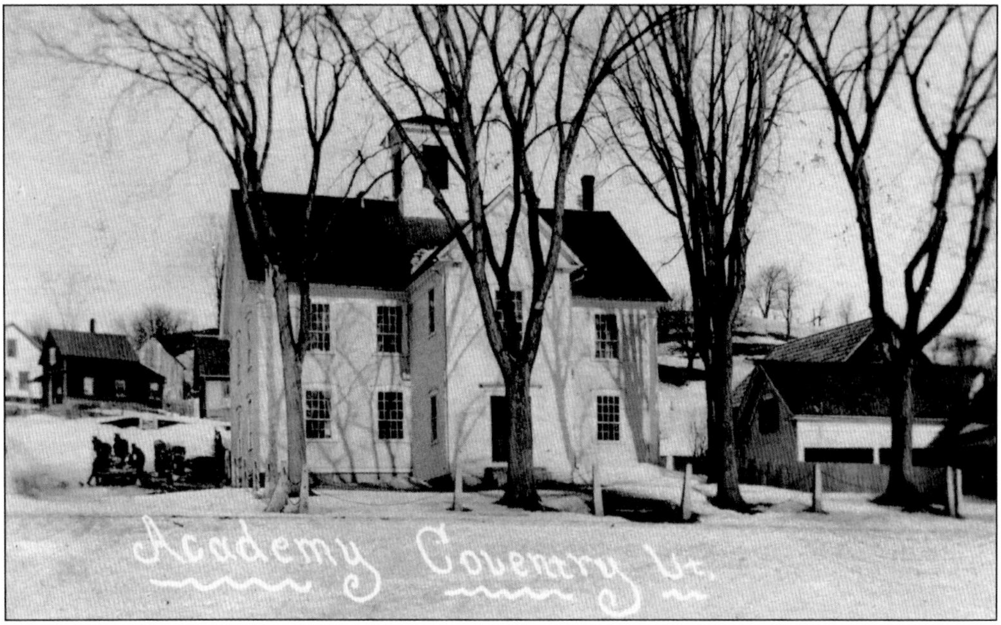

Coventry Academy, established in 1859, was maintained by rentals of school lands and by the town. It continued as such until it closed in 1872. The elementary school used the building until it burned in 1915. Since that time, Coventry has sent its high school students to other schools and pays their tuition. (APC.)

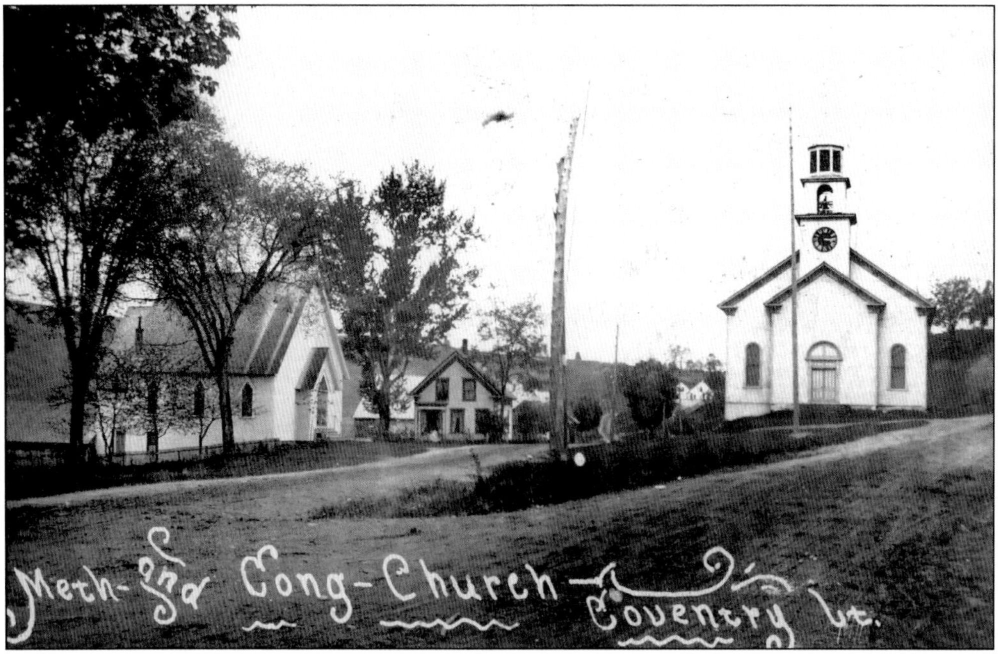

These two churches served the community of Coventry in the 1800s. The church on the right was the Congregational church built in 1830 by Elijah Cleveland. The Methodist church on the left was built in 1877, with seating for 300 people. The congregations combined in 1919 and continued meeting at the Congregational church. The Methodist church was sold to the Coventry Grange and is now a private home. (APC.)

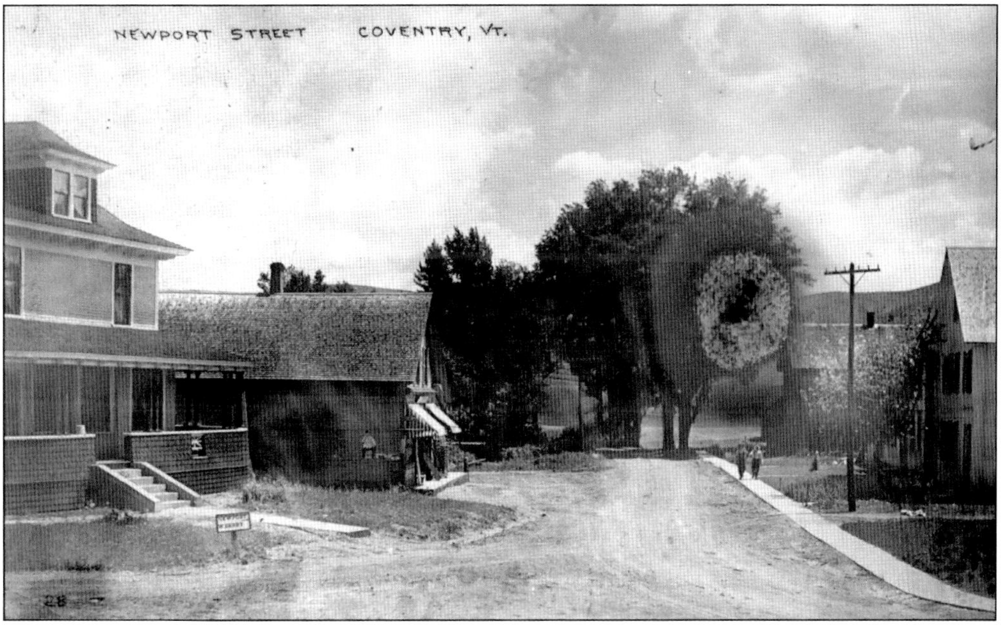

This road, called Newport Street in the picture, is now the northern part of Main Street in Coventry Village. The road curves to the left near the trees on its way to Newport. The house at the front left was built for the Thurber family after their store and original home were destroyed by fire. (APC.)

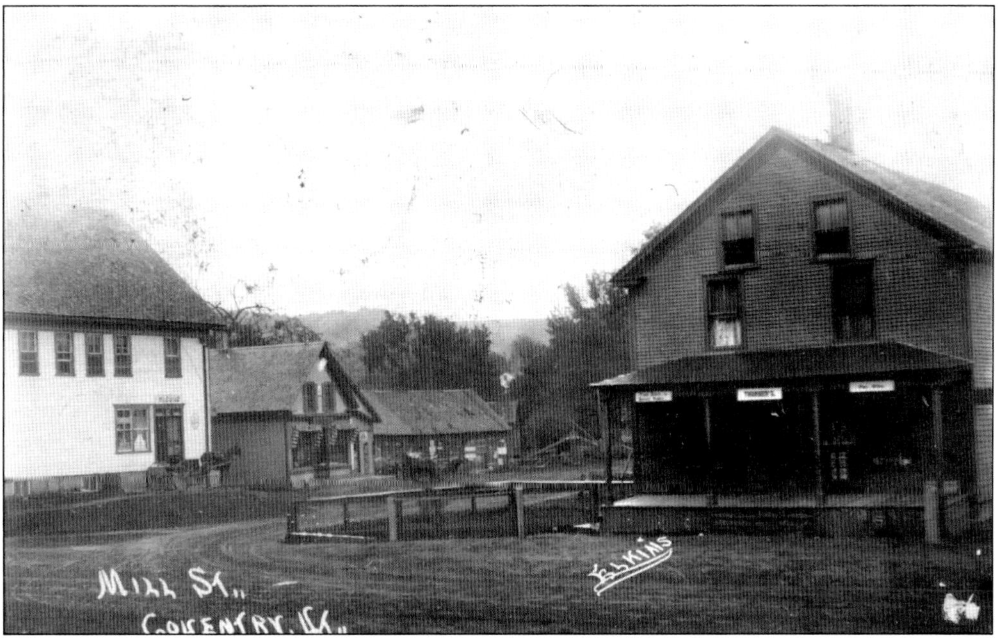

The label on this picture is misleading: the road at the center is Main Street Coventry, with Newport Street leading off to the right. The building on the right was Thurber's General Store, which was destroyed by fire on July 26, 1913. A hotel, where A.D. Thurber and family lived, was also destroyed. The house on the left was later moved to the location of the old store. (APC.)

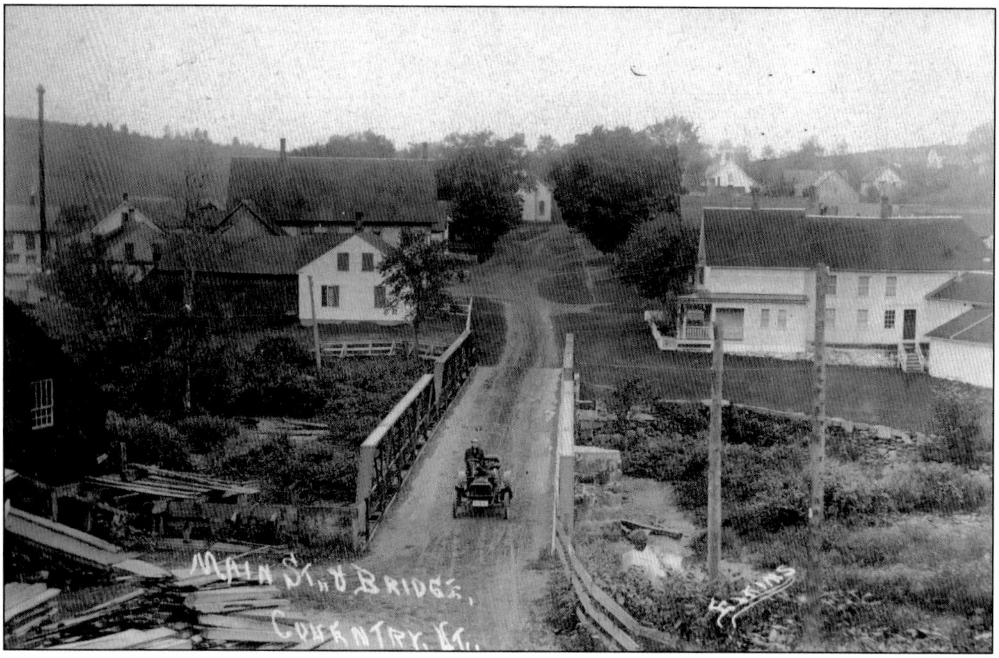

This bridge in Coventry Village was built to cross the Black River near where the tannery and gristmill were located. The bobbin mill that was in production in the early 1900s was closed in 1960, and the bridge was shut down. The road is now a dead end. (APC.)

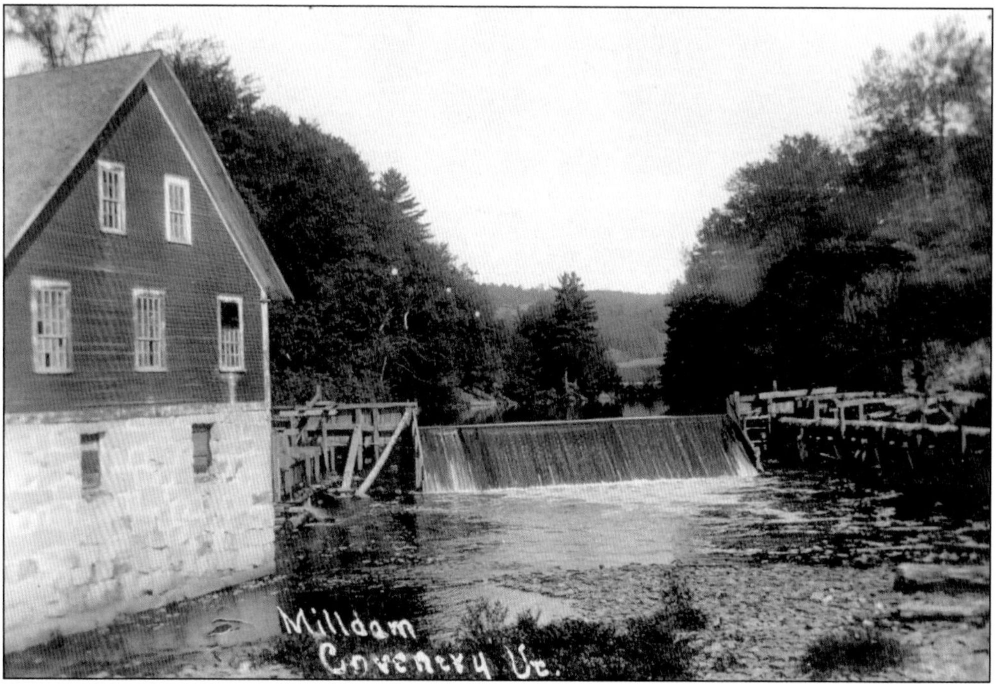

Coventry Falls, as it was situated next to the Black River, once had four working mills. In 1859, there were two sawmills, a gristmill, a starch mill, and a tannery on the river. The gristmill was built by Elijah Cleveland in 1827. The tannery, which was built in 1825, was changed to a bobbin mill in the 1900s. (APC.)

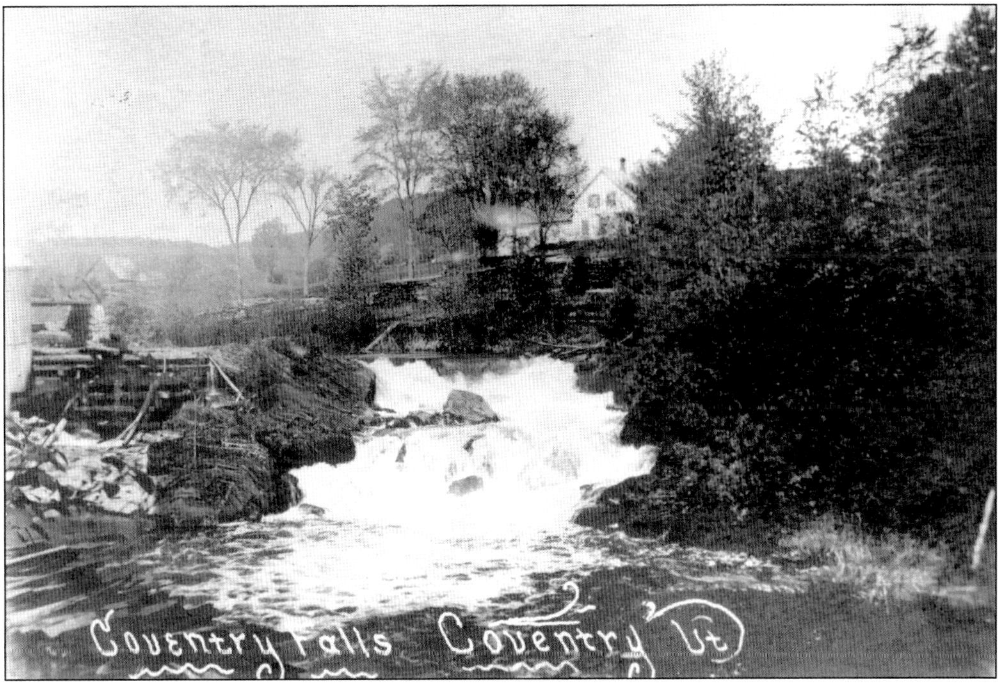

To the west of the village of Coventry was an area called Heermanville, on the upper falls of the Black River. The Heerman family used the water of the river to power the sawmill they built in 1822. (APC.)

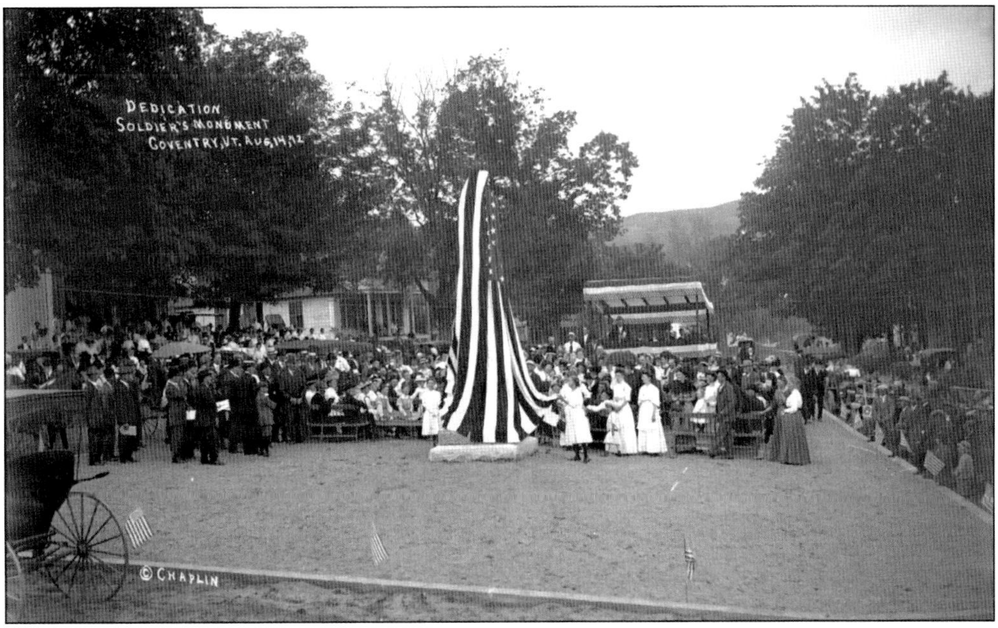

On August 14, 1912, Coventry celebrated the dedication of a monument in the town common. Judge Riley E. Wright—who resided in Baltimore, Maryland, but grew up in Coventry and served in the Civil War—donated the monument in memory of the Coventry soldiers who served in the military. The women holding the flag in this picture are Lucy Hancock and Dorothy Niles, granddaughters of veterans. (RCC.)

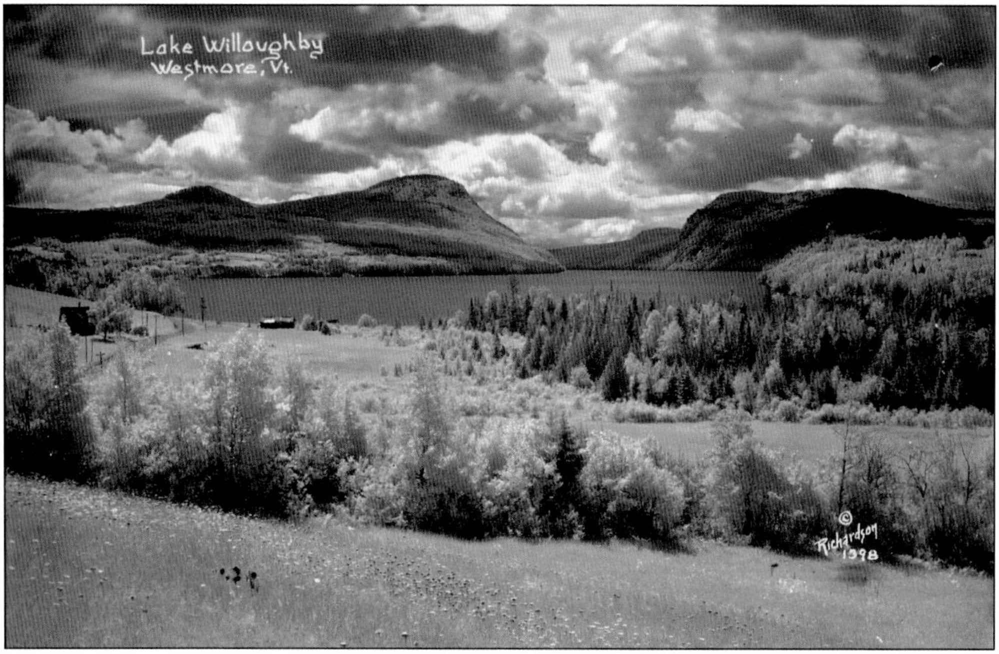

This is the image most people think of when they hear the name Willoughby Lake. The town of Westmore was settled in 1800 and was initially called Westford. Because of the beautiful lake and mountains, Westmore has been a popular summer destination. The two mountains, Pisgah and Hor, tower over the lake, much like a Scandinavian fjord. (RCC.)

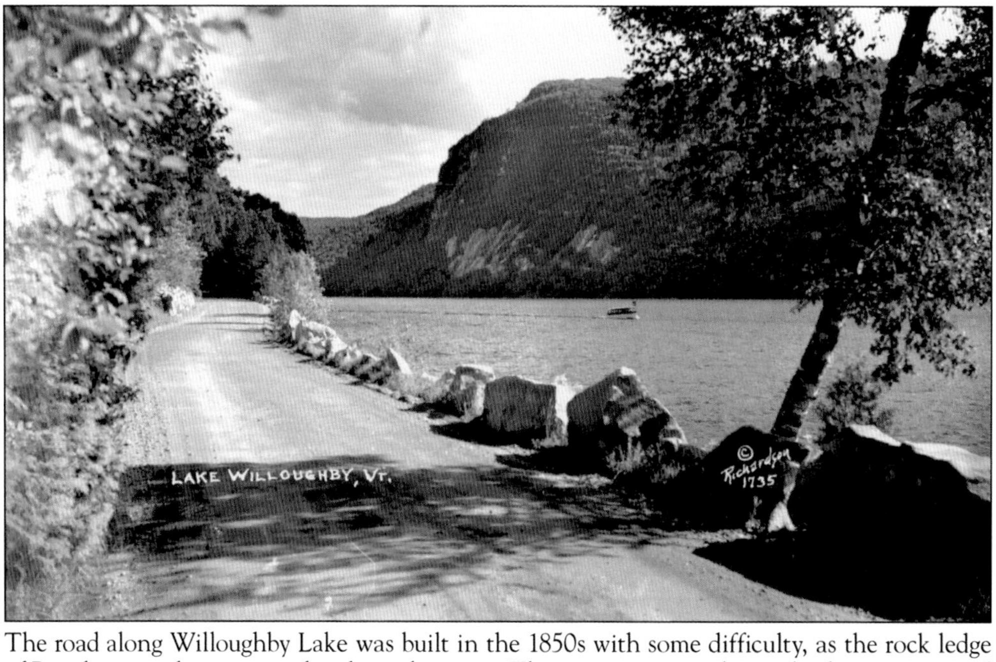

The road along Willoughby Lake was built in the 1850s with some difficulty, as the rock ledge of Pisgah came almost immediately to the water. This was one spot where a bridge was required to get around the large jut of rock. Peter Gilman, who owned Gilman Tavern, was hired to build the road, and when the town money ran out, he spent his own. This road is now a state highway. (RCC.)

Franconia Notch in New Hampshire was not the only mountain with a naturally occurring rock face. Mount Hor, one of the two surrounding Willoughby, had a rock face referred to as the Dutchman. If looking closely, it can be found in this picture. (RCC.)

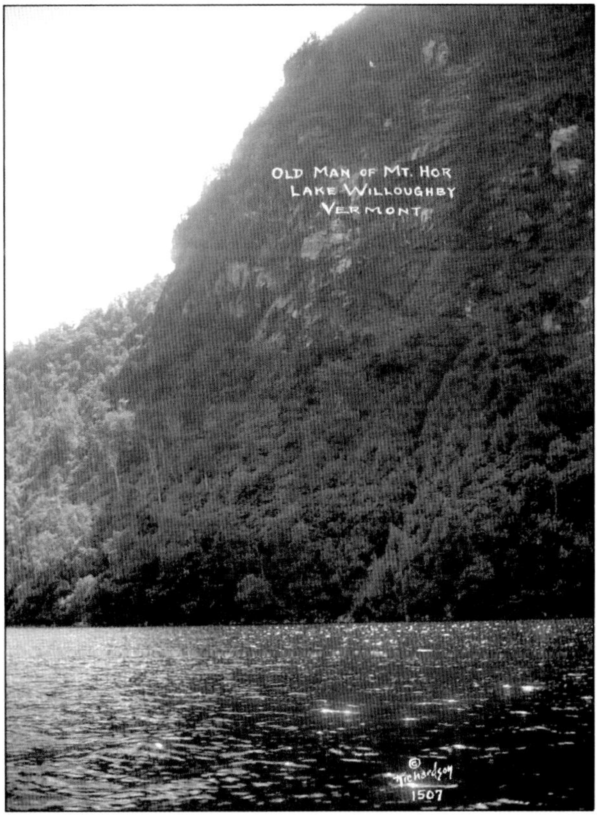

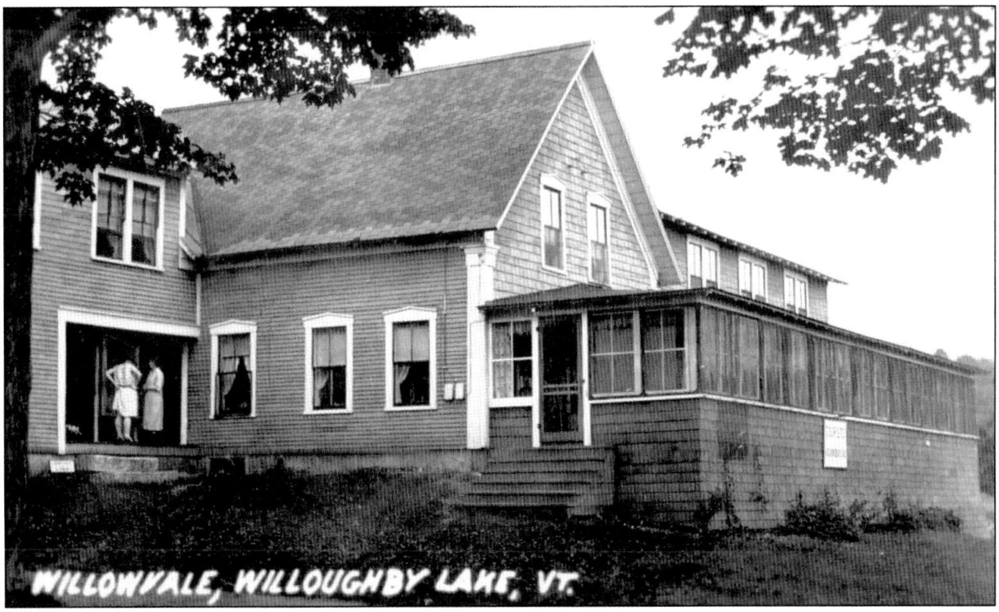

This was the Willowvale Inn in Westmore during the early 20th century. Robert Frost stayed on the property in 1909. Doc Harter, the man who owned Songadeewin, a girls' camp in Westmore, purchased the property and renamed it WilloughVale Inn Cabins and Restaurant. WilloughVale Inn still rents out rooms at this spot along the lake, but the building has been rebuilt. (APC.)

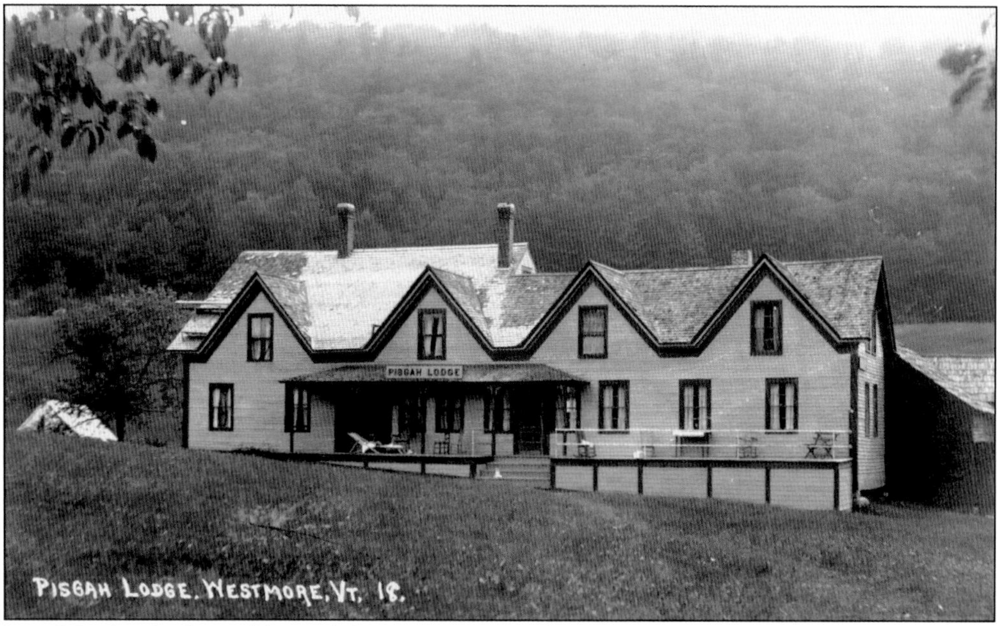

Pisgah Lodge, built as additional sleeping rooms for the Willoughby Lake House hotel across the road, survived the fire that destroyed the Lake House in November 1904. The Lake House had been a popular hotel, opening seasonally to hold balls and other social events. When the Lake House burned, Pisgah Lodge continued as a hotel until interest waned. Then, in September 1971, it too was destroyed by fire. (APC.)

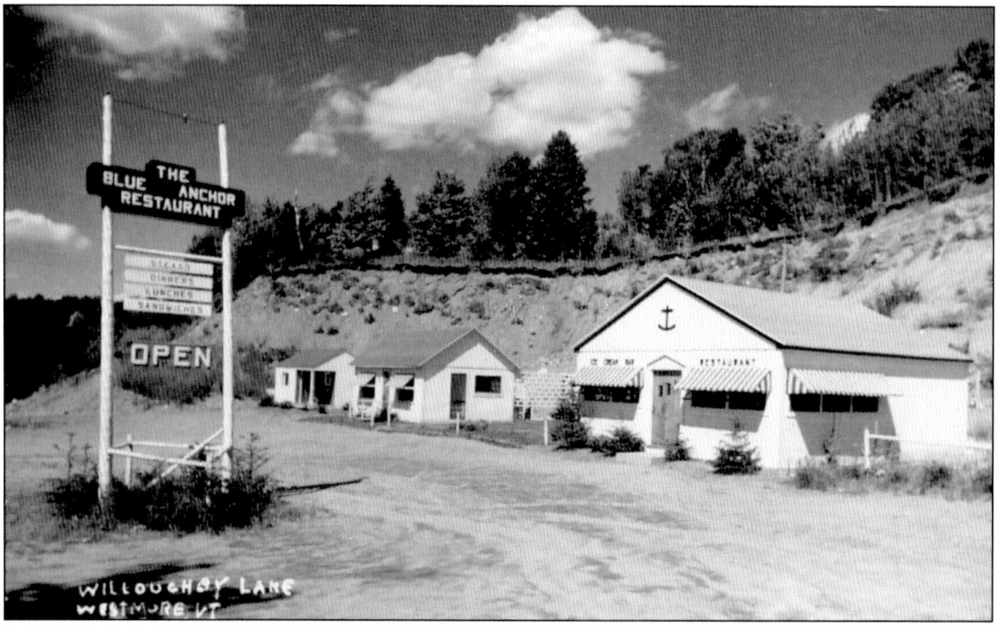

The Blue Anchor restaurant in Westmore, owned by Bill and Anna Johnson, was built in 1948. Located on land carved out of a sandpit, the seasonal restaurant served breakfast, lunch, and dinner, offering booth and counter service. Anna's Sunday turkey dinner was a popular meal. Cabins added in 1949 are still operated by the Johnson family today. The restaurant closed and then was torn down in 1963. (APC.)

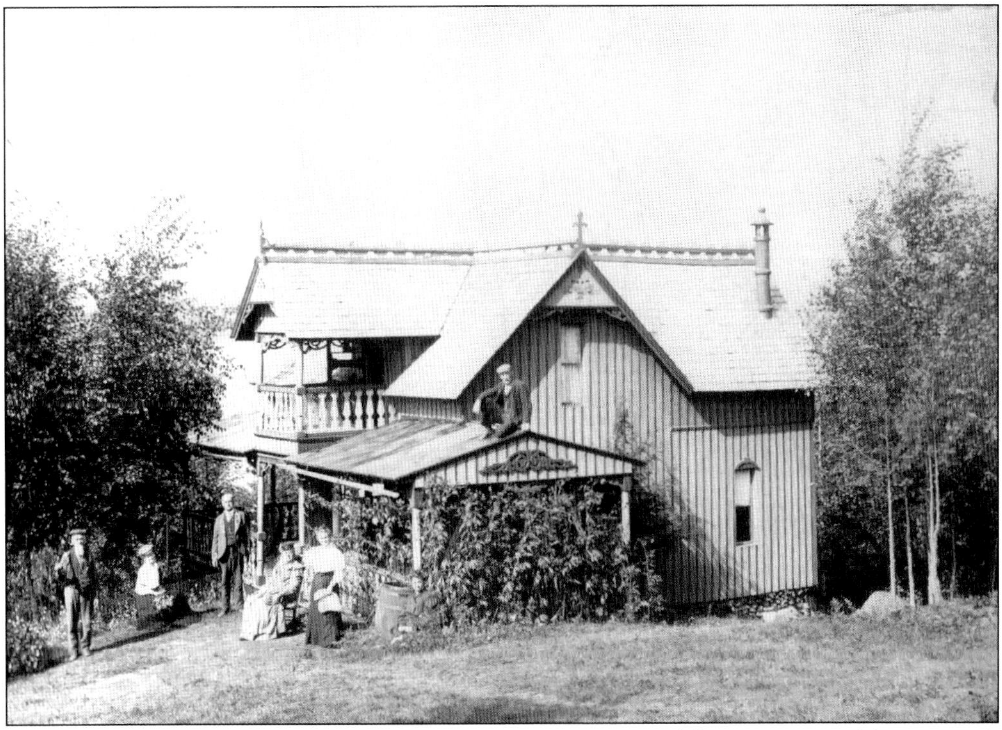

Camps on Willoughby Lake have long been a tradition. Some of them are quite elaborate, such as this one, dated 1905 and owned by R. Perry Porter of West Burke. From left to right are Daniel Skinner, Mrs. R. Perry Porter, R. Perry Porter, Mrs. Daniel Skinner (in chair), Mrs. Porter's sister, Mrs. George Craig (on ground), and George Craig (on roof). (OCHS.)

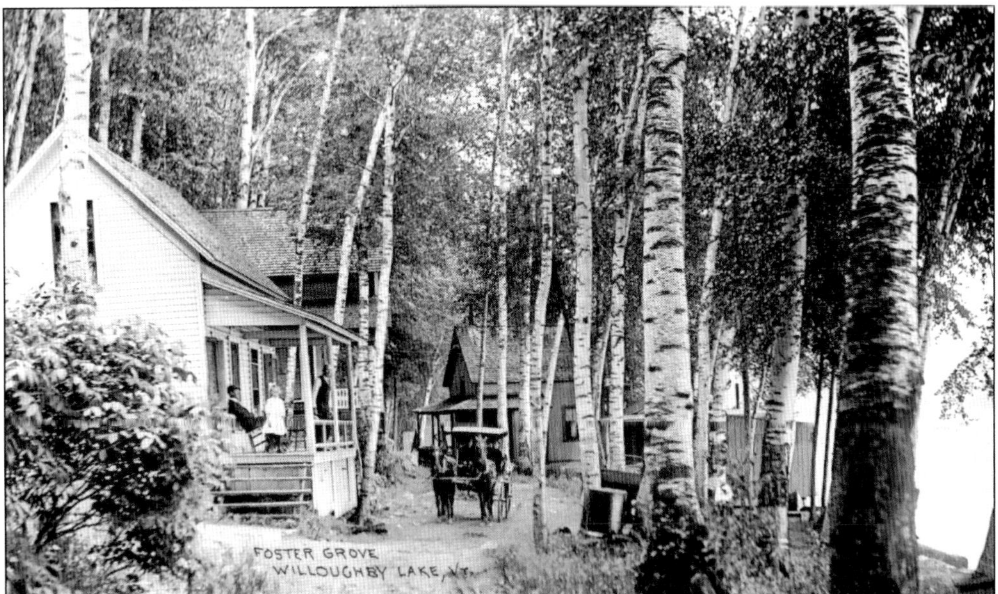

Foster Grove was the name given the area of cottages surrounded by birch trees that sprang up on the east side of the lake, with F. H. Foster having a grand cottage there. The cottages were considered an ideal location for a quiet summer stay. (APC.)

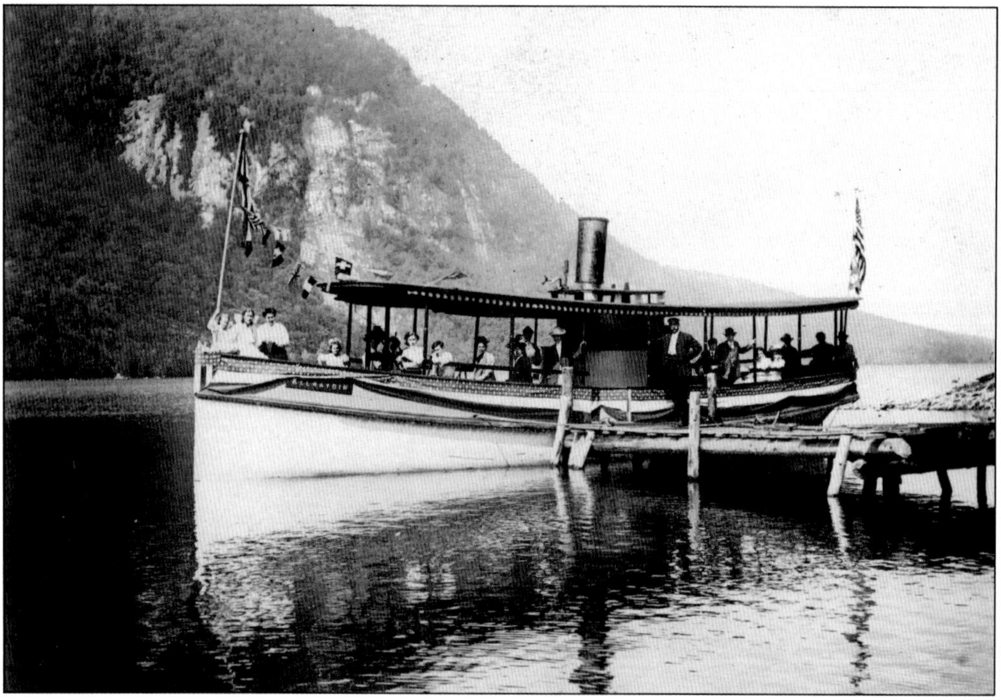

Traveling Willoughby Lake on steamboats was just as popular as visiting the local hotels. The *Keewaydin* was the last steamboat on the lake, as well as the last boat captained by Rufus Averill. The ship burned so much fuel that supplies were needed at each stop along the lake. Steamers were no longer being used by the end of the *Keewaydin*'s run. (APC.)

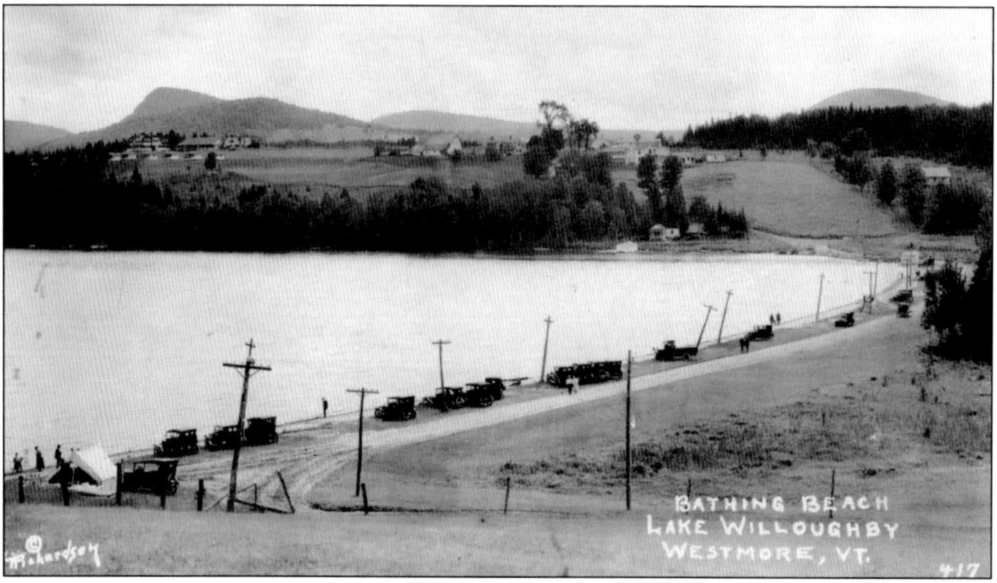

In the 1850s, Lake Willoughby was filled with large trout called muskellunge, some weighing as much as 34 pounds. The North Beach was a popular swimming area for the locals in Orleans County. On the hill to the left of the picture is the Songadeewin Camp, a girls' camp. Songadeewin, meaning "gentle wind," had accommodations for 75 to 120 campers. Activities like canoeing, golf, and horseback riding were the norm. (APC.)

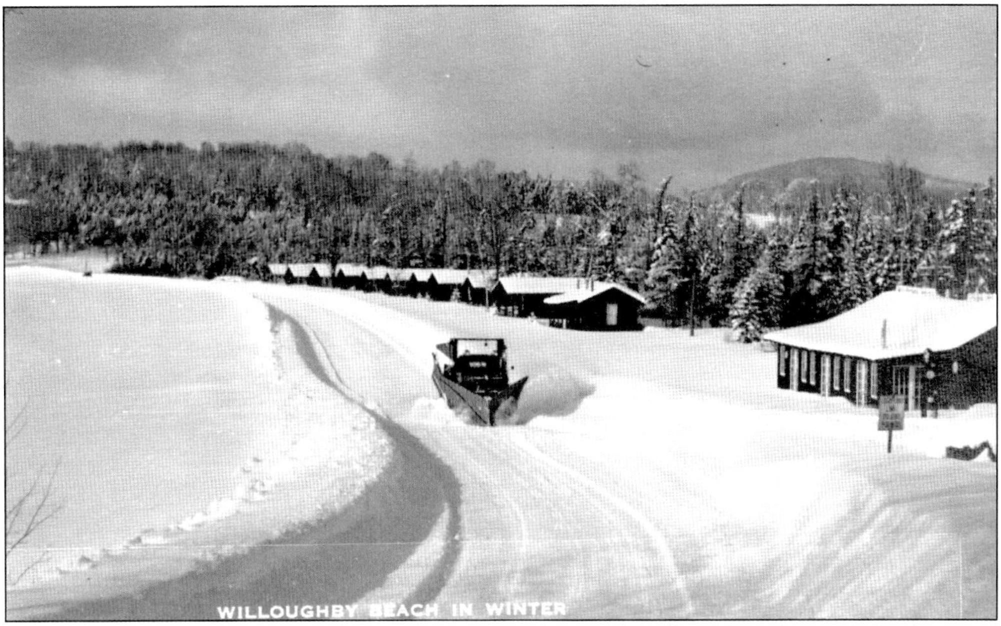

An early automotive snowplow is out clearing the road around Willoughby Lake. In the background are the summer camps used in the warmer months. (APC.)

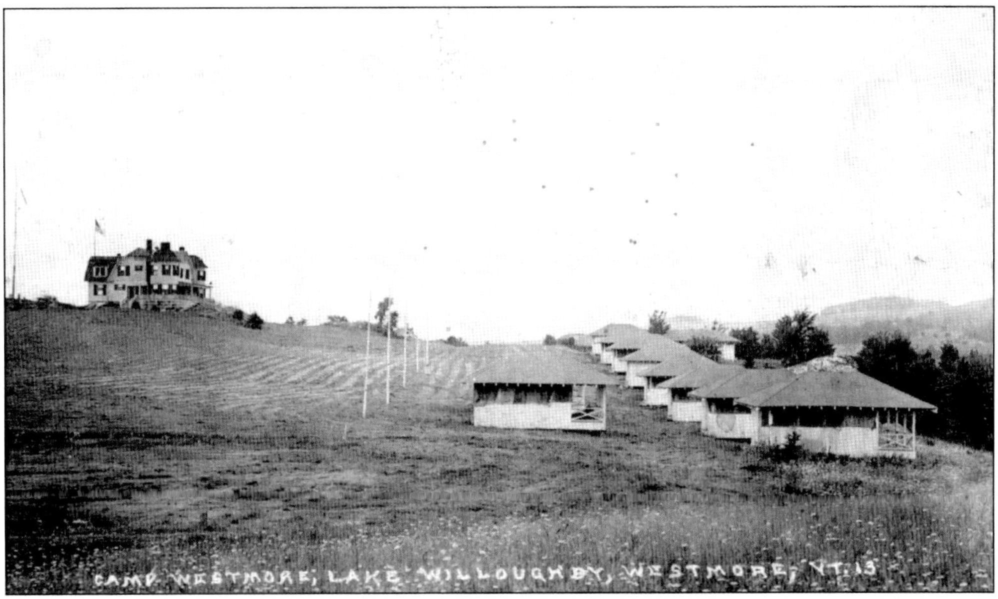

Built in the 1890s as a summer home for John G. and Ava Peene, Fox Hall became part of a popular camp known as Songadeewin in 1921, when Keewaydin Camps of Connecticut purchased the property. The last season of camp was held in 1976. In the 1990s, a local theater group named Outfoxed began their shows in Fox Hall. A few years later, they renamed themselves QNEK, and today they perform at the Haskell Opera House in Derby Line. Fox Hall is now a private home owned by Ken and Sherilyn Pyden. (APC.)

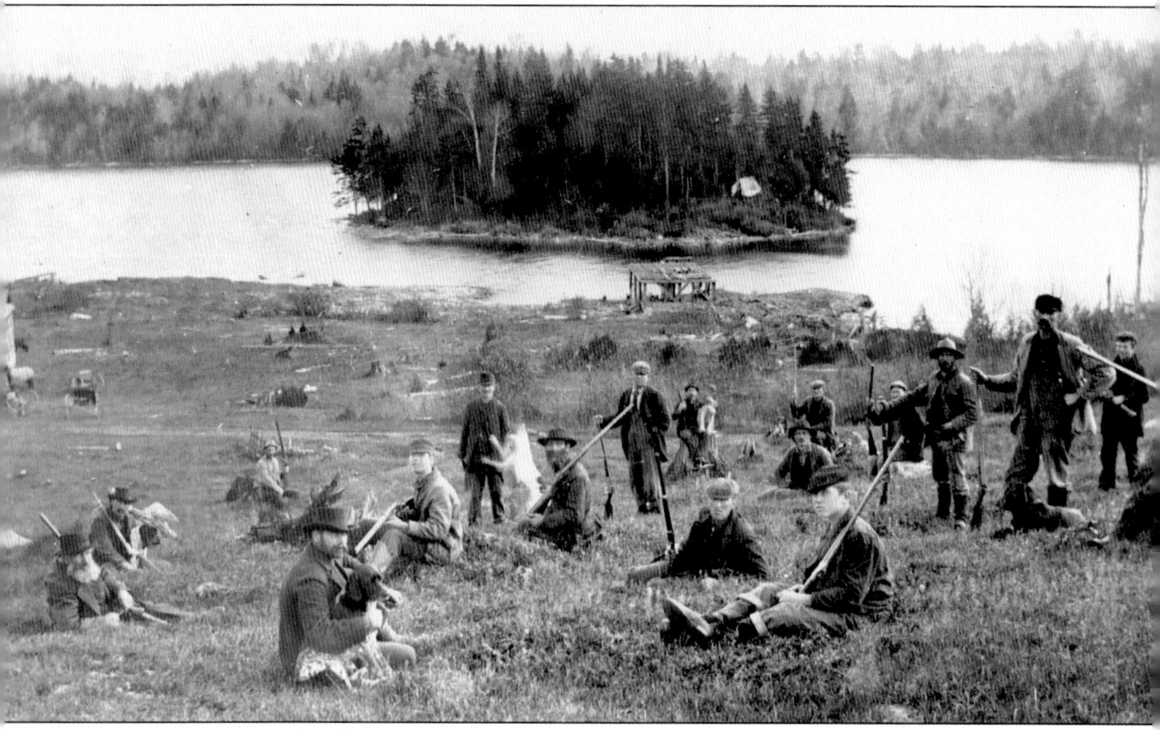

A few miles east of Willoughby Lake is Long Pond, a large pond with an island at one end. This hunting party camped out at the pond and brought their dogs to help them catch their bounty. Today there are many camps around Long Pond with access to boating and swimming. (OCHS.)

Four

Barton, Orleans, and Glover

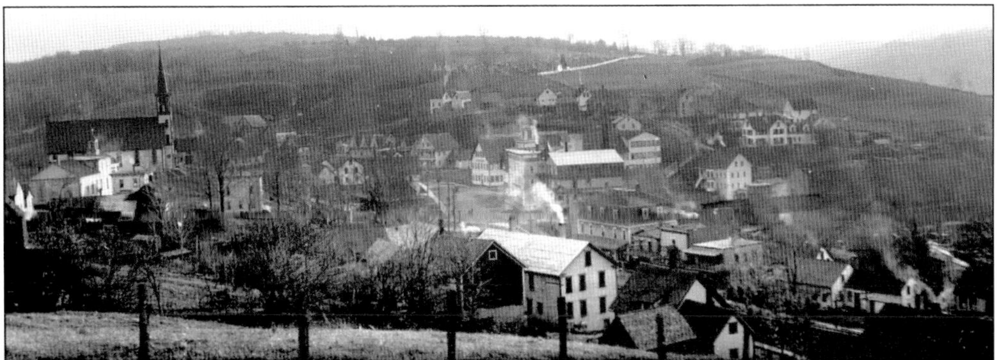

Barton was originally chartered with the name Providence after many of the grantees' hometown of Providence, Rhode Island, in 1789. Barton was incorporated in 1874, containing the village of Orleans, the village of Barton, and the town of Barton. Construction of the railroad started in 1858, with the first passenger arriving in 1863. (RCC.)

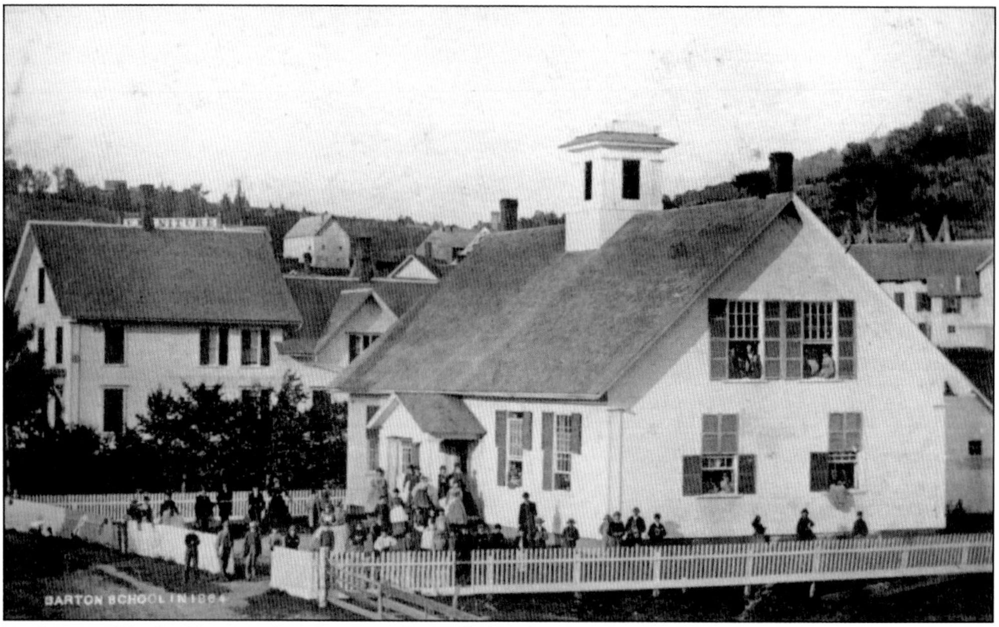

Built in 1852, the Barton Academy and Graded School in Barton Village was both primary and high school. Students had many strict regulations to follow: if a student was absent without excuse, tardy, or misbehaving, he would receive demerits. Every month the parents would be mailed a report on their children's progress and behavior. This picture was taken in 1864. (APC.)

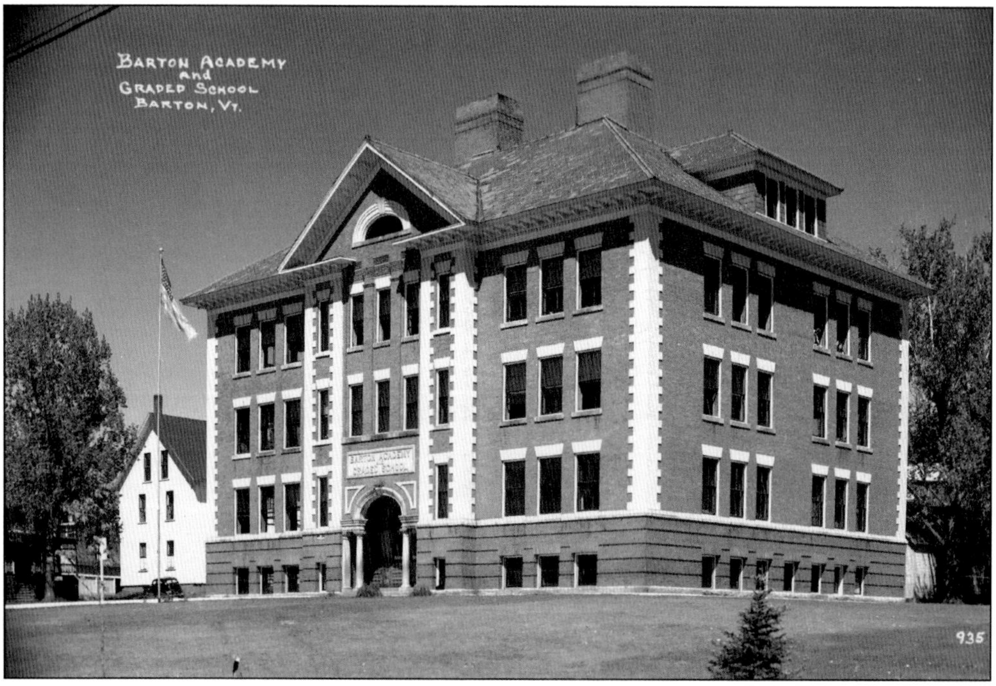

Barton Academy became an incorporated academy and grade school in 1886. This structure was completed in 1908, after the former school building became too small to accommodate the students. This was a high school for almost 60 years until 1967, when the students were transferred to Lake Region High School. (RCC.)

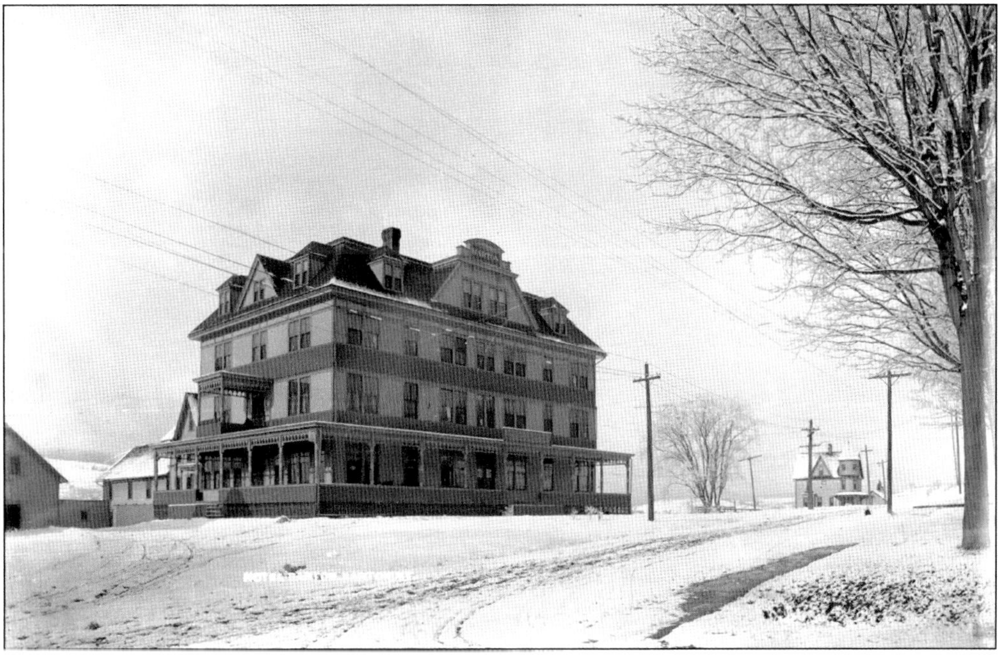

Opened in March 1896, the Hotel Barton had modern conveniences, such as electricity, steam heat, and toilets. Many elderly locals closed up their houses and moved into the hotel from the winter months until the warmer spring months. The hotel burned down in 1971, resulting in one fatality, an elderly woman who was asleep on the fourth floor. (RCC.)

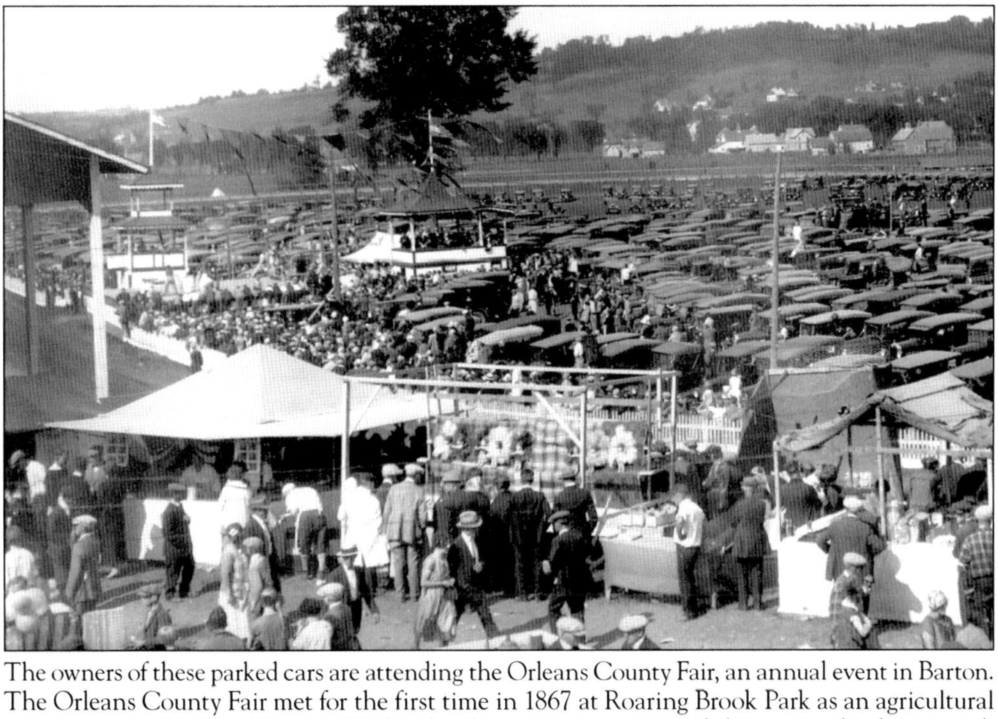

The owners of these parked cars are attending the Orleans County Fair, an annual event in Barton. The Orleans County Fair met for the first time in 1867 at Roaring Brook Park as an agricultural event sponsored by local farmers. Today, families can come to see exhibits, animal judging, truck pulls, and a demolition derby and have fun on rides like the Ferris wheel.

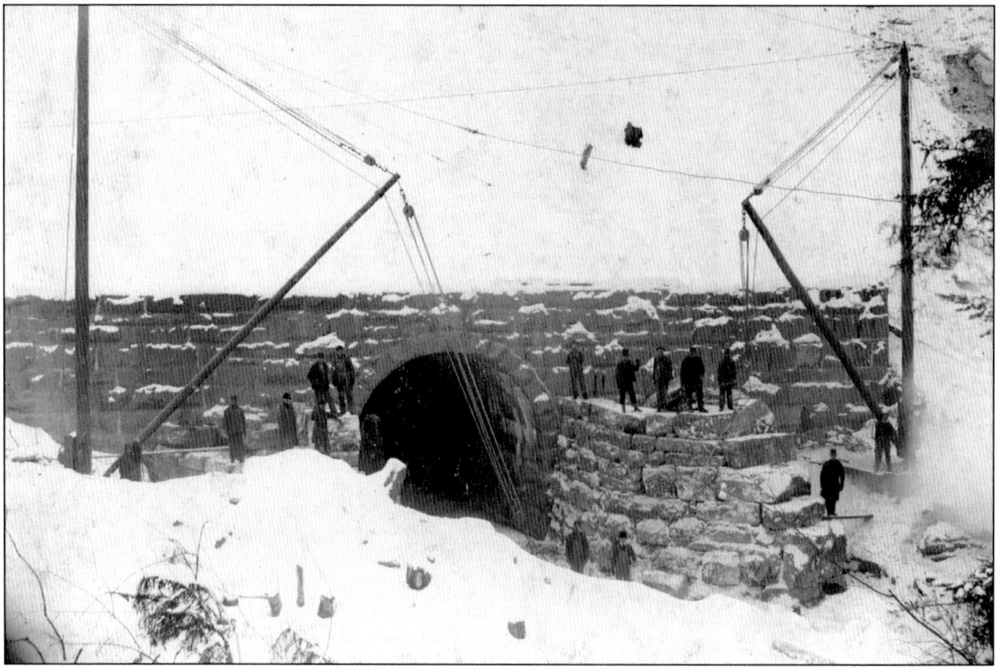

Charles Scott and a railroad group are working on a St. Johnsbury and Lamoille County Railroad bridge, called High Bridge, between Barton and Orleans. The water of Runaway Pond from Glover went through this valley in 1810, following the path of Barton River. (OCHS.)

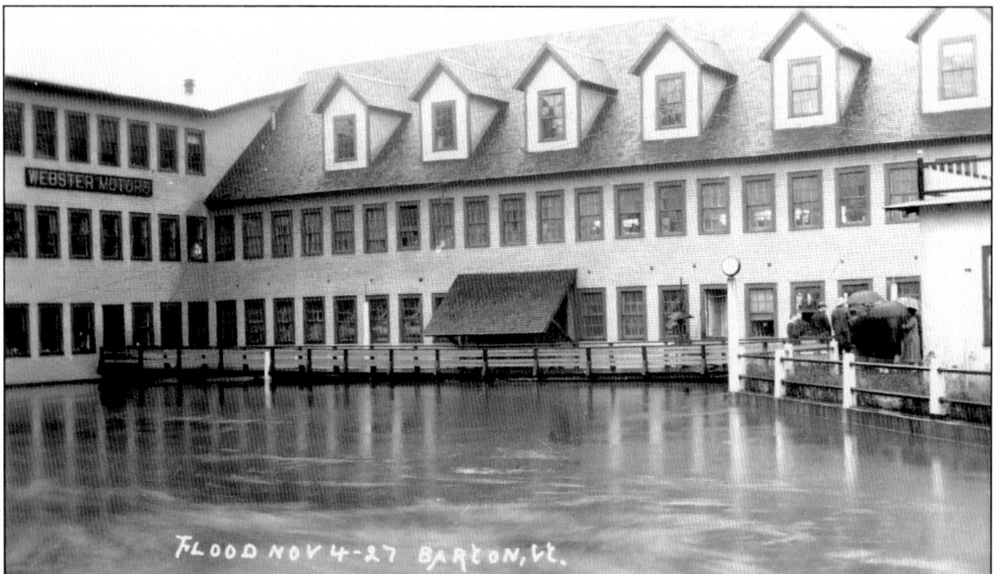

During the flood of 1927, the water of the Barton River quickly rose up to the Peerless Manufacturing building (pictured). The manufacturing plant prevented the water from draining out, and many feared the building would be pushed off its foundation. To prevent this and to allow the water to move freely, a portion of the foundation was removed. (APC.)

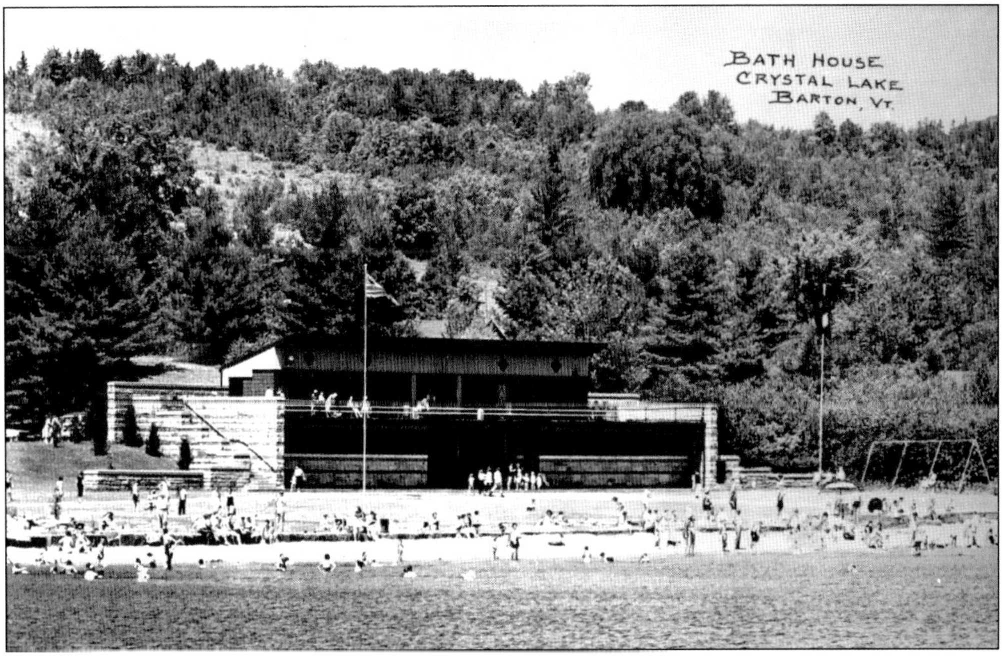

Along the natural sandy beach on Crystal Lake's northern shore, the Crystal Lake Bath House opened in 1942. As part of a public park, this structure had toilets, showers, lockers, and a concession stand for swimmers. The granite foundation was quarried locally along the lake. This historical building is still open today. (RCC.)

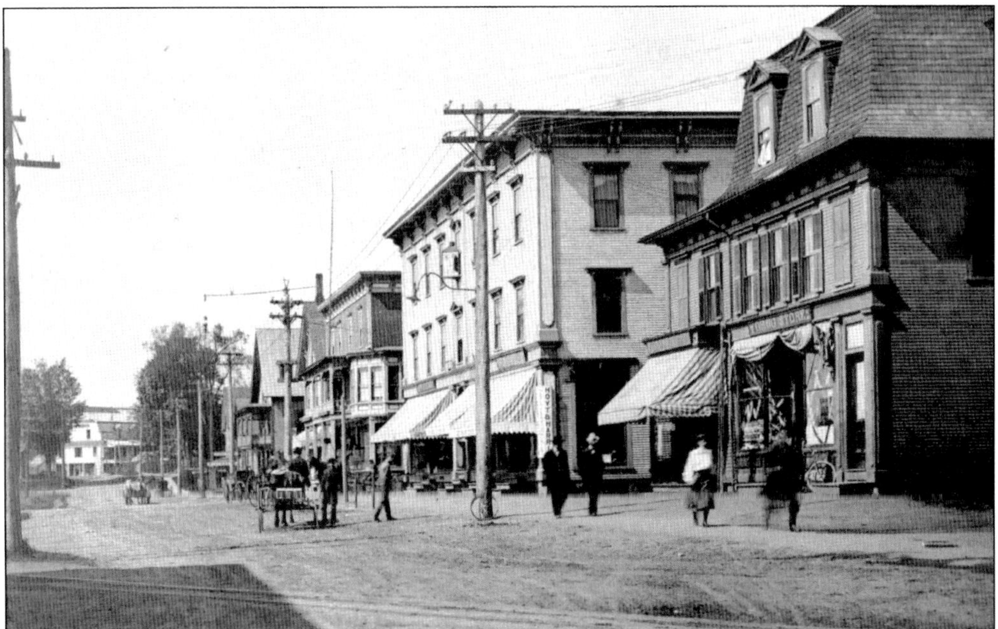
This view of Main Street, Orleans, formerly Barton Landing, shows the businesses in the downtown area. The drugstore on the right was owned by Henry Webster and then sold to Arthur Austin in 1905. Later, Webster's businesses, including the post office, were across the square from the Valley House. (APC.)

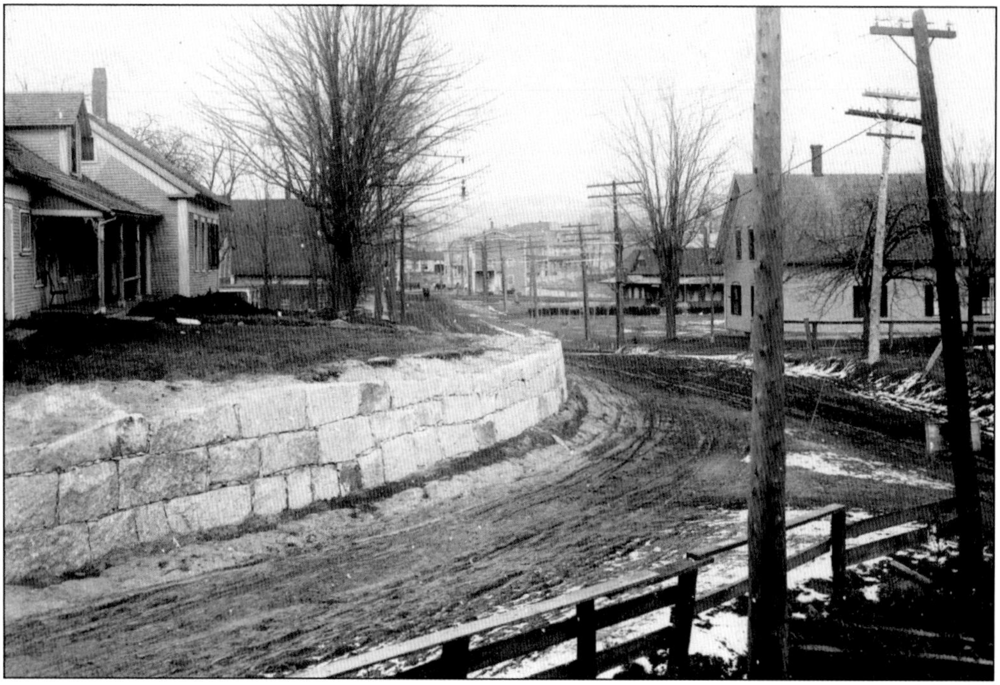

This is the curve of road that merges with Main Street in Orleans. The building at the left was the first schoolhouse in Barton Landing and was originally located across the street. Before the roads were paved through town, travelers had to ride through springtime mud and ruts. (APC.)

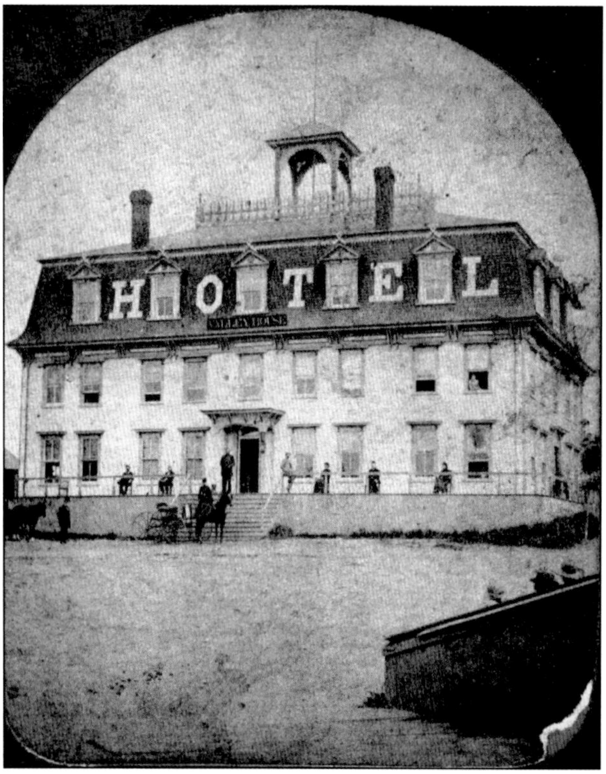

In Orleans, the Valley House, first a tavern in 1833 then an inn in 1875, suffered from fire numerous times throughout its history. It was finally destroyed by a fire in 1998. Written on the back of this picture is "Brown's Hotel, Barton Landing, VT." At the time the picture was taken, John H. Brown was the owner. He owned the Valley House from the late 1870s until 1891. (H. Brooke Paige.)

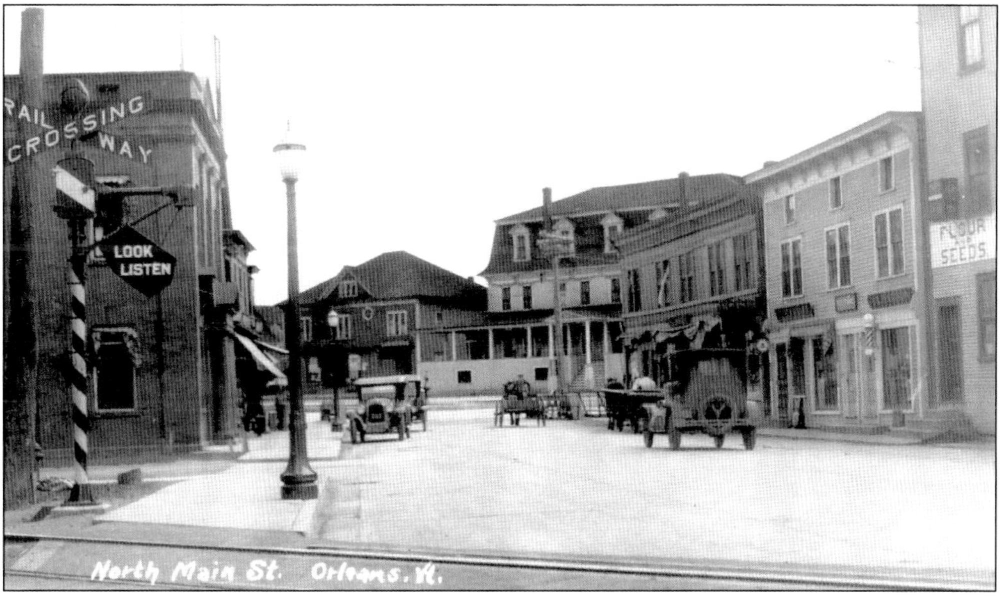

The end of Main Street in Orleans opened up into a small square in front of the Valley House, an immense hotel. (APC.)

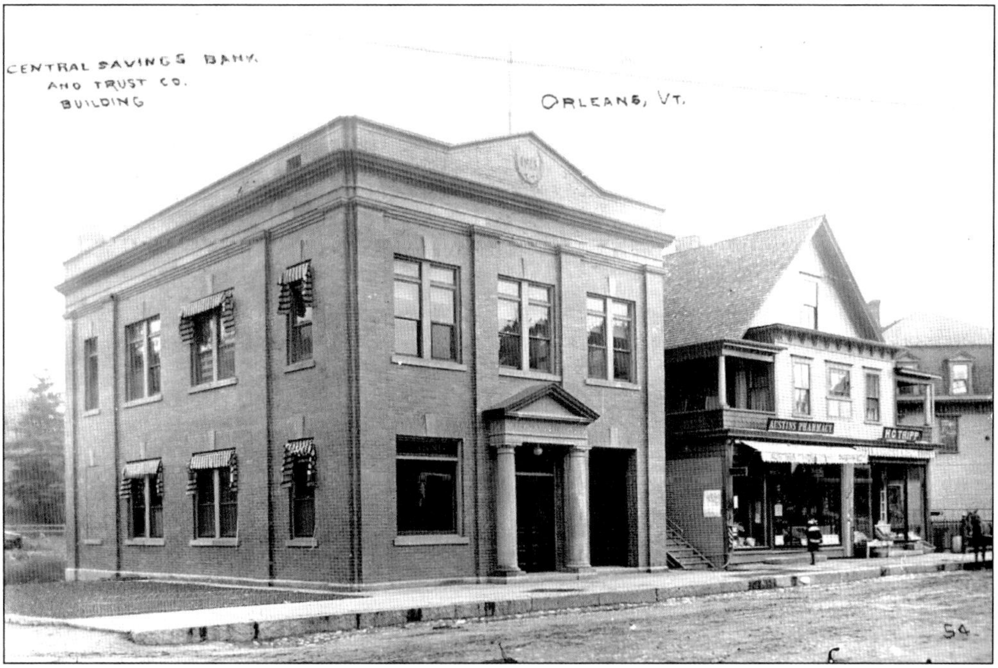

The first bank structure in Orleans was built in 1913. Previously, the Central Savings Bank and Trust Company was in the building next door, which was moved closer to the town square and the river to make room for the new structure. Today, the building is still used as a bank. (APC.)

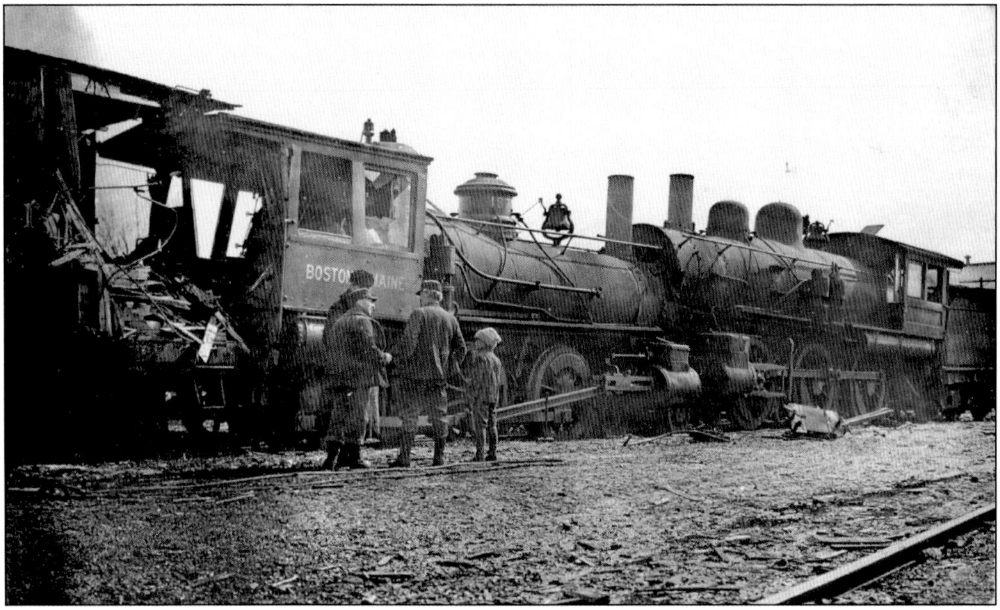

At 5 p.m. on March 12, 1913, two trains collided in Orleans just north of the veneer mill. A result of miscommunication, the northbound train was an extra freight that day, and the two trains were expecting to meet in Coventry. The crews jumped from the trains, except one brakeman, who was killed in the collision. The engines were so crushed together that it took hours to separate them. (APC.)

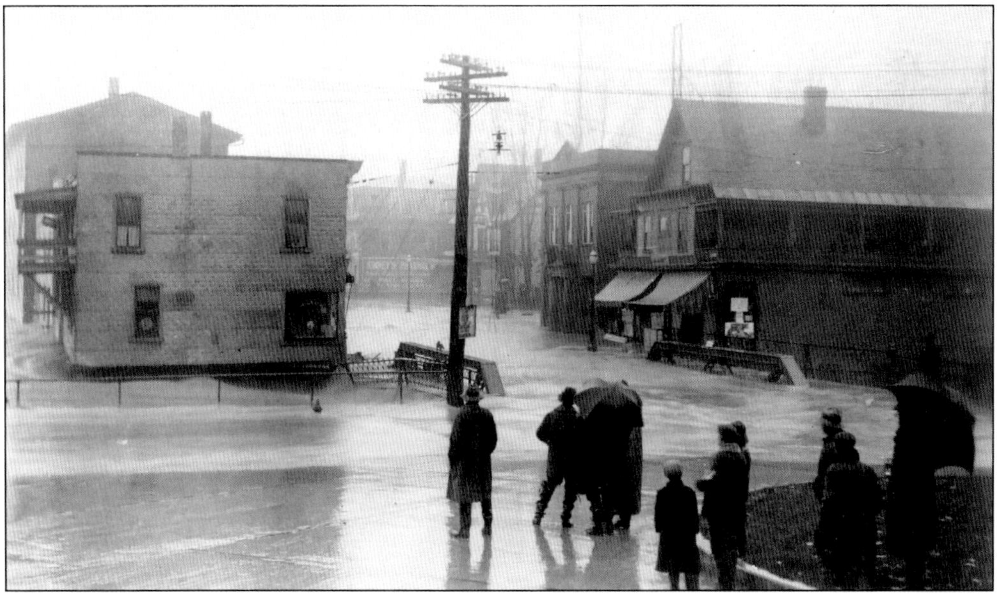

Spectators watch as the Barton River flows through the village of Orleans during the November 1927 flood. (APC.)

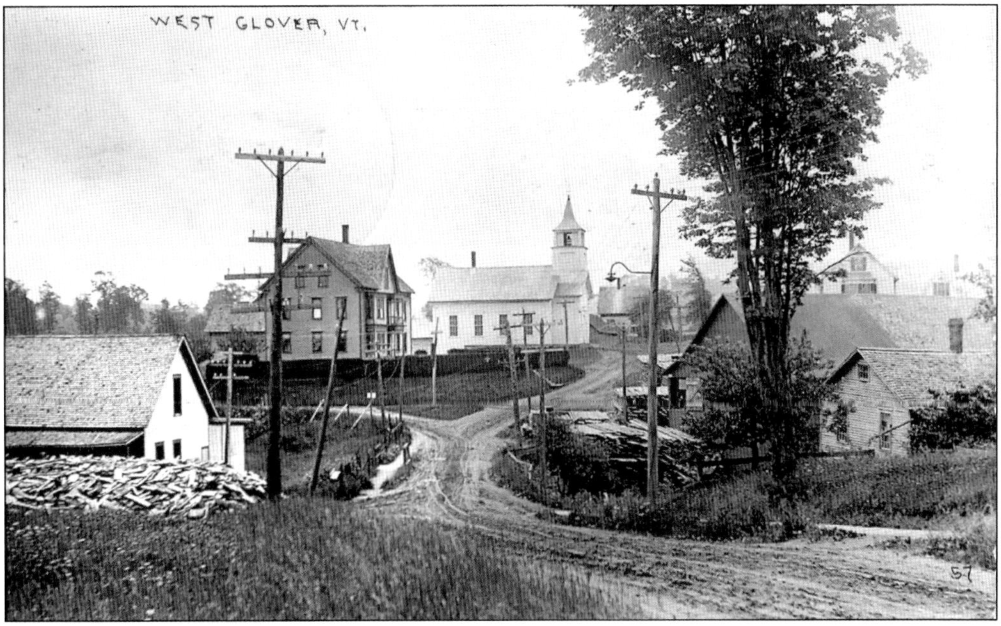

Glover, settled in 1798, contains two villages: Glover and West Glover. The church in this picture of West Glover still stands, though it was not originally here. It was built in 1832 in the Parker Settlement and then pulled by oxen to this location. (Glover Historical Society.)

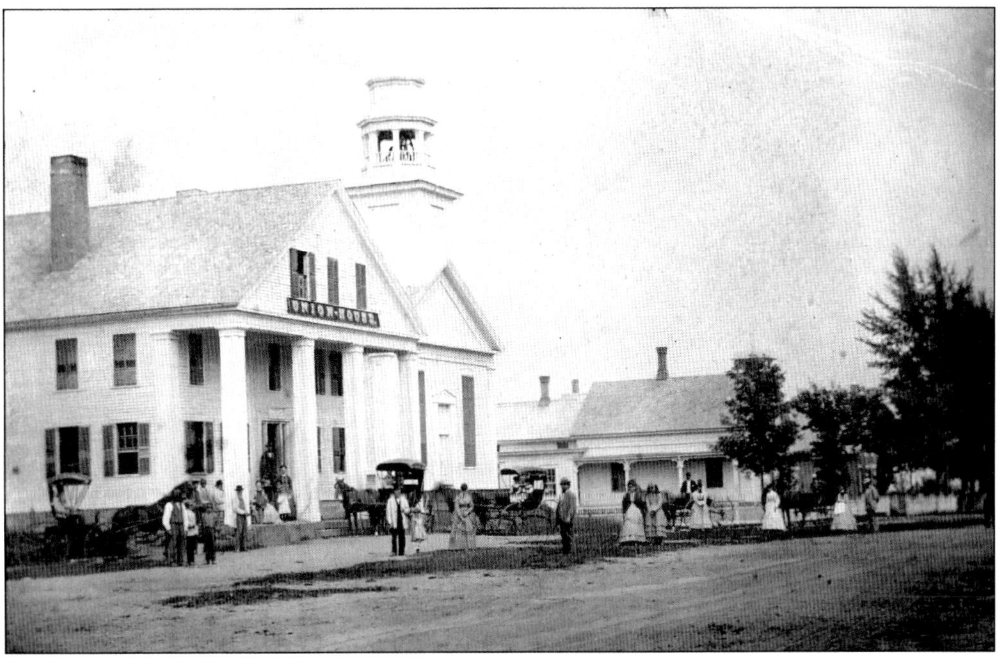

This building was erected as the Union House hotel in Glover Village in 1830. It was the largest hotel in town and was known for its social balls on various special occasions. Across the road from the hotel was a horse barn, where the stagecoach driver could collect fresh horses for his rig. Since the 1950s, the building has been used as a nursing home. (OCHS.)

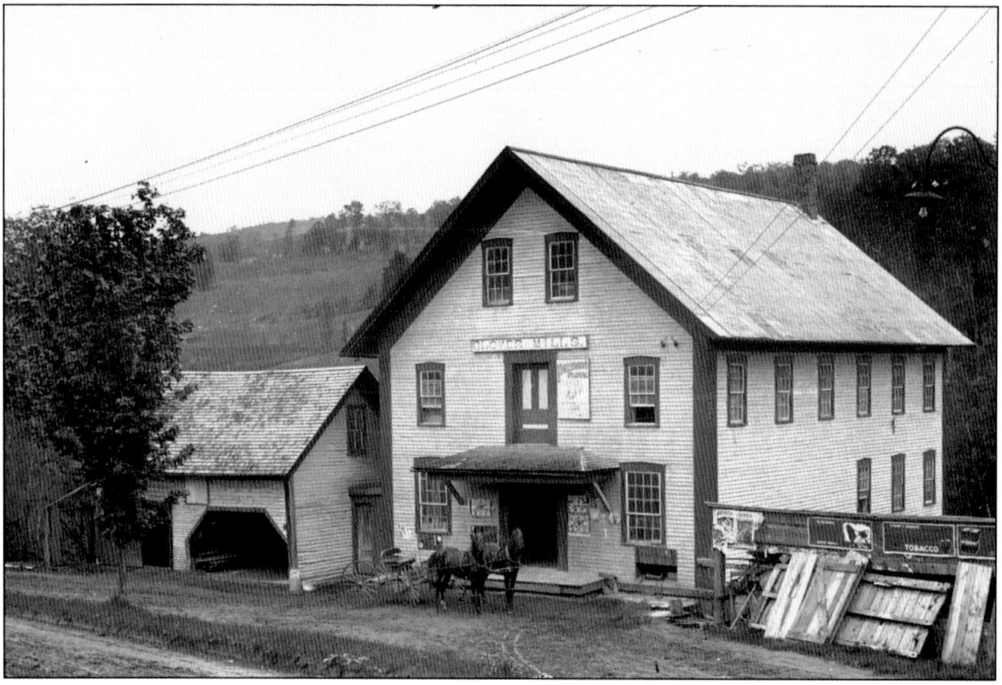

The Glover Grist Mill was one of three gristmills in Glover. The owners created a log dam to provide water power to the mill. In the winter, children would skate on the frozen dam pond. The gristmill burned in 1908, and the dam was destroyed in the flood of 1927. (RCC.)

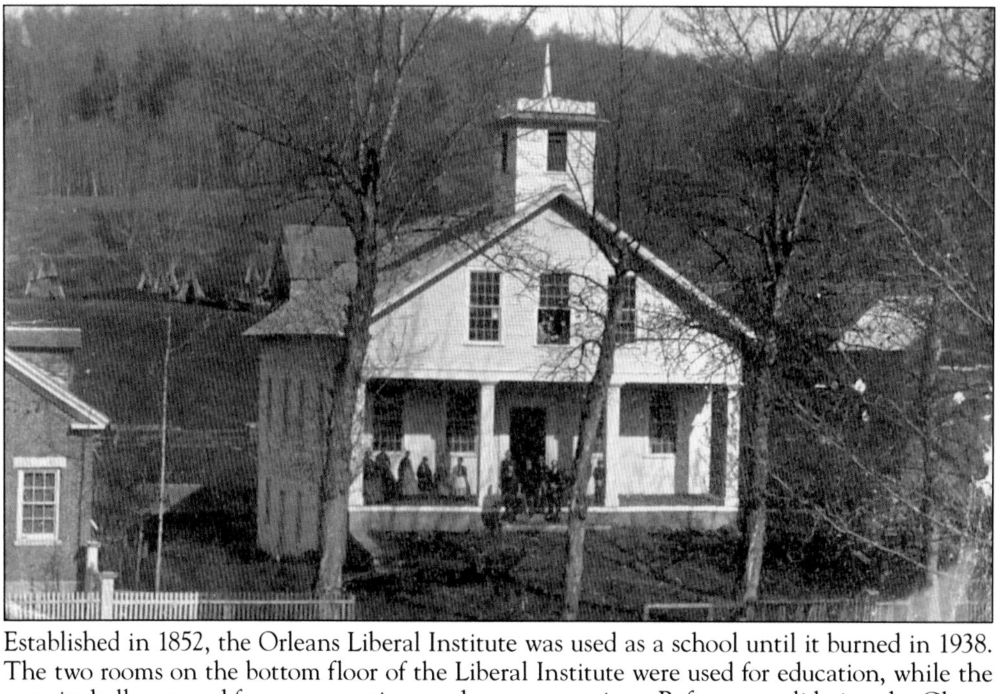

Established in 1852, the Orleans Liberal Institute was used as a school until it burned in 1938. The two rooms on the bottom floor of the Liberal Institute were used for education, while the upstairs hall was used for town meetings and grange meetings. Before consolidating the Glover school system into this one building, students were taught in 14 different districts. This picture was taken about 1890. (Glover Historical Society.)

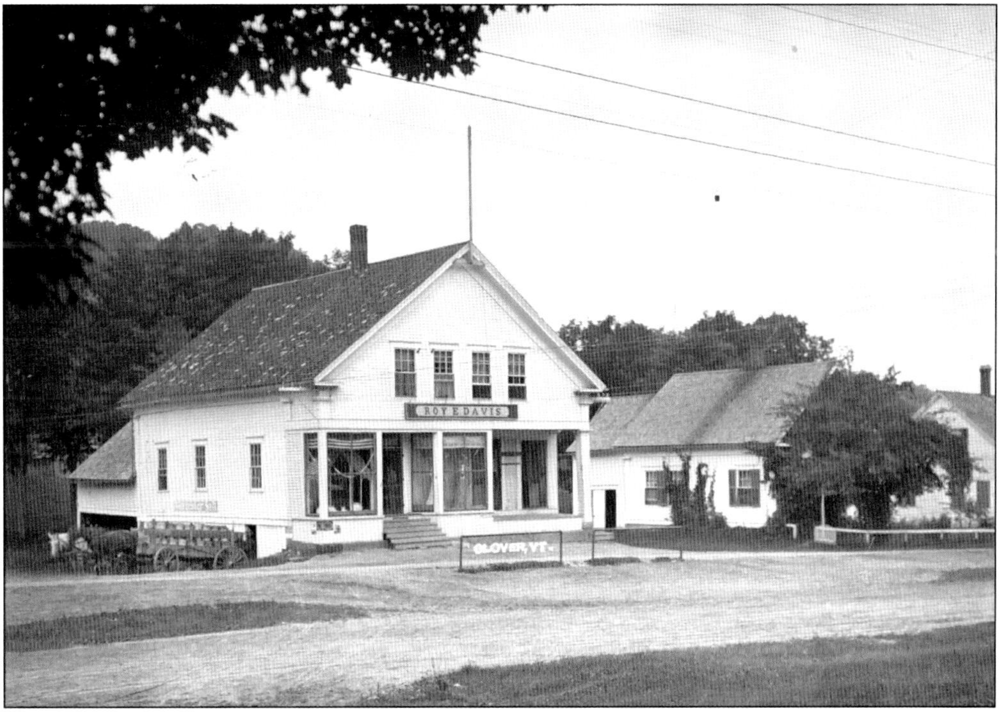

In 1840, a general store owned by Simonds and Conant (above) opened in Glover Village. It passed through a few hands until the early 1900s. In 1908, the building, owned by Roy E. Davis, burned in the fire that destroyed most of Glover's business section. He rebuilt (below) and reopened his store. Again it passed through a few hands, such as Dale Walcott and Carroll Lyon in 1919, until 1967, when the Currier family, including James and Gloria, purchased it and renamed it Currier's Market. The store is still in existence today. (Above, RCC; below, APC.)

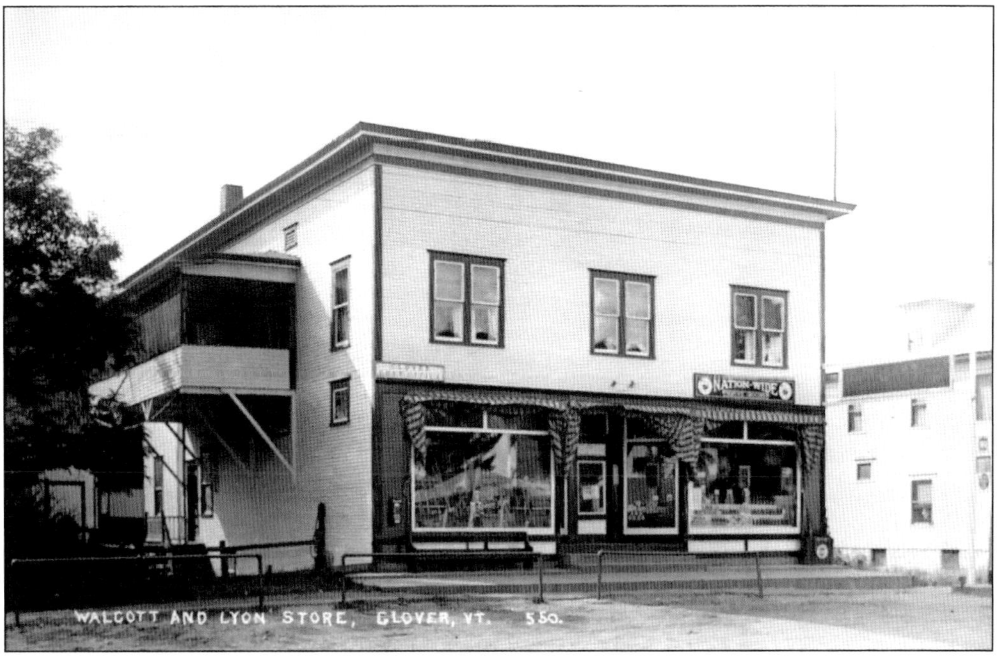

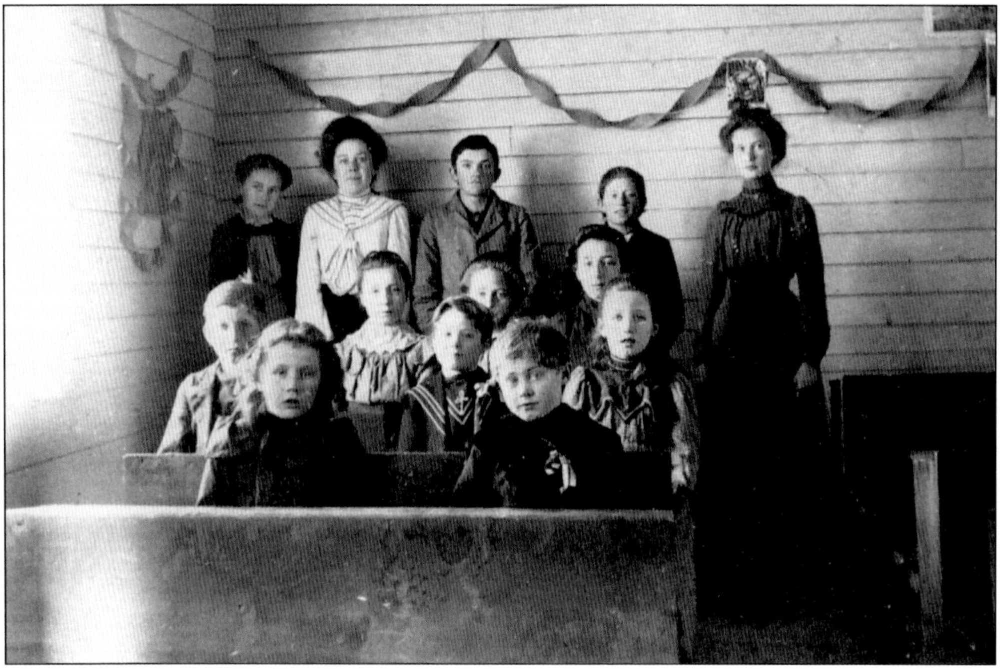

This picture, taken around 1902, shows the pupils and teacher of Maples School in Glover. One-room schoolhouses were common in this district with 10 schools. The teacher in this picture is Mabel Thorpe, and many of the students were from the Lewis and Salmon families. (Glover Historical Society.)

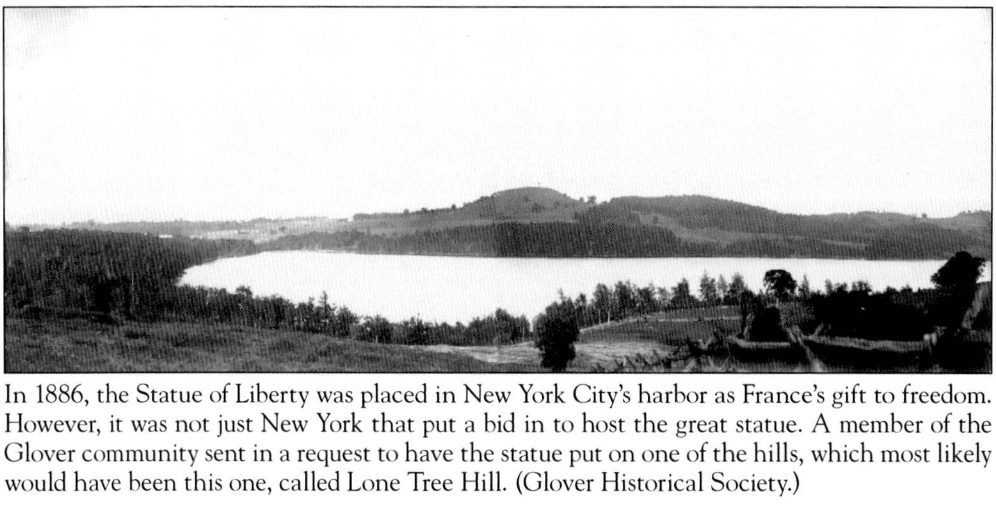

In 1886, the Statue of Liberty was placed in New York City's harbor as France's gift to freedom. However, it was not just New York that put a bid in to host the great statue. A member of the Glover community sent in a request to have the statue put on one of the hills, which most likely would have been this one, called Lone Tree Hill. (Glover Historical Society.)

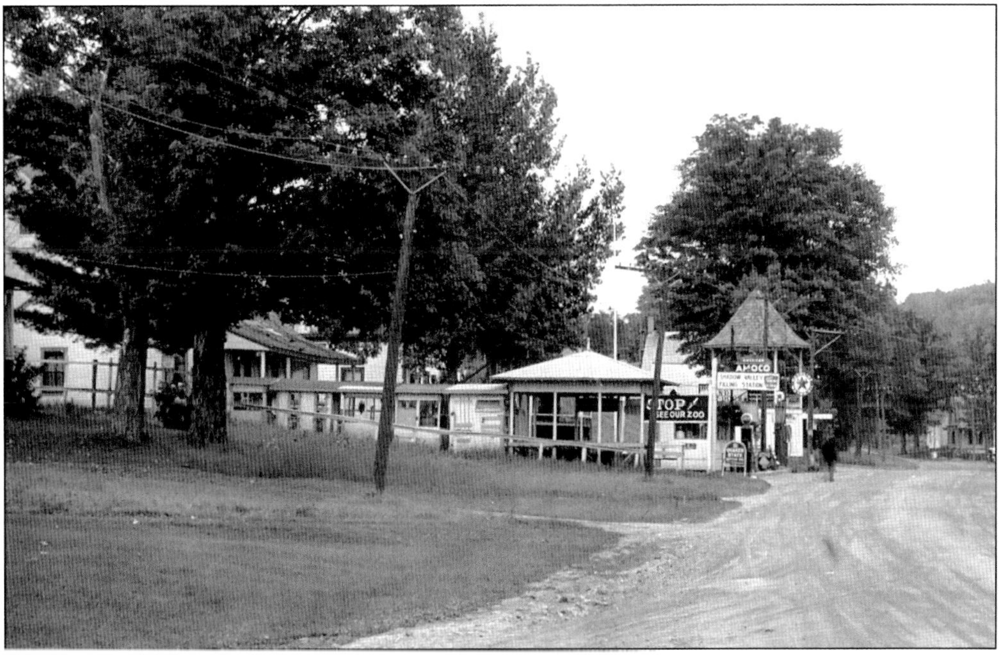

In the 1920s, Wesley Drew built a shack in the village of Glover to sell tobacco and chewing gum, and then he put in a gas pump. He also ran Drew's Zoo, which boasted a bear that would drink from a soda bottle, an African red monkey, raccoons, and a bobcat, among many other animals. The zoo closed down after World War II. (Glover Historical Society.)

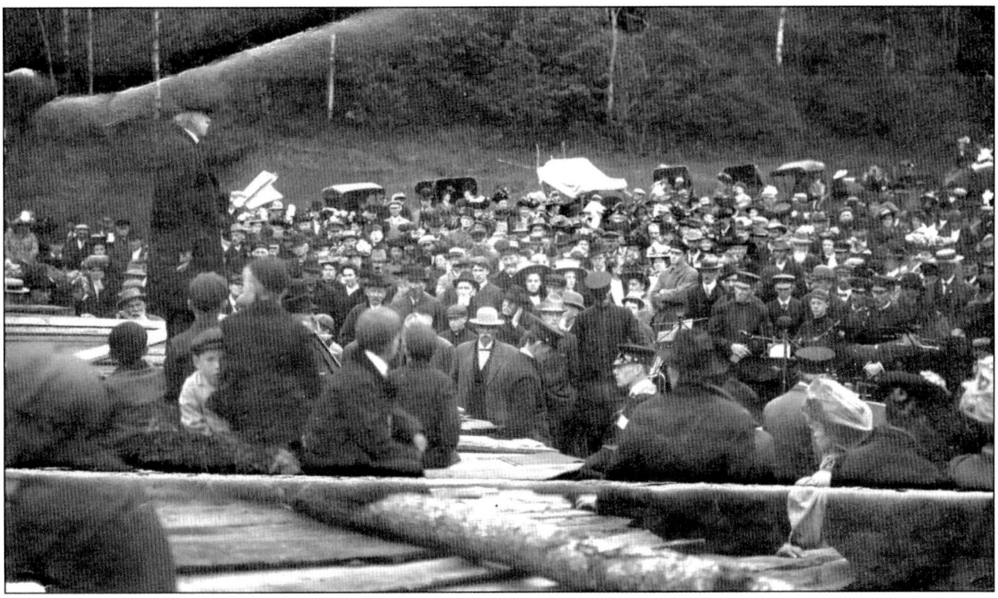

The community of Glover gathered on June 6, 1910, to remember the Runaway Pond disaster. Due to a lack of water in the summer of 1810, the townspeople of Glover dug a channel at the outlet of a large pond so the water would run the mill downstream. They did not realize the ground they were digging was similar to quicksand. It gave way, and the entire pond poured out. In a matter of six hours, the water had disappeared. Today the marshy remains are known as Runaway Pond. (Glover Historical Society.)

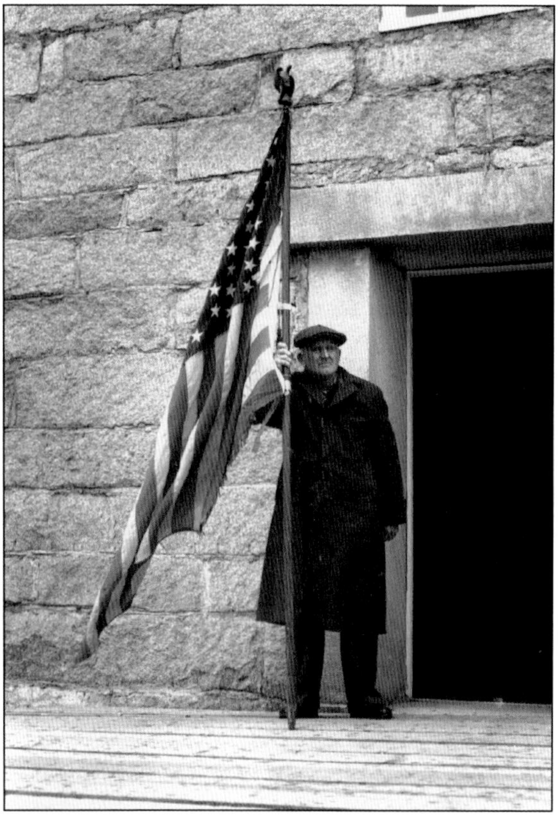

Harry Phillips, Glover's favorite poet, stands here on Old Stone House Day in 1962 with the American flag he had carried in Memorial Day parades for more than 30 years. The flag was a gift to the Masonic post of Glover in the 1920s, and when the post disbanded, Phillips saved the flag from destruction. Harry Phillips wrote the *History of Glover and Runaway Pond*. (OCHS.)

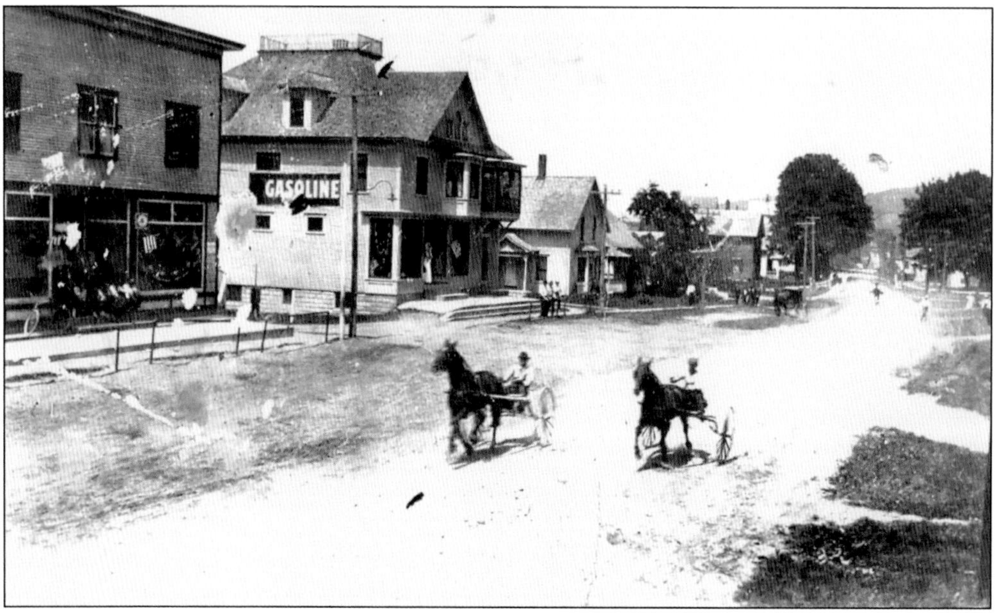

Horse racing was quite the sport in Glover in the 1920s. The Glover Driving Club was all about racing down Main Street in Glover, turning at the taxidermist shop, and letting loose at the bridge for a quarter of a mile through the village. The Glover Driving Club competed with the Lyndonville Club every year. They raced in the summer and winter. (Glover Historical Society.)

Five

Craftsbury and Greensboro

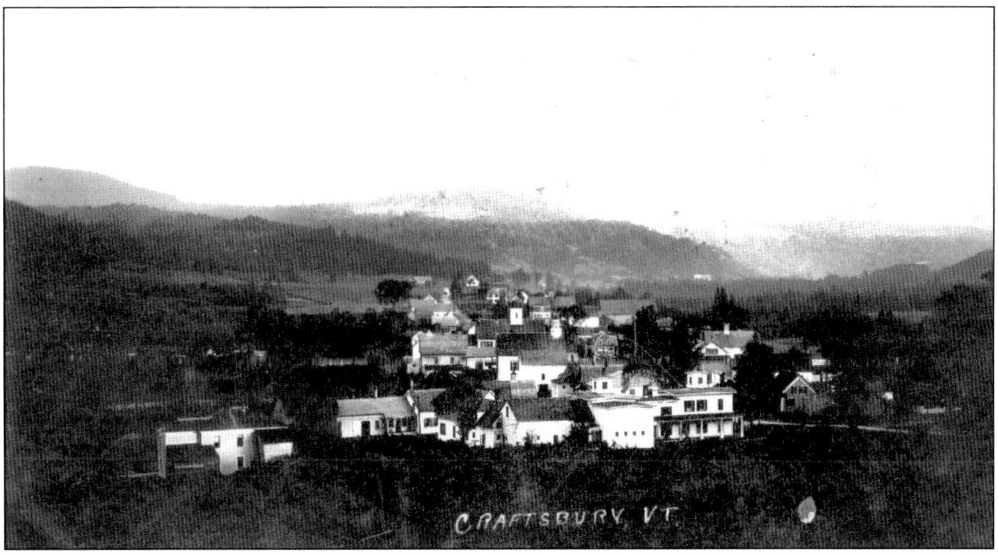

The first settler in Craftsbury, originally known as Minden, was Col. Ebenezer Crafts from Sturbridge, Massachusetts. A former Revolutionary War soldier, Crafts arrived in 1789. The next year, the town changed its name to Craftsbury to honor him. (APC.)

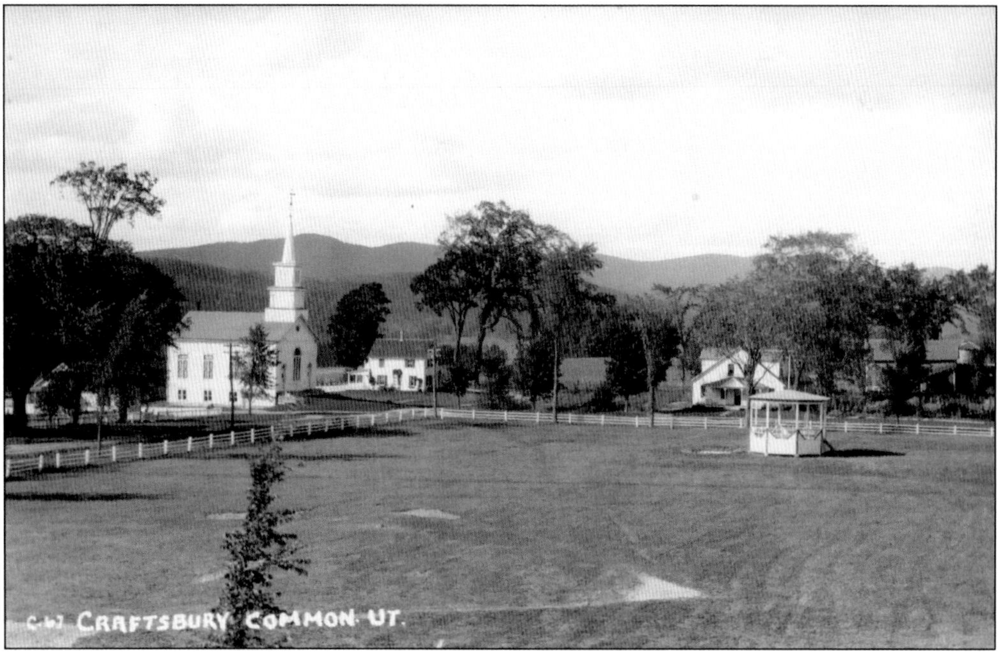

Craftsbury Common, the first settlement in Craftsbury, was established as a hill town, where the air was clearer with no wetlands. The land shown in the center of the picture was used by the townspeople to graze cattle and plant community crops. Two towns in Orleans County have this distinct, square common: Craftsbury and Irasburg. (Craftsbury Historical Society.)

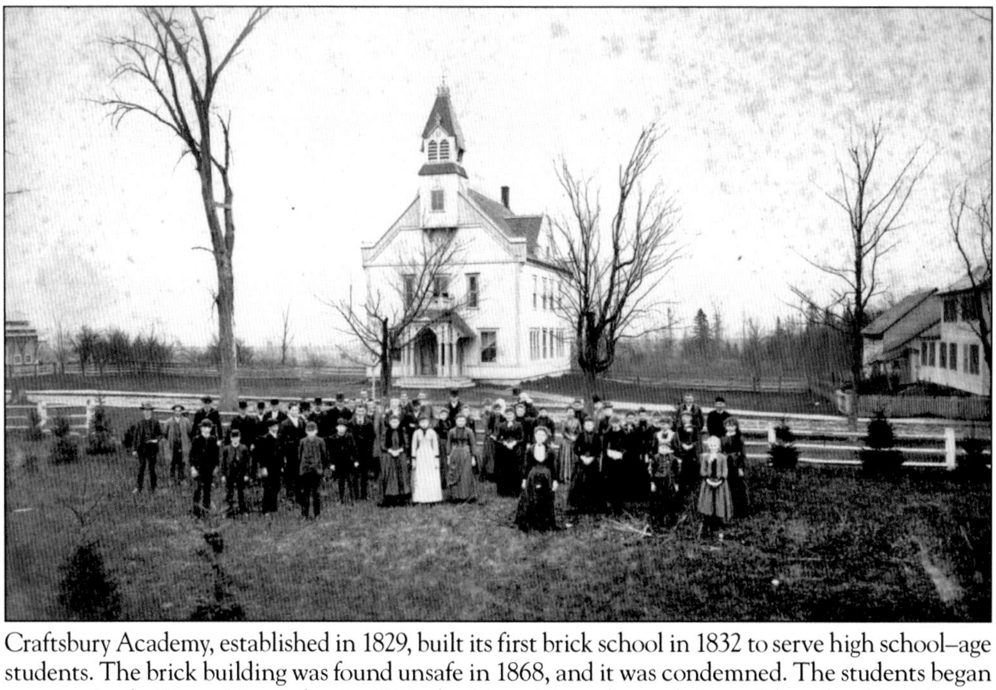

Craftsbury Academy, established in 1829, built its first brick school in 1832 to serve high school–age students. The brick building was found unsafe in 1868, and it was condemned. The students began meeting in the Town House, but in 1879, the Town House burned down. The school building in the center of this photograph was erected in the same area as the Town House. This picture is dated around 1890. (Craftsbury Historical Society.)

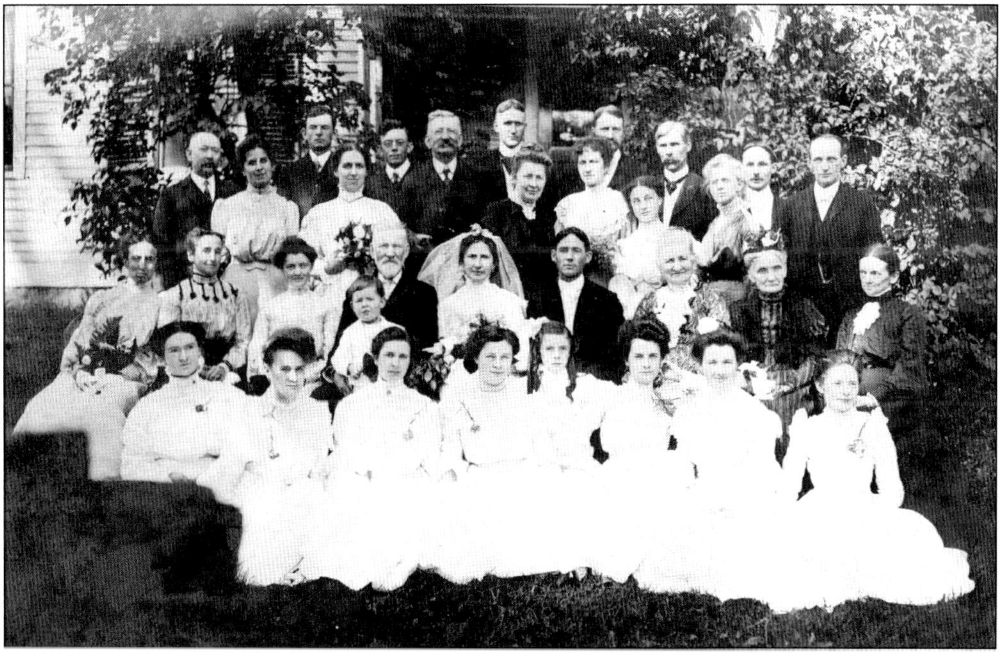

This is a picture of a wedding party in September 1904 in North Craftsbury. The bride is Mary Crafts Paddock, daughter of Augustus and Mary Paddock. She married Frank Hazen, a minister. Most of the people in this group are members of the Dustin and Paddock families, descendants of Ebenezer Crafts. (Craftsbury Historical Society.)

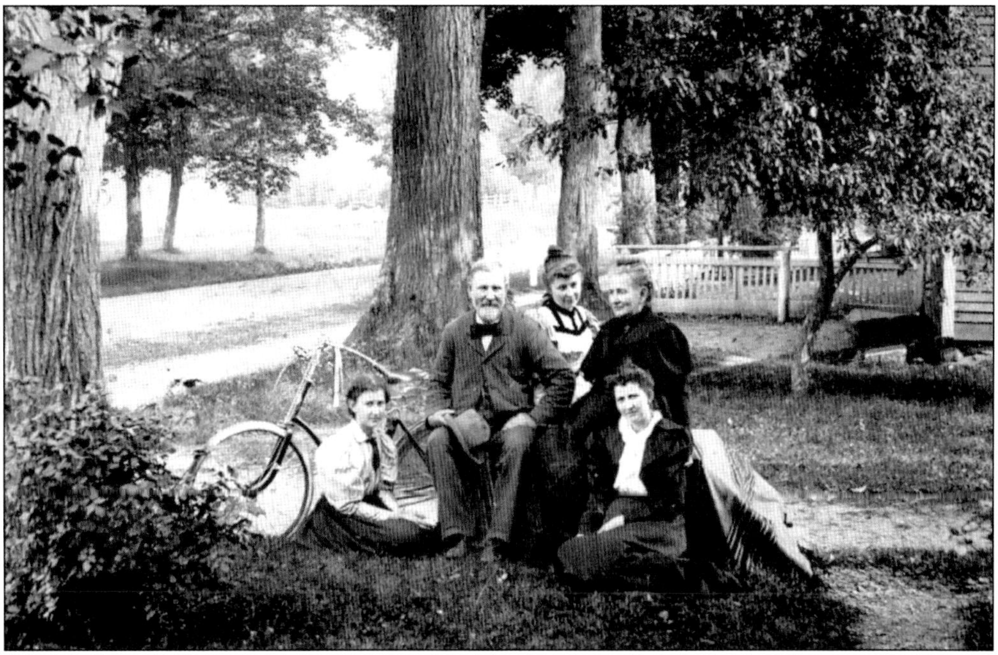

Augustus Paddock sits with his wife and daughters in front of his house around 1900. Augustus and his wife, Mary, were cousins, both descendants of Ebenezer Crafts. He was a Civil War veteran who served in the 1st Vermont Cavalry. His wife died of yellow fever while visiting her eldest daughter, who was a missionary in India. (Craftsbury Historical Society.)

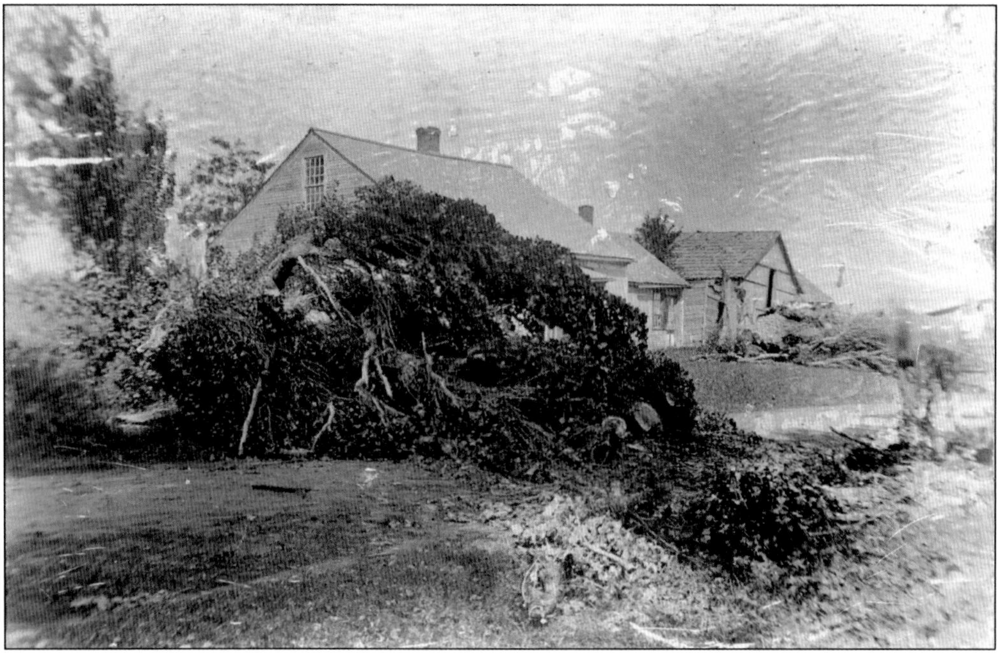

On September 4, 1898, a destructive storm blew through and took down numerous trees in Craftsbury. The *Orleans County Monitor* called it a "terrible cyclone." One resident of the town, Martin Johnston Jr., was knocked unconscious for 24 hours after he received an electric shock during the storm. (Craftsbury Historical Society.)

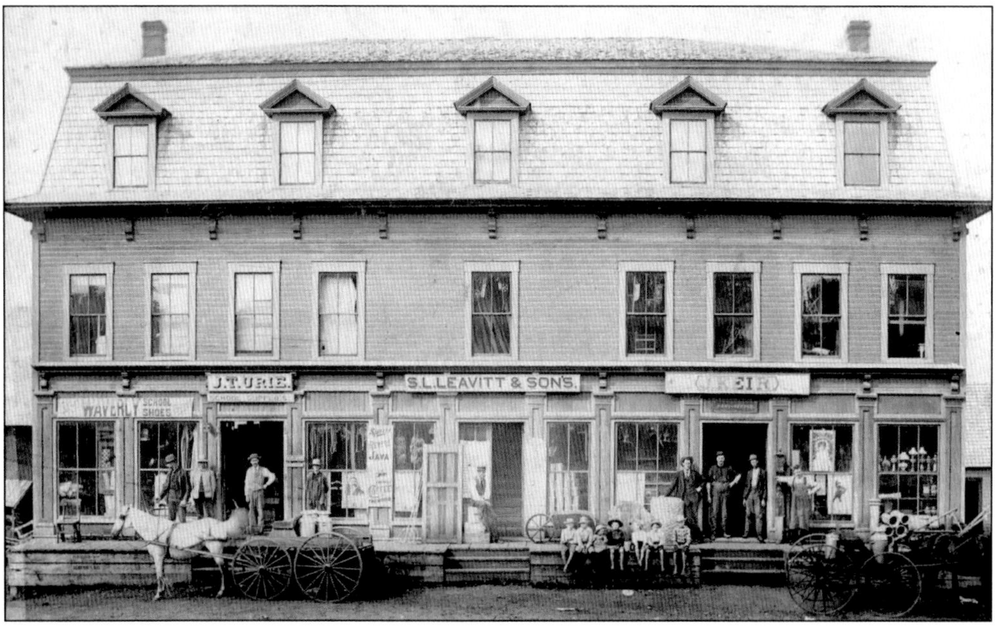

This building was known as the Leavitt Block in Craftsbury Village. Stephen Leavitt ran a general store here in the late 1800s. John Keir operated a tin shop that sold stoves and maple sugaring equipment, and the post office was also located in his shop. J. Urie ran a general store that specialized in school supplies. (Craftsbury Historical Society.)

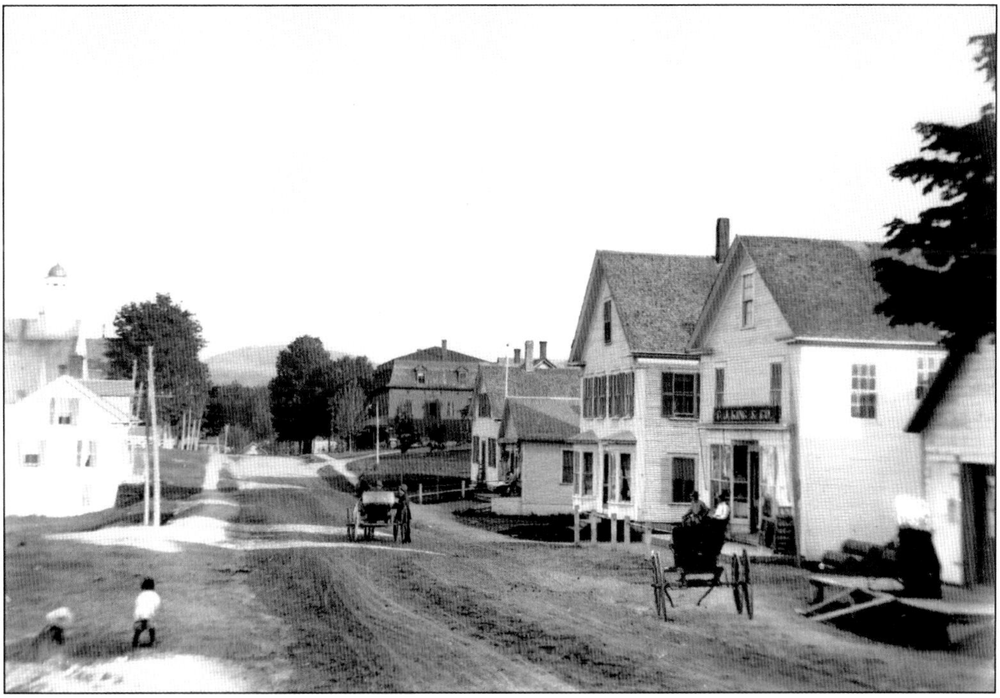

Here is Main Street in Craftsbury village looking south early in the 1900s. The area suffered two major fires shortly after this picture was taken. The C. J. King & Company store is now the local Masonic hall, complete with a slightly charred interior attesting to how close it came to going up in smoke as well! (RCC.)

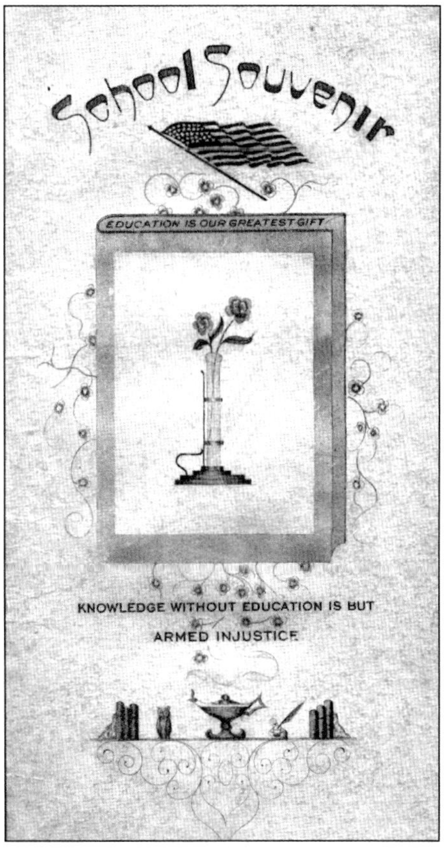

The Village School in Craftsbury used this pamphlet to list the student names in 1930 as well as provide poetry for reader enjoyment. The teacher that year was Cora B. Wylie. (Craftsbury Historical Society.)

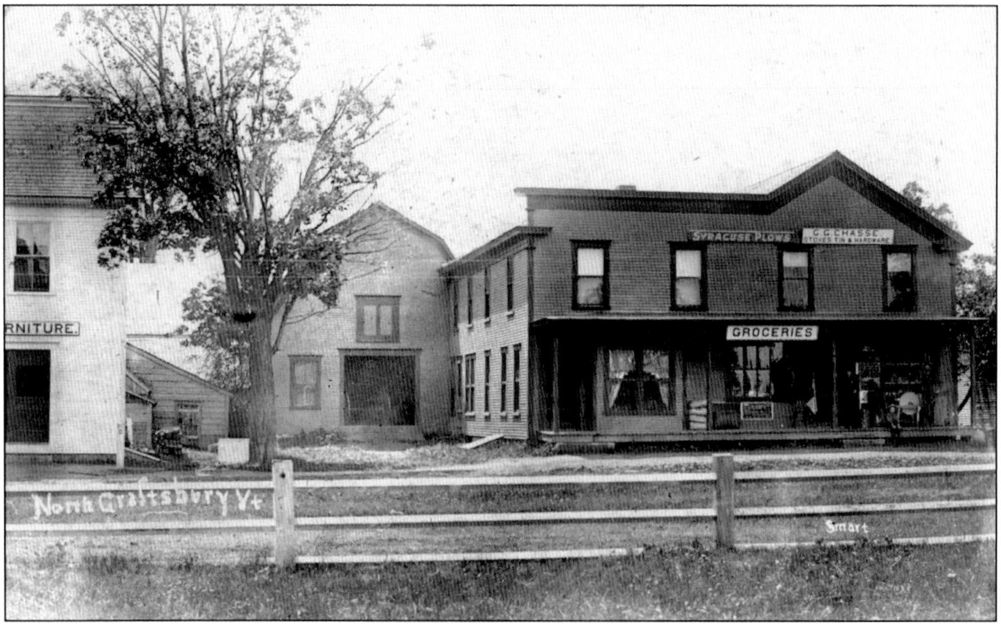

G.G. Chasse's Groceries and Hardware store was located in North Craftsbury, also known as Craftsbury Common. On December 30, 1935, these buildings were destroyed by fire. Named the Farrar Block after the building's owner, it contained a general store, post office, the Farrar private residence, and the residence of Craftsbury Academy's principal, Daniel Dyer. The fire started from an unobserved stove in the car shed. (APC.)

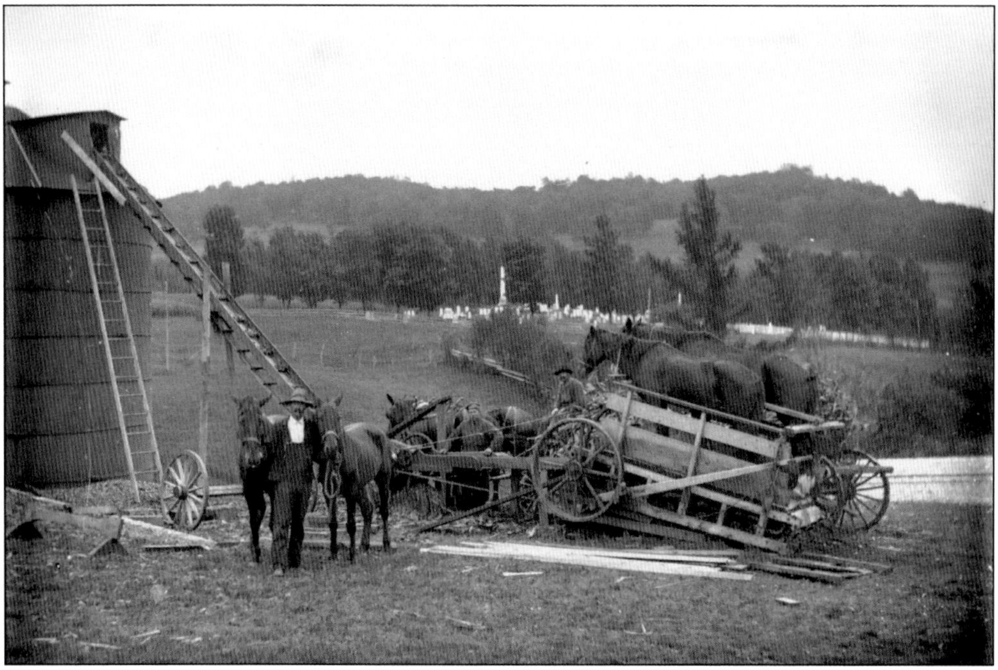

In East Craftsbury, these farmers at the Brassknocker Farm are using a horse-operated corn cutter and then filling their silo. The East Craftsbury Cemetery is just behind on the next hill. (Craftsbury Historical Society.)

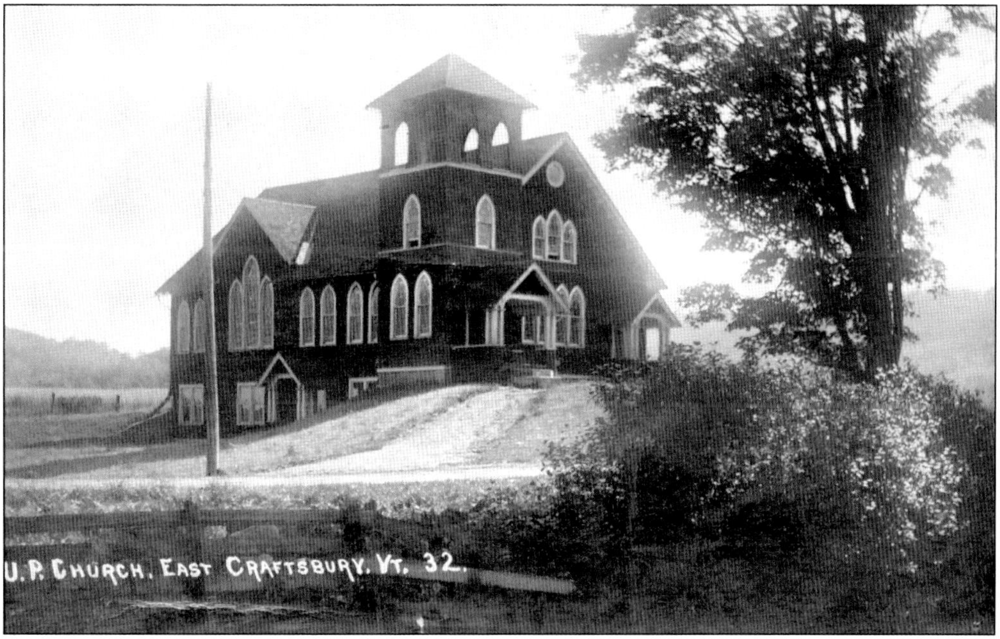

East Craftsbury was settled mainly by immigrants from Scotland, who were Presbyterian in denomination and were referred to as the Covenanters. The United Presbyterian church above was dedicated on January 26, 1910. This was the second building for Presbyterians in Craftsbury. (APC.)

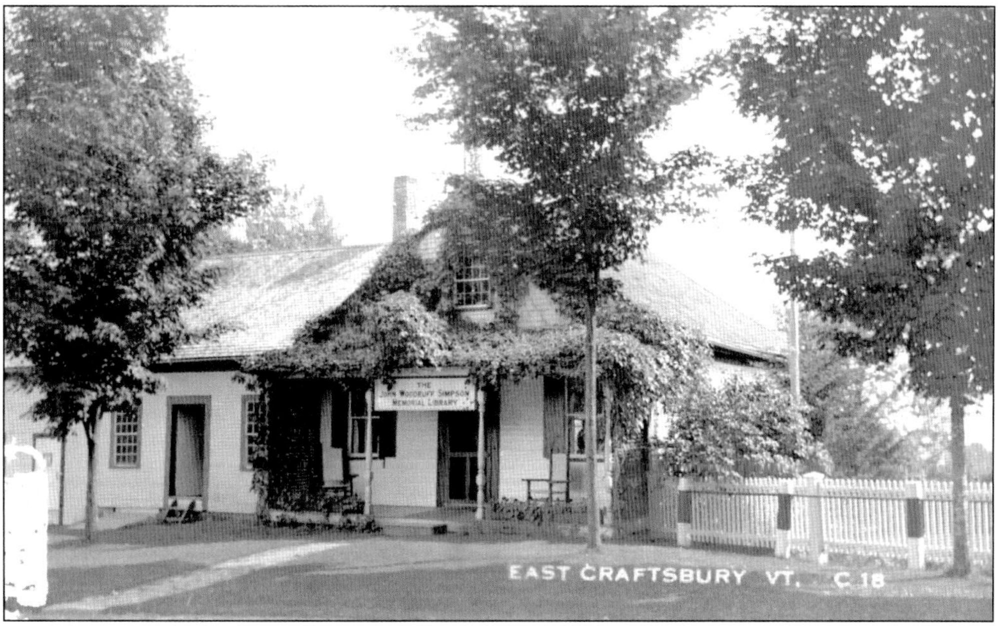

James Simpson and his son George ran a general store in this building in East Craftsbury from 1847 to 1914. Jean W. Simpson, granddaughter of James, founded the library on July 2, 1921, in memory of her father, John Woodruff Simpson. Born in East Craftsbury in 1850, John went on to be a distinguished lawyer in New York. (APC.)

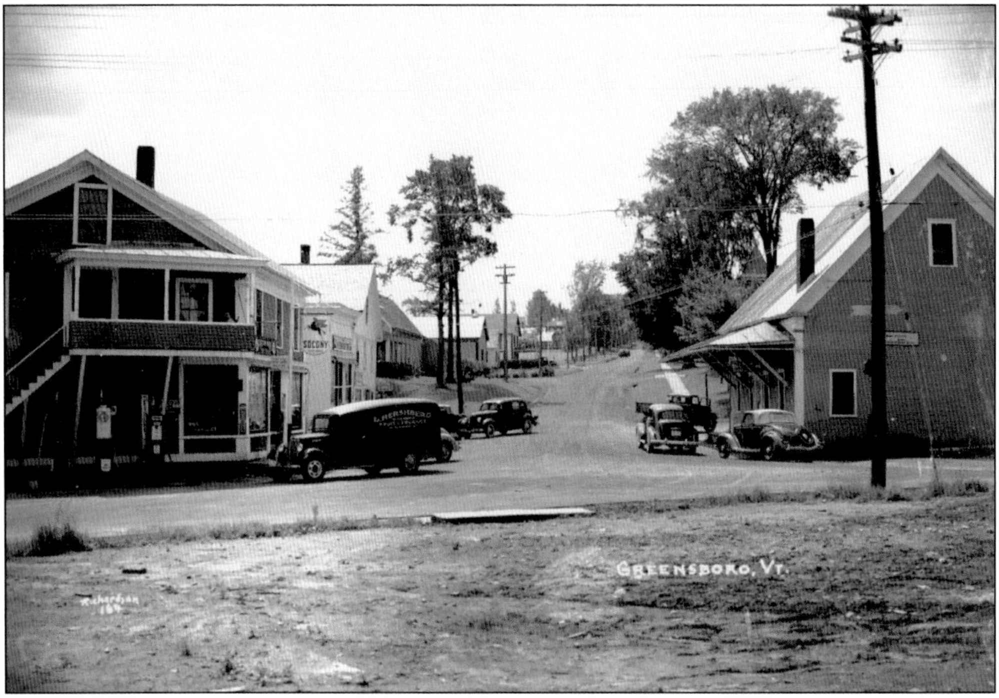

Facing south on Main Street (also known as Hinman Road) in Greensboro around 1940, this image shows the mill on the right and the general store on the left. Greensboro was chartered in 1781, but settlers did not arrive until the 1790s. The Bayley-Hazen Military Road, the first road in Orleans County, traveled through the outskirts of town. The Hinman Road was built next, in 1791. (RCC.)

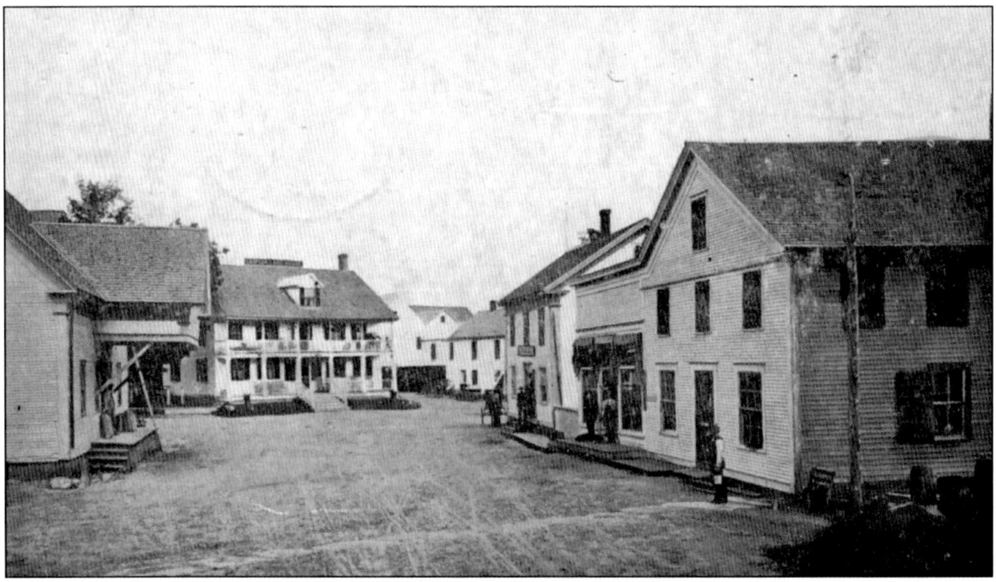

Taken before 1910, this photograph shows the view of Greensboro looking north on Hinman Road into the center of the village. A general store, now Willey's Store, is visible on the right, and a gristmill can be seen on the left. The Caspian Lake House, in the center background, served business travelers and visitors who came to enjoy the summer months at Caspian Lake. (APC.)

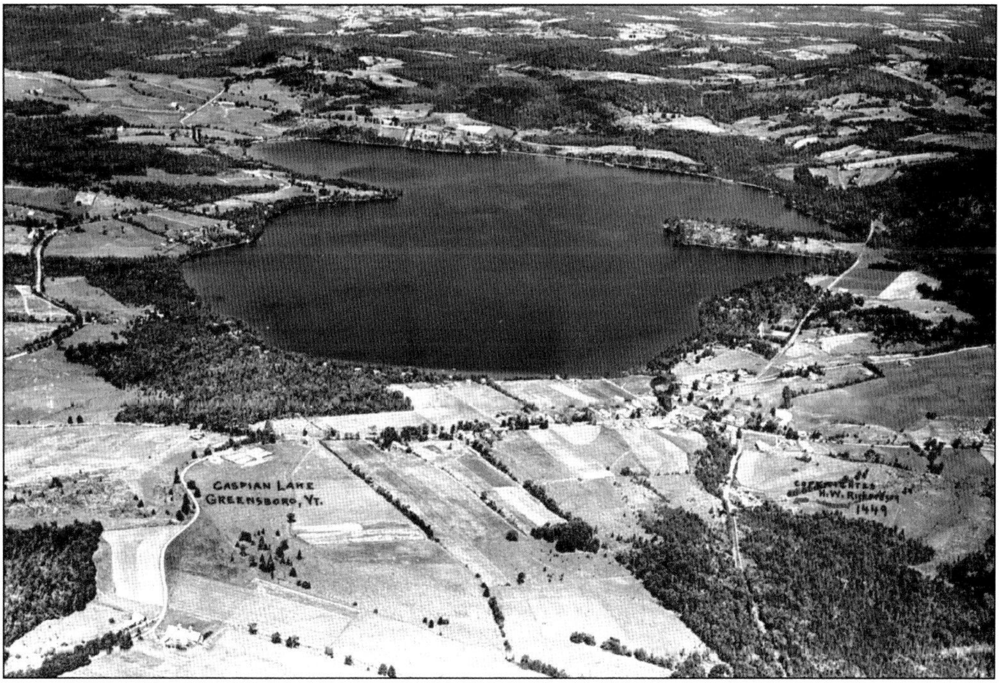

Greenboro's Caspian Lake and the five other ponds within the town limits were created from glaciers, and all stretch north and south in the direction of the ice movement. Caspian Lake brought campers to Greensboro as early as the 1880s, and it became a favorite vacation place for clergymen, professors, and writers from all over. The population of the town more than doubled each summer. (RCC.)

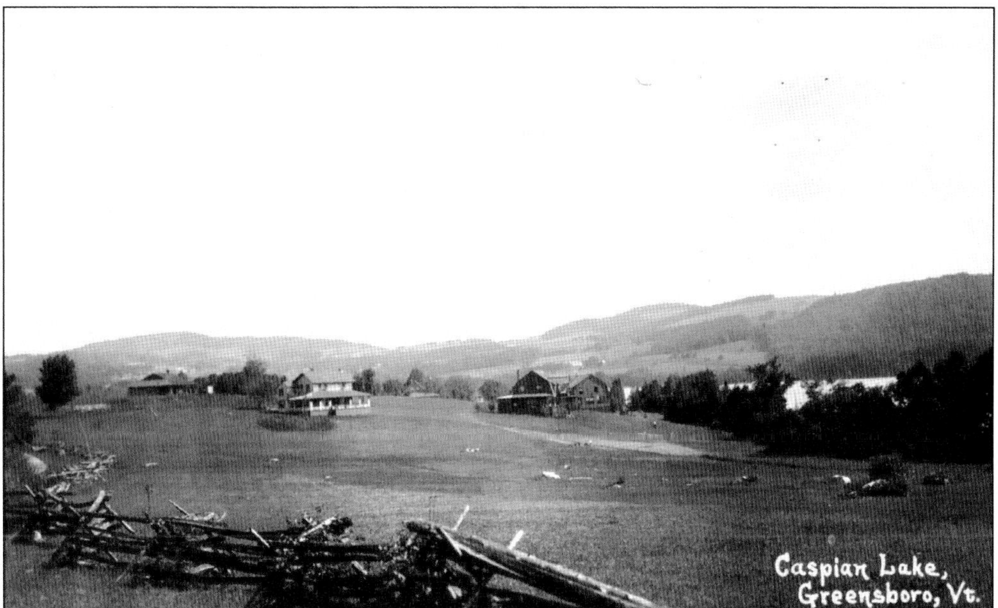

The area of Caspian Lake, Greensboro, has always been a summer attraction for visitors. Many residents of Greensboro were seasonal, arriving and departing with the summer months. Two of the famous summer residents were author Wallace Stegner and Margaret Mead. (APC.)

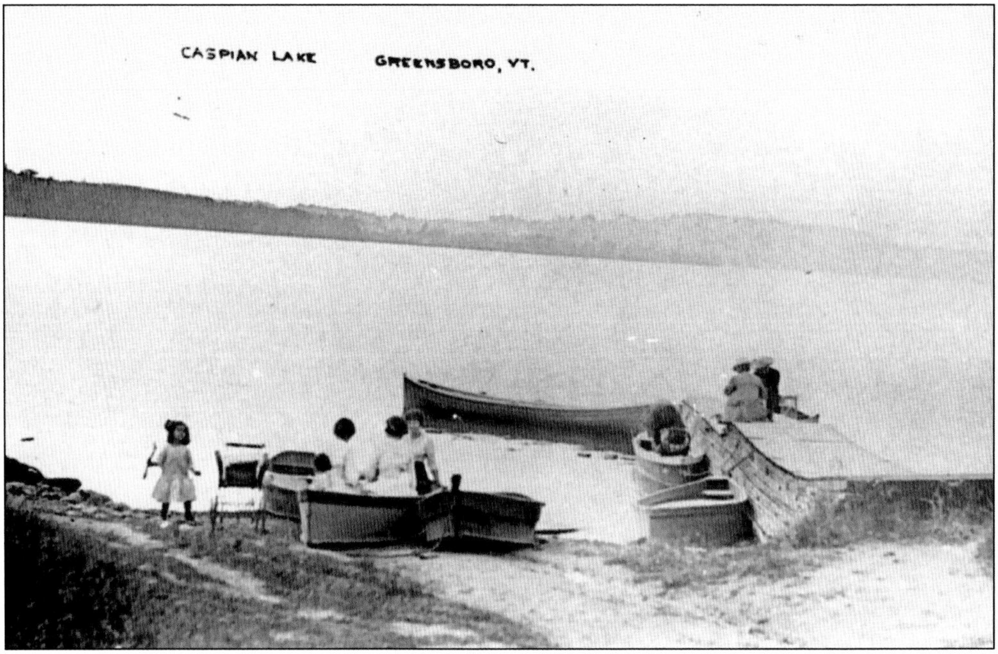

This is the public dock at Caspian Lake around 1910. Boating, swimming, and fishing were favorite pastimes at the lake in summer. In the winter, ice was harvested for iceboxes and food storage in the summer. (Greensboro Historical Society.)

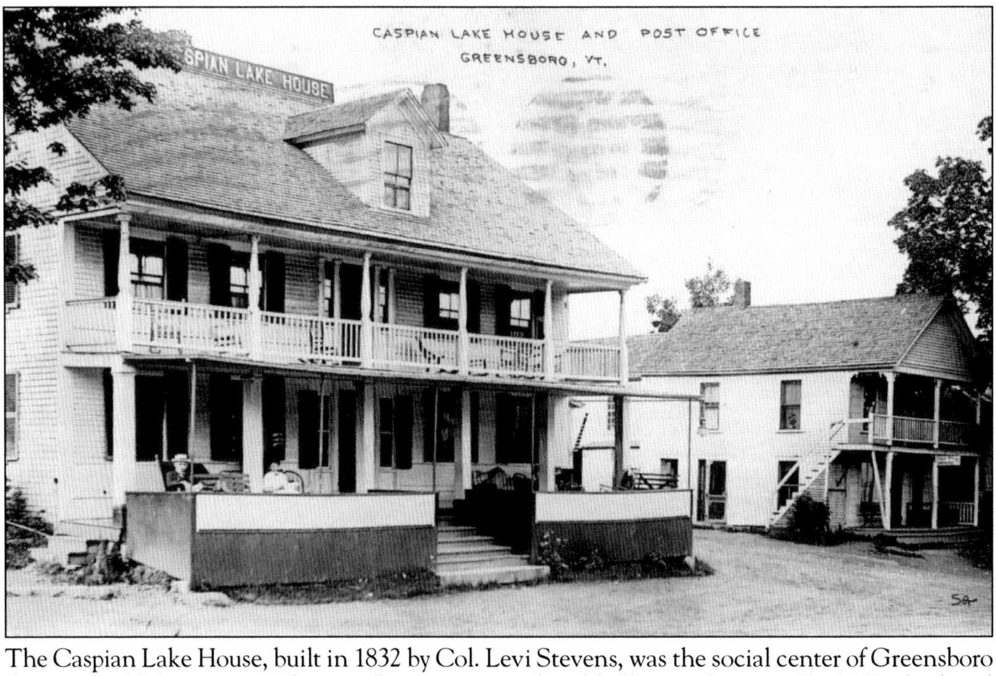

The Caspian Lake House, built in 1832 by Col. Levi Stevens, was the social center of Greensboro during the 19th century. The top floor accommodated ballroom dancing. By 1919, the hotel became seasonal, closing every winter and opening for summer guests. The post office was located next door. (APC.)

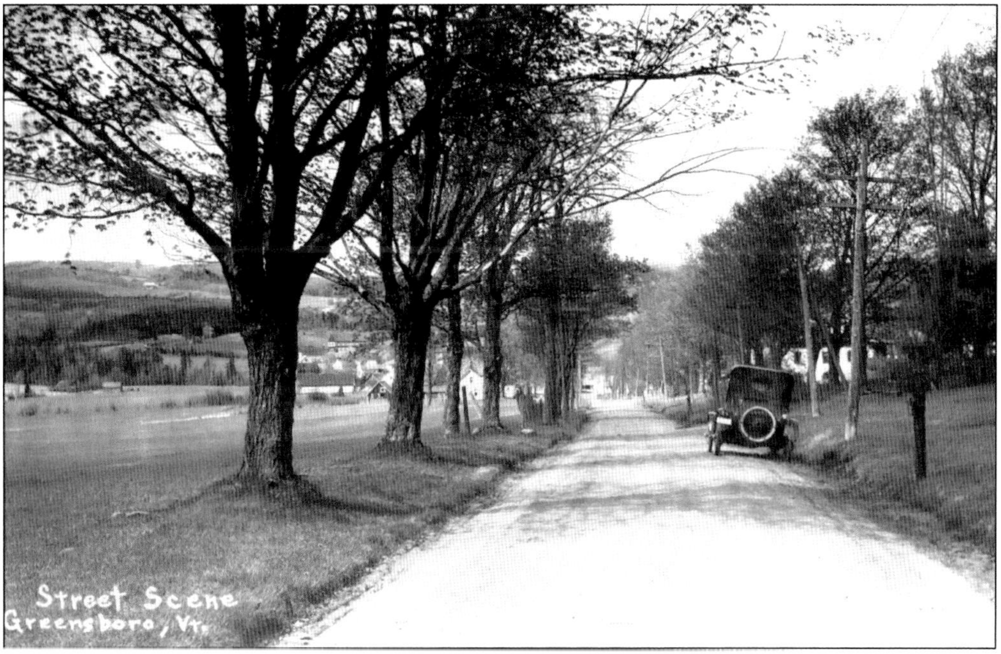

From an extension of Main Street (now called Breezy Avenue) Greensboro, a person could see Caspian Lake on the left and the village straight ahead. (APC.)

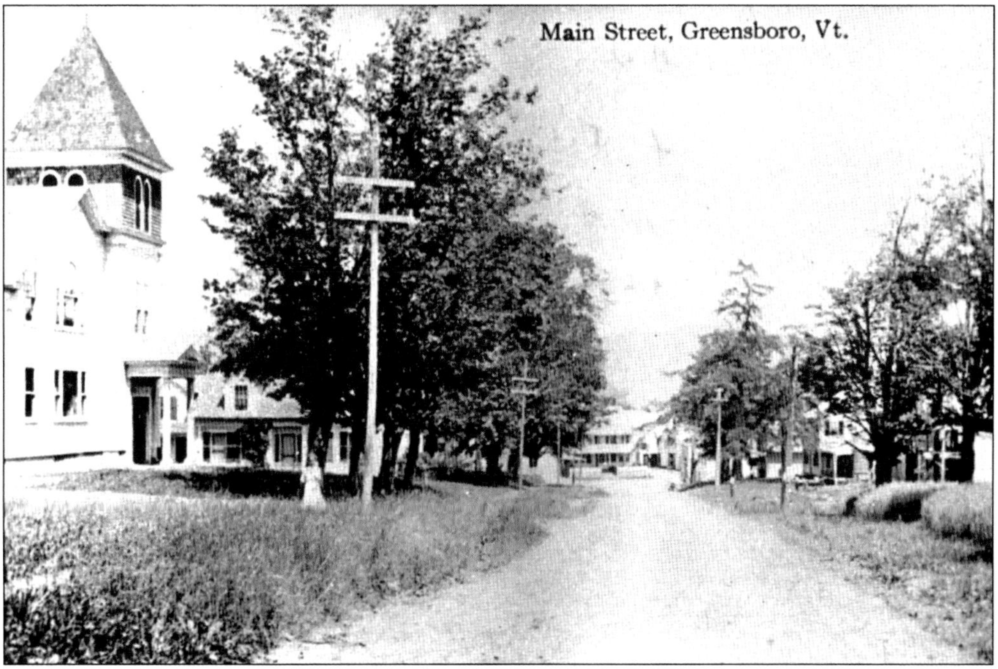

Electricity came to Greensboro at the start of the 20th century, but Main Street remained a dirt road well into the 1950s. There was a sidewalk that made walking around town easier during mud season. Telephone lines went up in 1910. At the left of the picture is the Presbyterian church, which was just outside the village. (Greensboro Historical Society.)

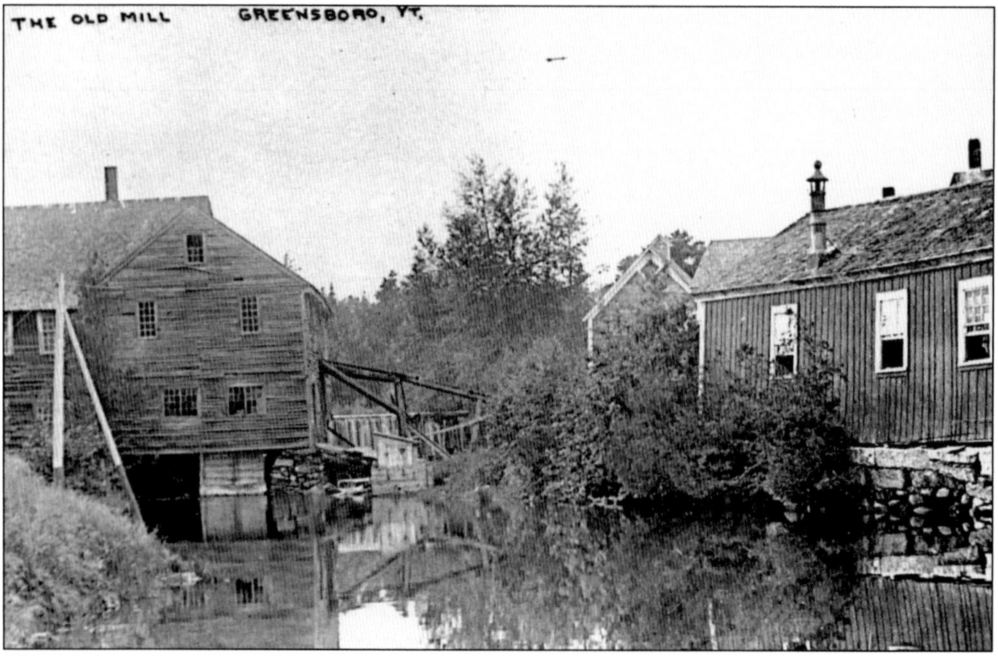

The Cutler and Goss woodworking factory, (on the left) between Caspian Lake and the village, made sashes, blinds, butter tubs, and coffins in the late 1800s. The blacksmith shop is on the right. (Greensboro Historical Society.)

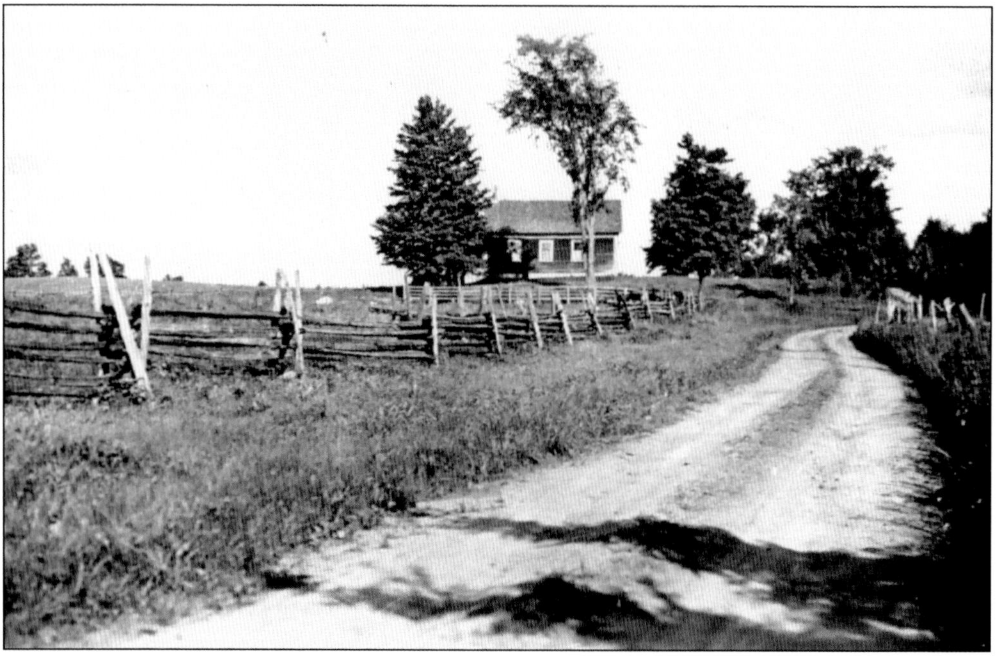

The Young School at Campbell Corner, at the northwest point of Caspian Lake, was one of 12 school districts in Greensboro in the 1830s. It closed in the mid-1930s. (Greensboro Historical Society.)

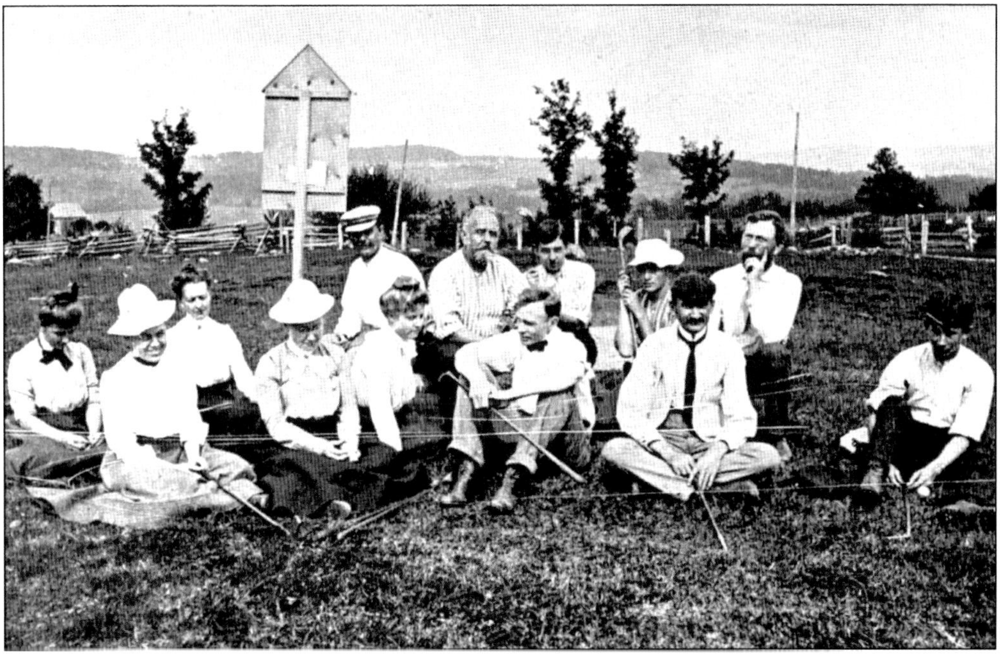

The game of golf was introduced to Greensboro in 1898. These golfers played their game in a cow pasture, which was the case for many years. The man in the center of the picture is Bliss Perry. (Greensboro Historical Society.)

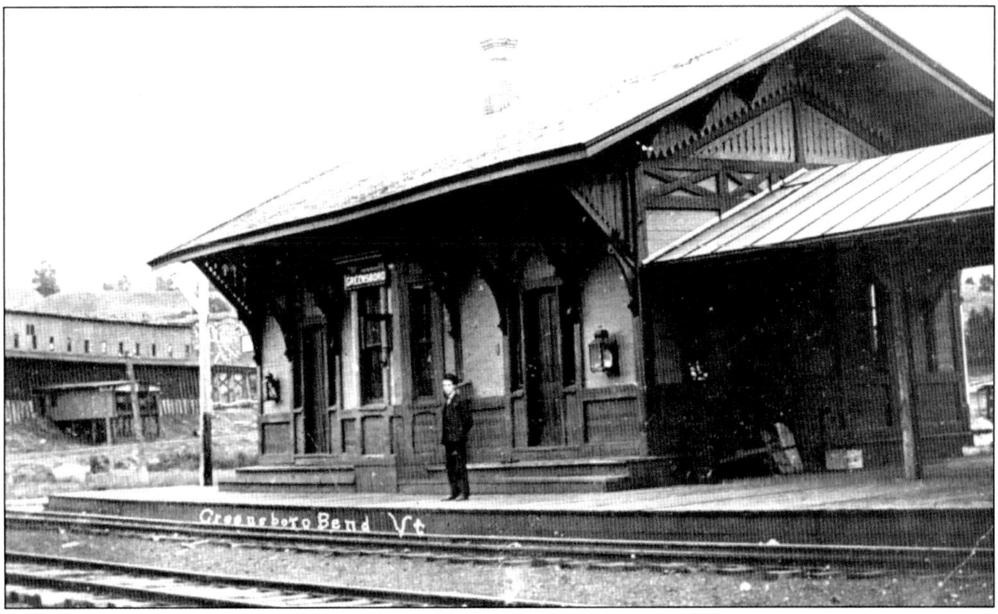

Thanks to the railroad, the village of Greensboro Bend grew in the 1870s. Before the arrival of the locomotive, the area was a swamp with only two residents. The St. Johnsbury and Lake Champlain Railroad traveled west to east, with an 18-mile loop around Greensboro Bend. With four passenger and two freight trains a day, the railroad made Greensboro a bustling community. (Greensboro Historical Society.)

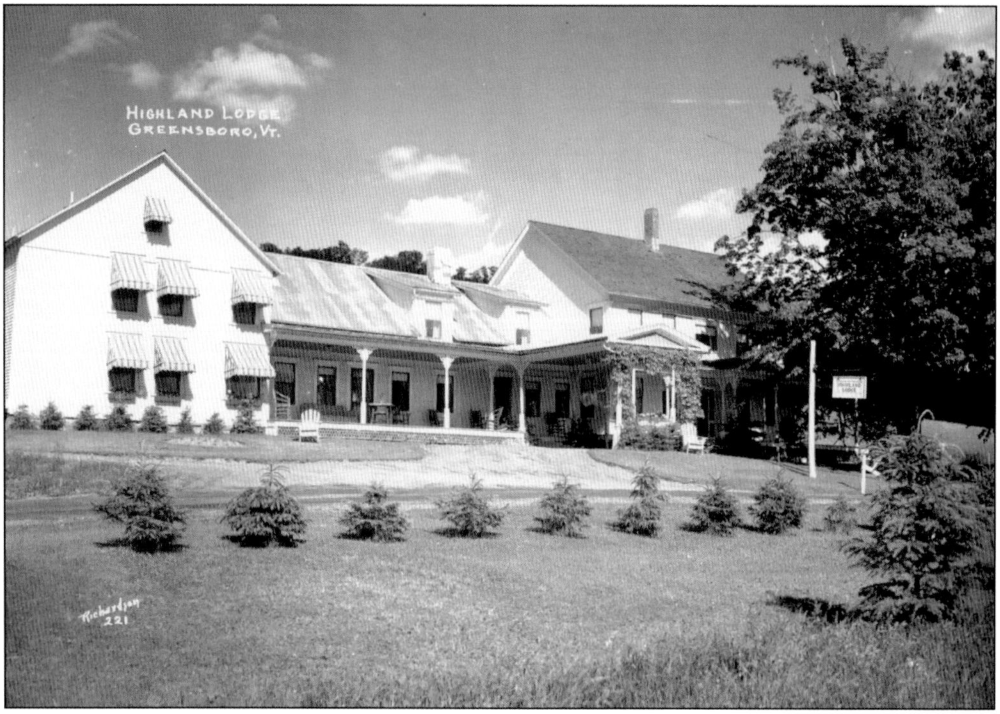

Three local men established the Highland Lodge in the 1920s. The building was the former farmhouse of the Fred Goodrich family. The structure was added to and converted into boarding rooms. The lodge closed sporadically, such as during World War II, but it always reopened and is still operating today as a hotel. (RCC.)

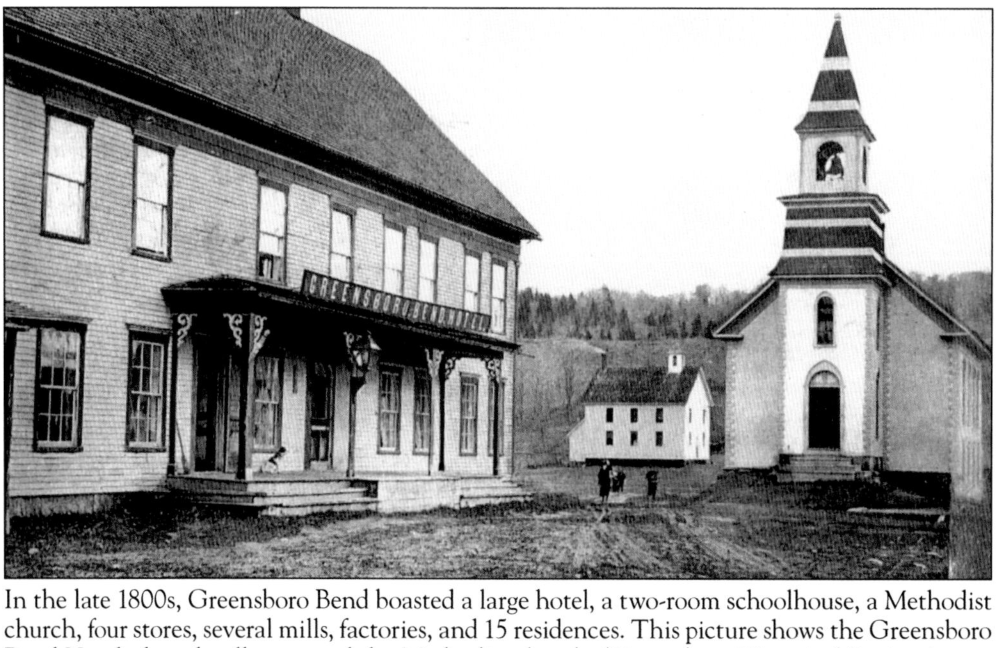

In the late 1800s, Greensboro Bend boasted a large hotel, a two-room schoolhouse, a Methodist church, four stores, several mills, factories, and 15 residences. This picture shows the Greensboro Bend Hotel, the schoolhouse, and the Methodist church. (Greensboro Historical Society.)

Six

Albany, Irasburg, and Lowell

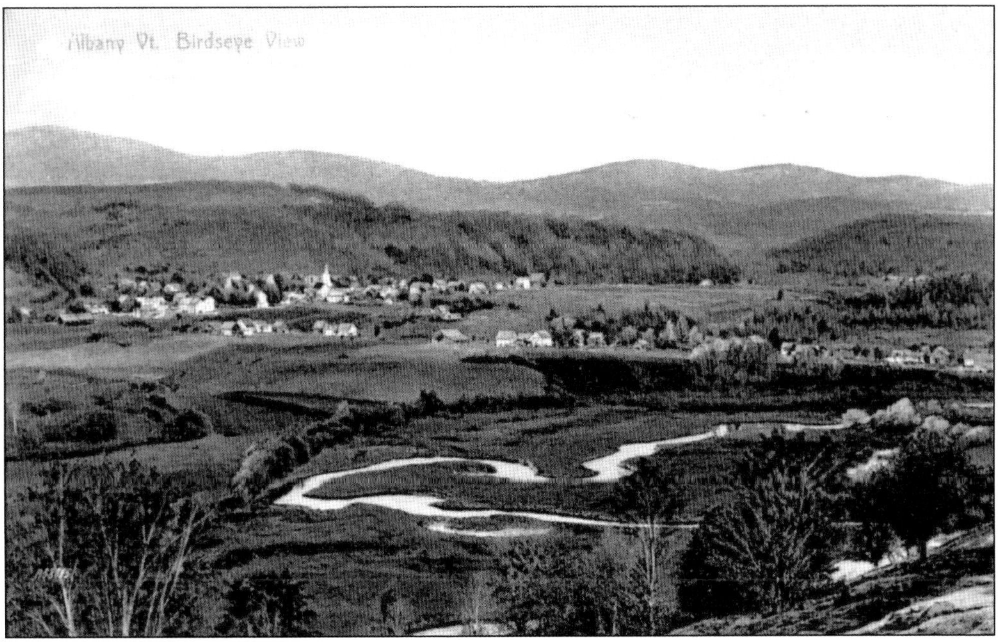

Once called Lutterloh, the town of Albany is in the southwest corner of Orleans County. The Black River winds through the eastern part of town. Lutterloh was organized on March 27, 1806, and the name was officially changed to Albany in 1815. There were four different neighborhoods in Albany: West Albany, Albany Center, East Albany, and South Albany. (APC.)

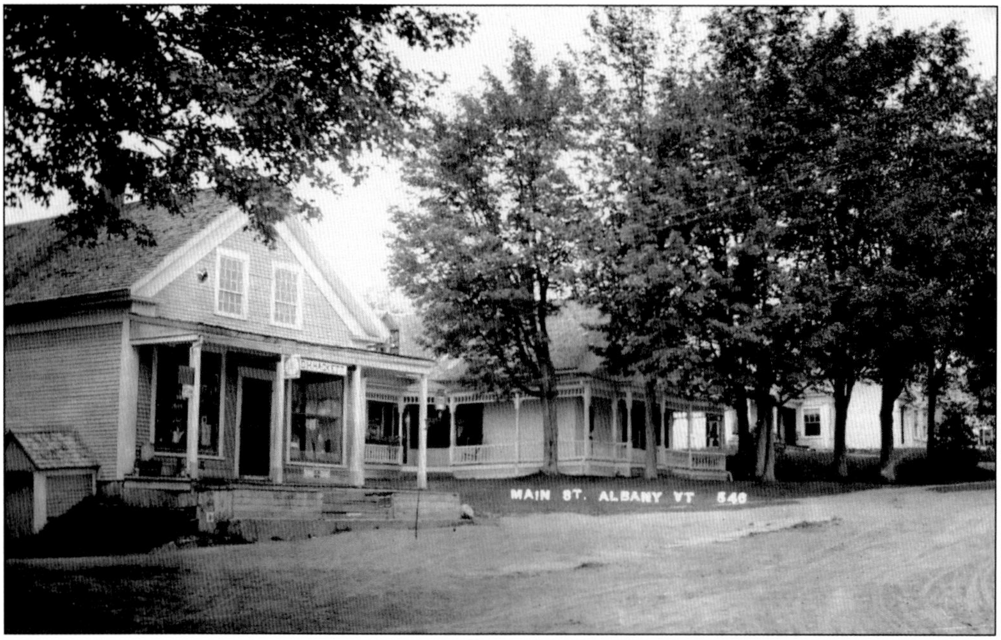

The Hackett store on Main Street in West Albany (the building on the left) opened in 1911 and was owned by Dana and Mattie Hackett. Their son Lloyd attended Middlebury College in 1930 but returned to his hometown during the Great Depression to run a potato farm. Lloyd ran the store until it closed in 1966. (APC.)

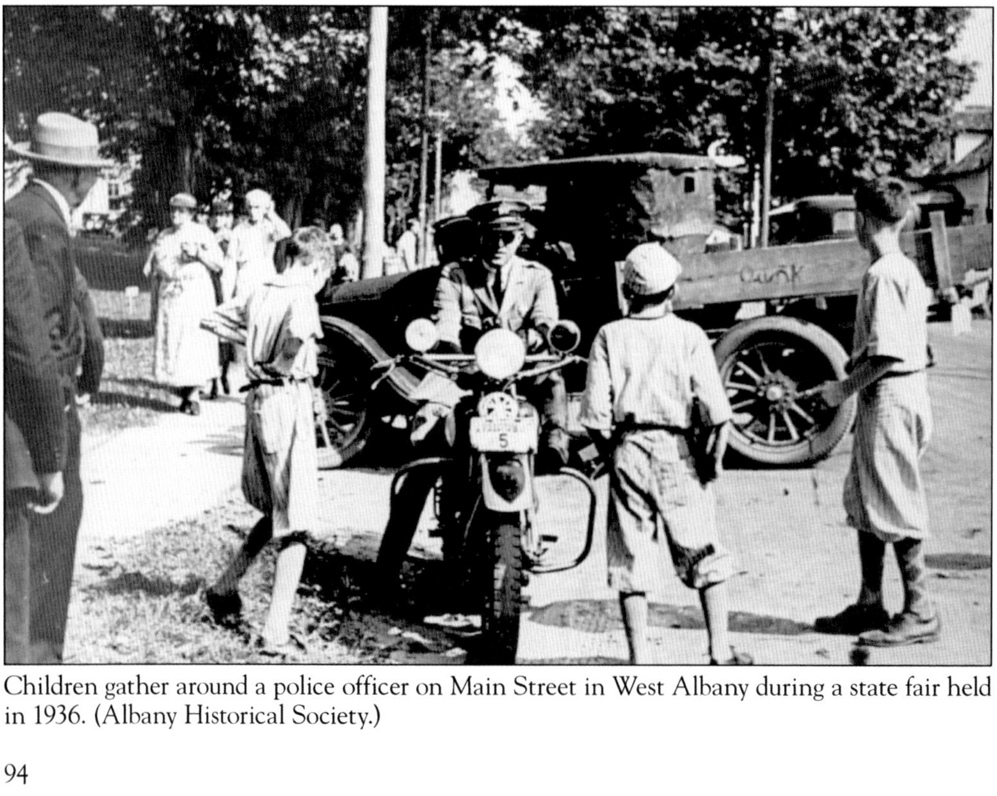

Children gather around a police officer on Main Street in West Albany during a state fair held in 1936. (Albany Historical Society.)

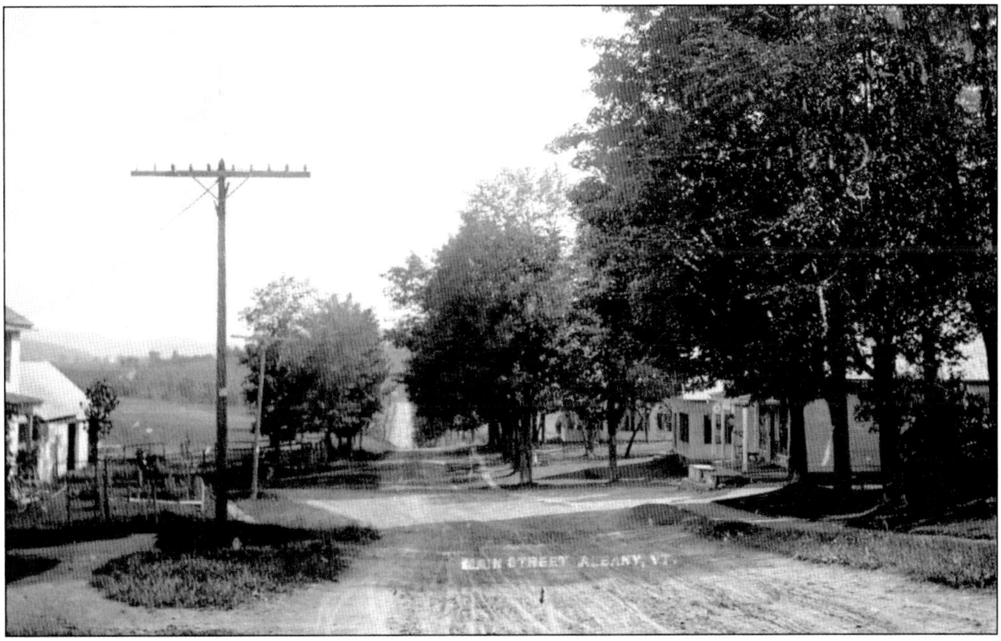

This is Main Street, Albany, heading south toward Craftsbury. Branching off to the left is Water Street. At the other end of Water Street is the Black River, where residents of Albany operated a sawmill. (APC.)

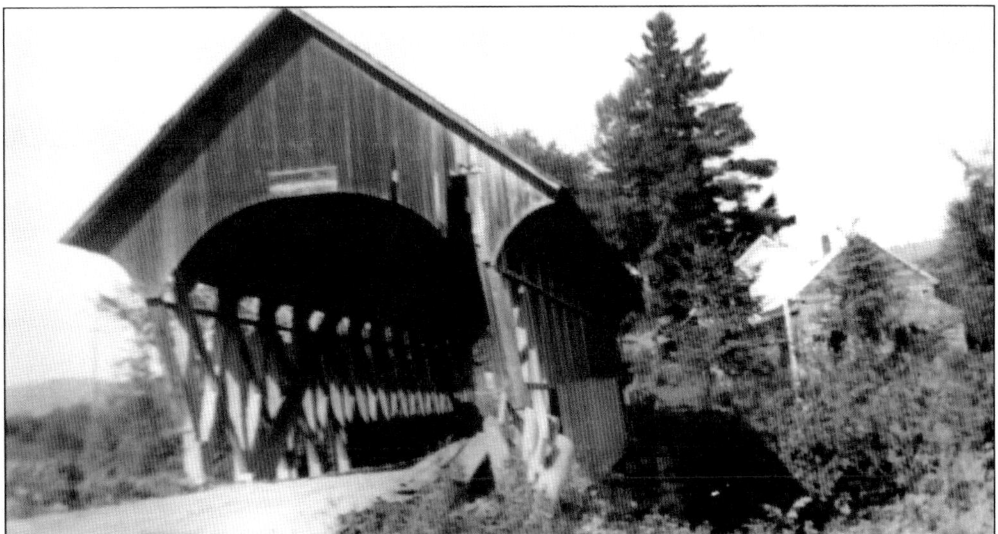

One of the last covered bridges in Albany, this one could be found in the western part of town on Water Street. It was nearing the end of its life in 1947, when this picture was taken. (Albany Historical Society.)

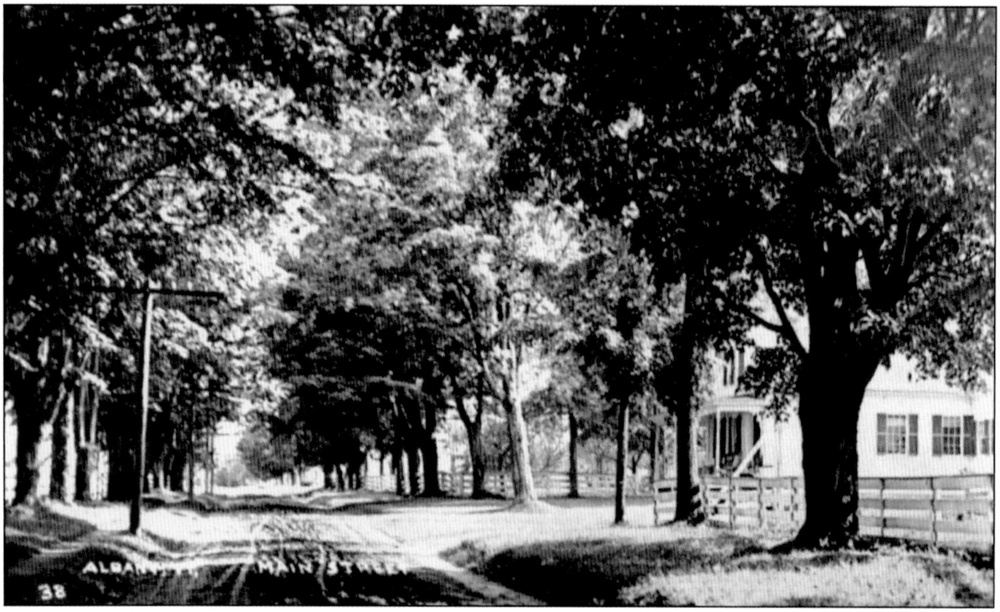

Main Street in Albany Village, called West Albany, was once lined with many trees, including great elms. Today the trees no longer line the road. (Albany Historical Society.)

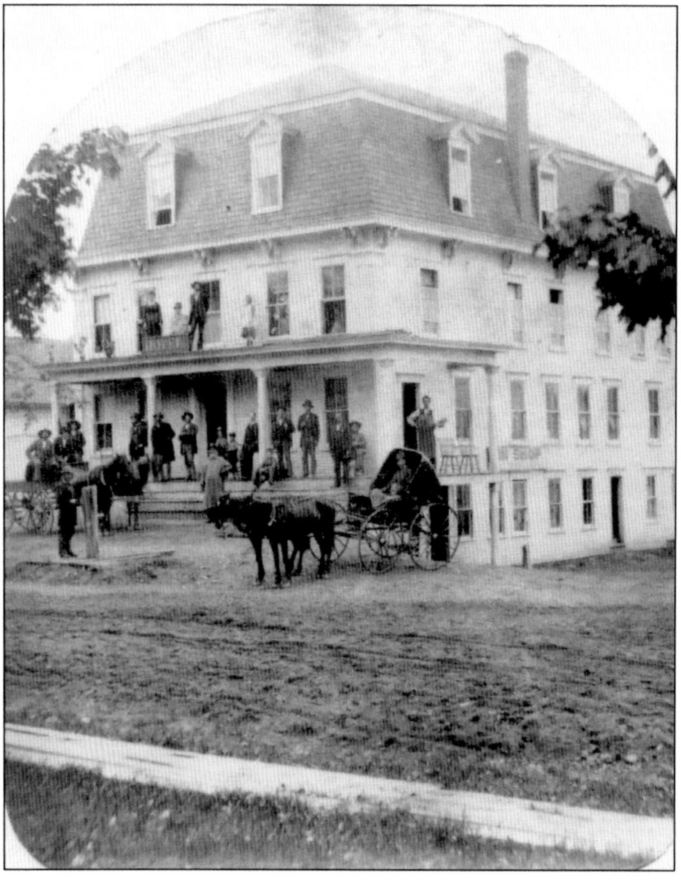

In 1868, Jeremiah and Alice Darling moved from Elmore, Vermont, to Albany, where they started a hotel. The Darling Hotel contained a millinery shop run by Alice Darling and a tinsmith shop. The building was on Main Street in the village. It burned in the 1880s, and the Darlings opened a second hotel across the street from the original. The new hotel was called the Albany House. (Richard Petit.)

A page from the Darling family's Albany House hotel guest book shows that the town enjoyed travelers from many places, including a variety show that performed in the hotel hall on January 26, 1888. The Whittier's Variety Show was named after H.W. Whittier, an illusionist and ventriloquist who performed with a contortionist named Eugene Merou. (OCHS.)

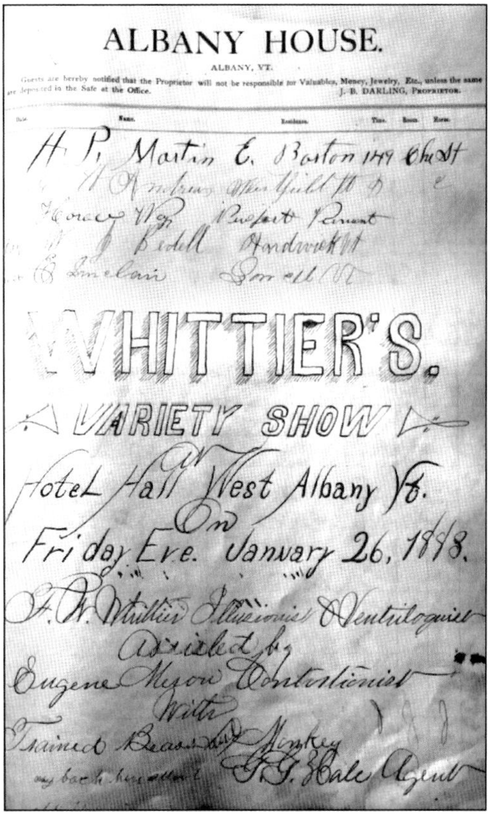

ALBANY HOUSE.

ALBANY, VT.

Guests are hereby notified that the Proprietor will not be responsible for Valuables, Money, Jewelry, Etc., unless the same are deposited in the Safe at the Office.

J. B. DARLING, PROPRIETOR.

H. P. Martin E. Boston 149 Che St

WHITTIER'S.

VARIETY SHOW

At Hotel Hall West Albany Vt.

On Friday Eve. January 26, 1888.

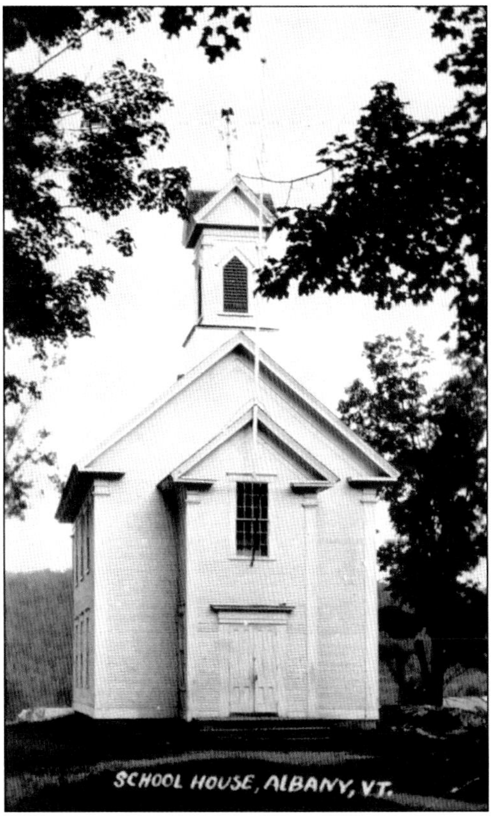

Originally built in 1855 as a single-story schoolhouse and expanded in 1880, the school building in Albany Village was used for the younger students as well as the high school students. The two age groups took turns using the building every other term. (Albany Historical Society.)

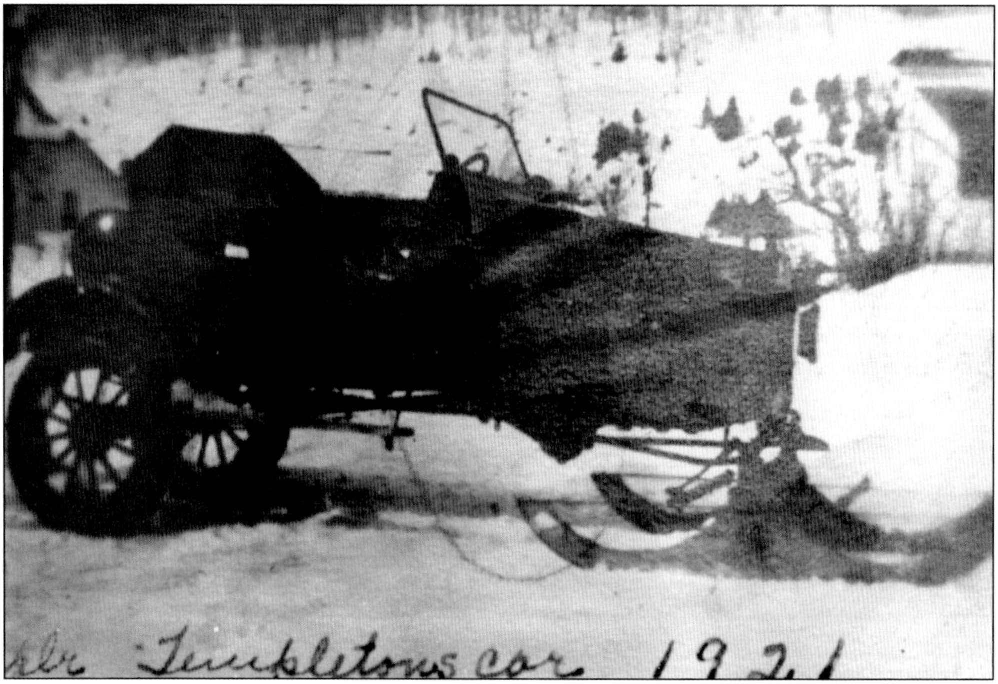

In 1921, the main roads through Albany were still covered in deep snow during the winter. The town physician, Dr. Templeton, added sleighs to the front of his automobile to make his travels easier. (Albany Historical Society.)

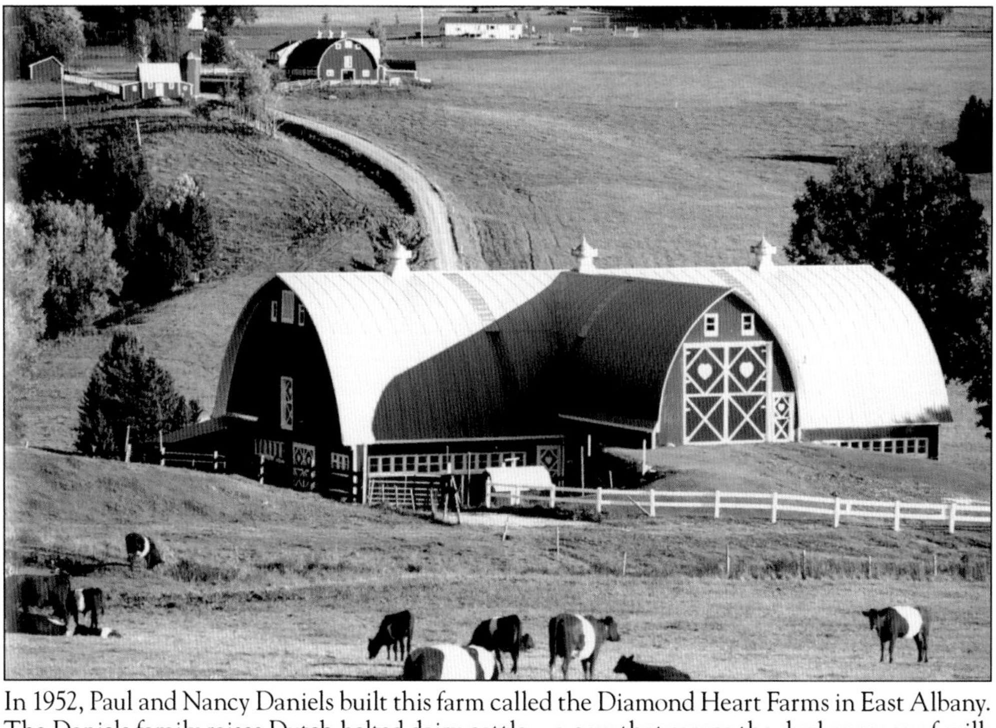

In 1952, Paul and Nancy Daniels built this farm called the Diamond Heart Farms in East Albany. The Daniels family raises Dutch belted dairy cattle—a cow that serves the dual purpose of milk and beef. (Paul Daniels.)

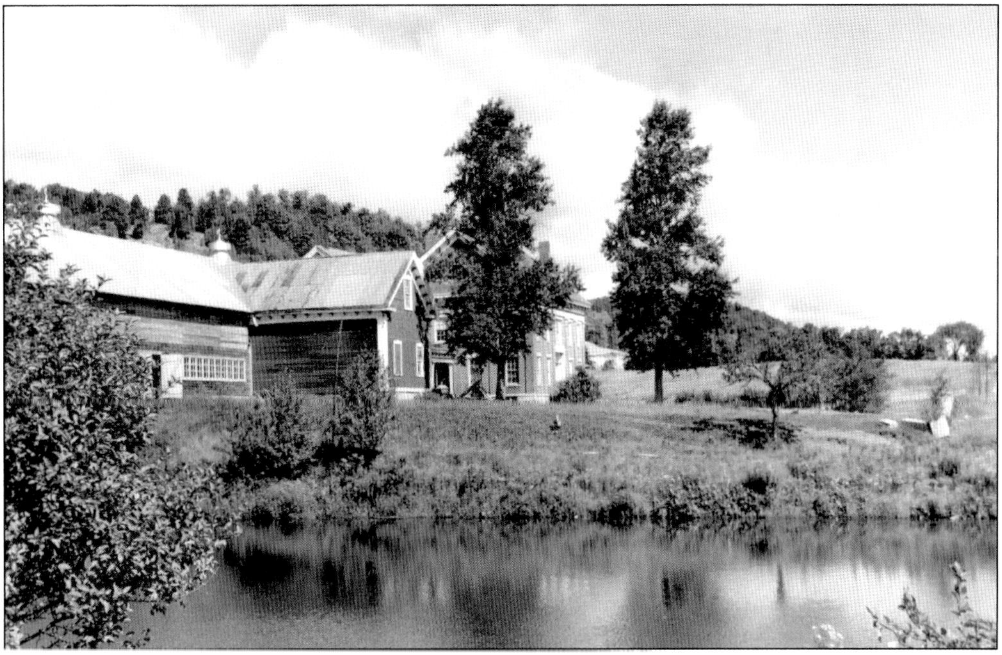

The Hayden House in southern Albany is a pre–Civil War mansion that was built in 1854 of brick fired in a kiln located a small distance from the house. William Hayden, a farmer and cooper, invested in a railroad contract in New Hampshire, acquiring great wealth. Local lore around town claims an unhappy mother-in-law put a curse on the family. (RCC.)

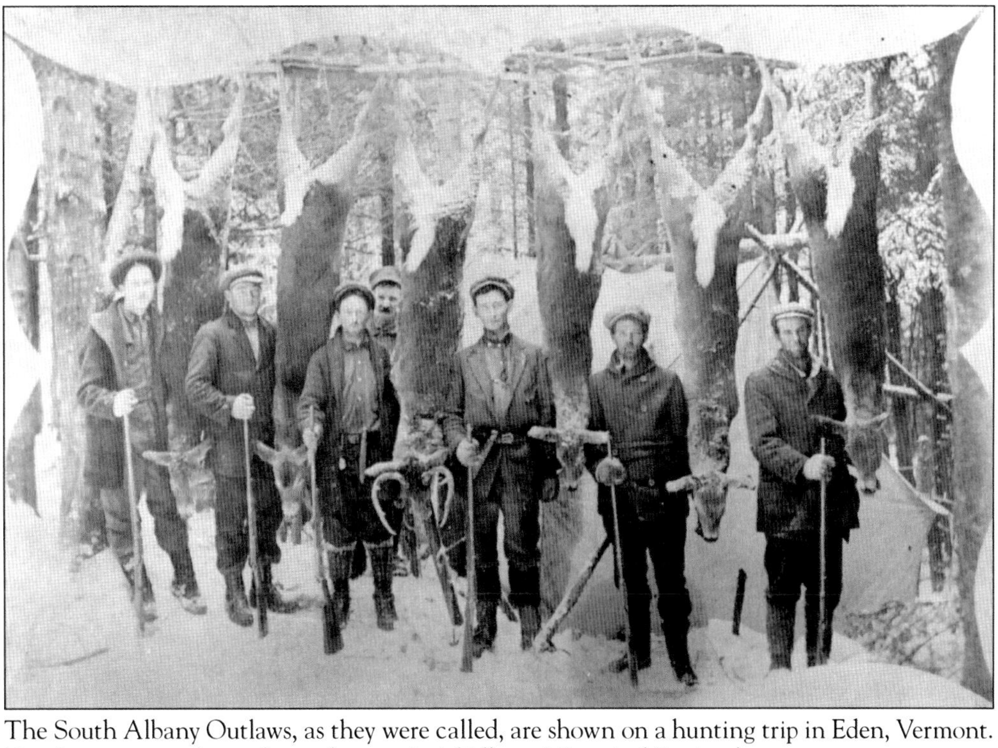

The South Albany Outlaws, as they were called, are shown on a hunting trip in Eden, Vermont. Nearly every man has a deer; what a prize! (Albany Historical Society.)

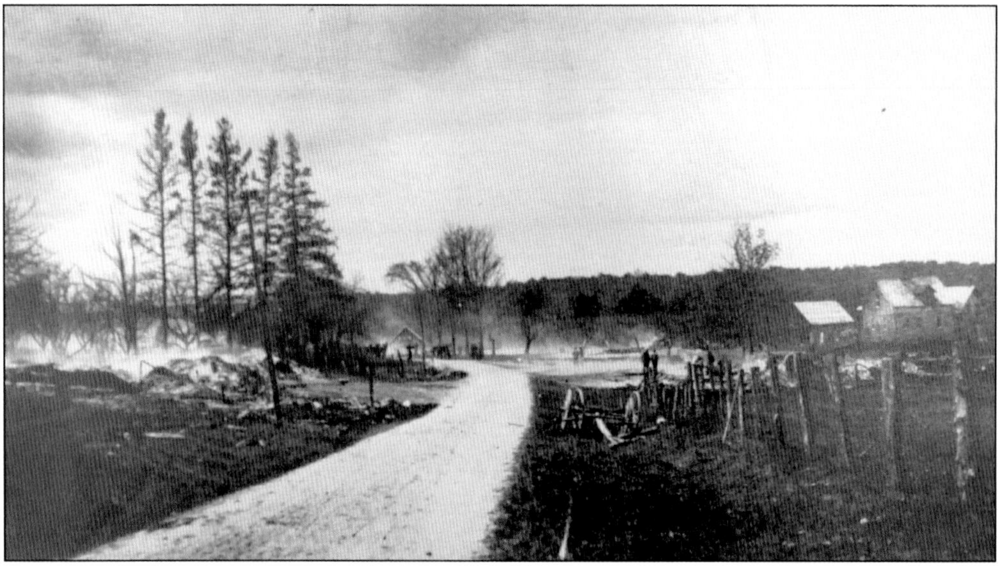

This picture shows the damage done to South Albany during the 1913 fire. The village of South Albany had many residences and successful stores. A man working at the Webster General Store was burning brush a little distance from the store. He lost control of the fire, and it quickly spread throughout the neighborhood. Nineteen buildings were destroyed. (Albany Historical Society.)

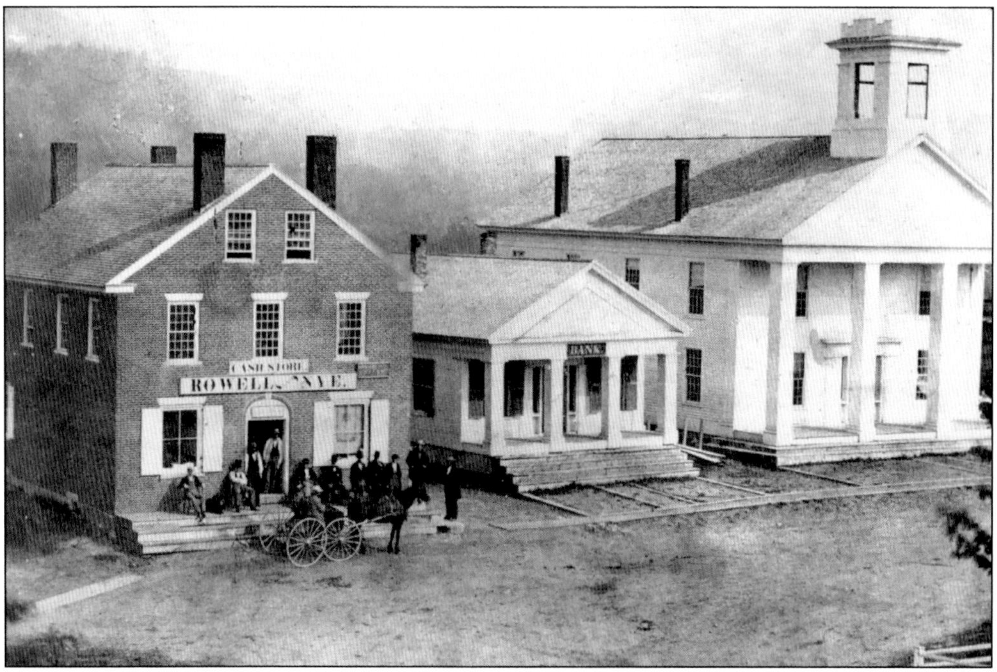

Labeled as the first picture of Irasburg in 1862, this image shows a general store owned by R.W. Nye, a bank, and a courthouse. Irasburg was made the county seat in 1812, so court was in session here until Newport became the county seat in 1884. The bank in the picture was established in 1832 and was the only bank in the county until 1851. (OCHS.)

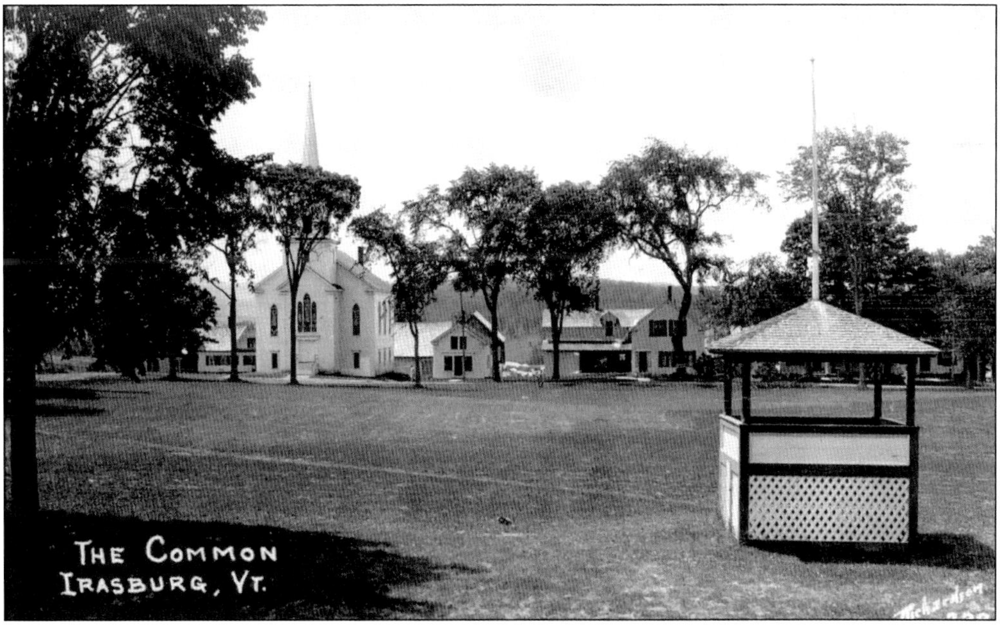

Jerusha Allen's 1816 deed for Irasburg provided a public highway and a town common. Four cast-iron balls marked the corners of the common. The common has been used for baseball games, skating rinks, and other community events. (APC.)

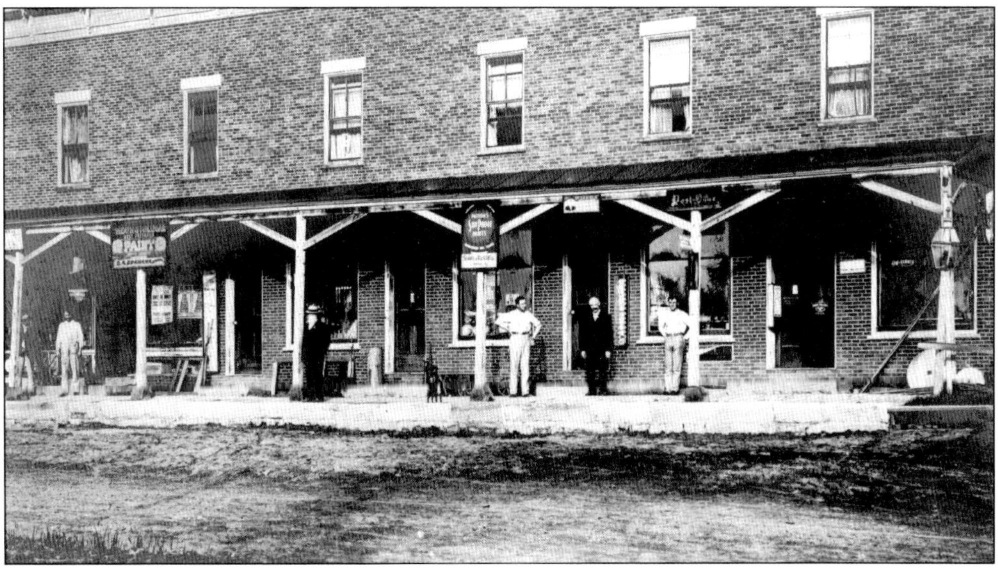

This building, erected around the town common, housed the Irasburg post office and the Sears and Russell General Store. Today, Ray's Market is in the north end of the structure, and the post office is still in the building. (APC.)

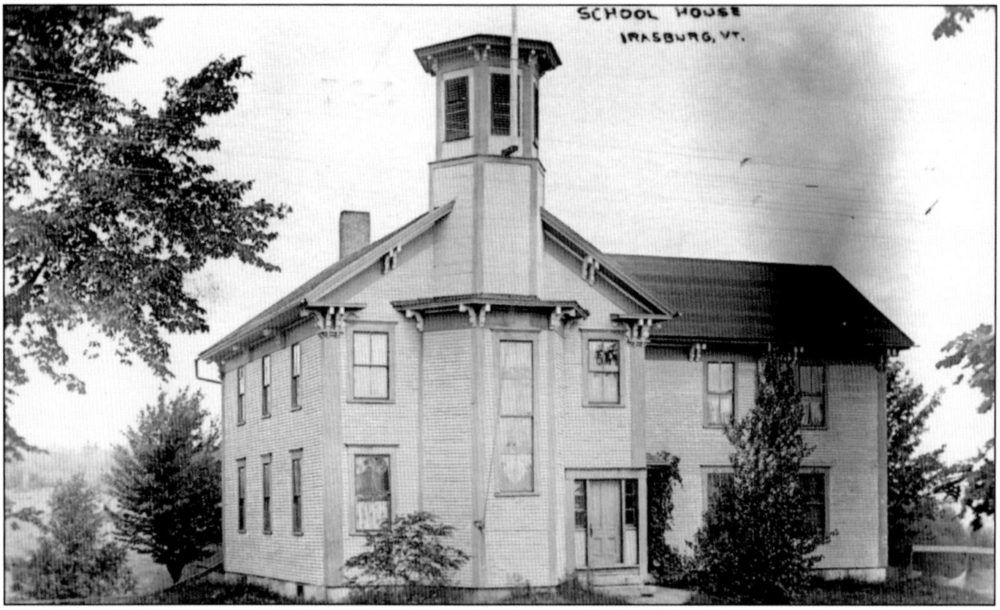

The Village School House in Irasburg was built in 1863 for younger and older students. The ell on the building housed the younger children. (APC.)

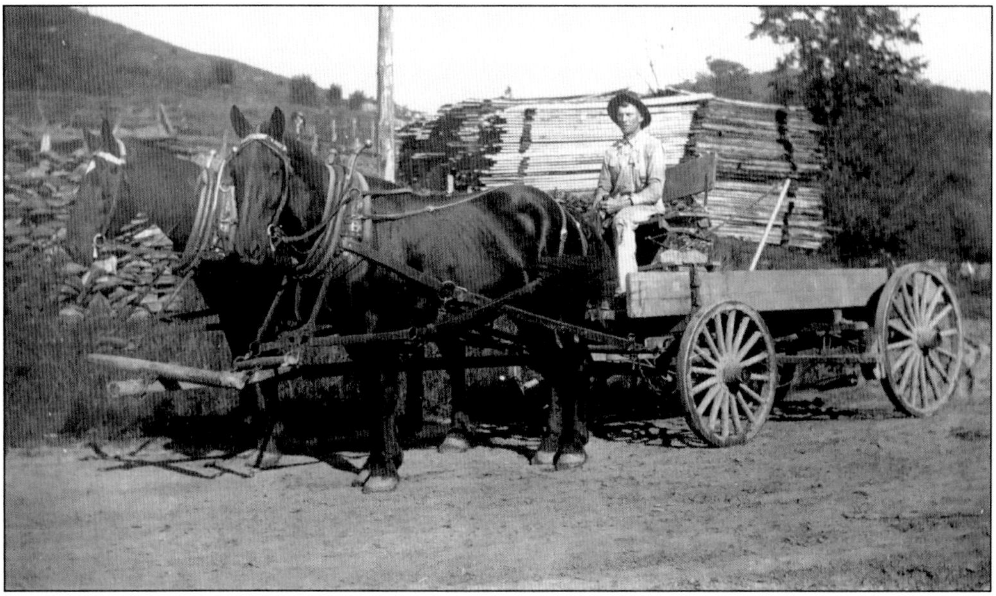

This man is transporting lumber from one of the sawmills on the Black River in Irasburg. In 1880, there were four mills on the Black River. (APC.)

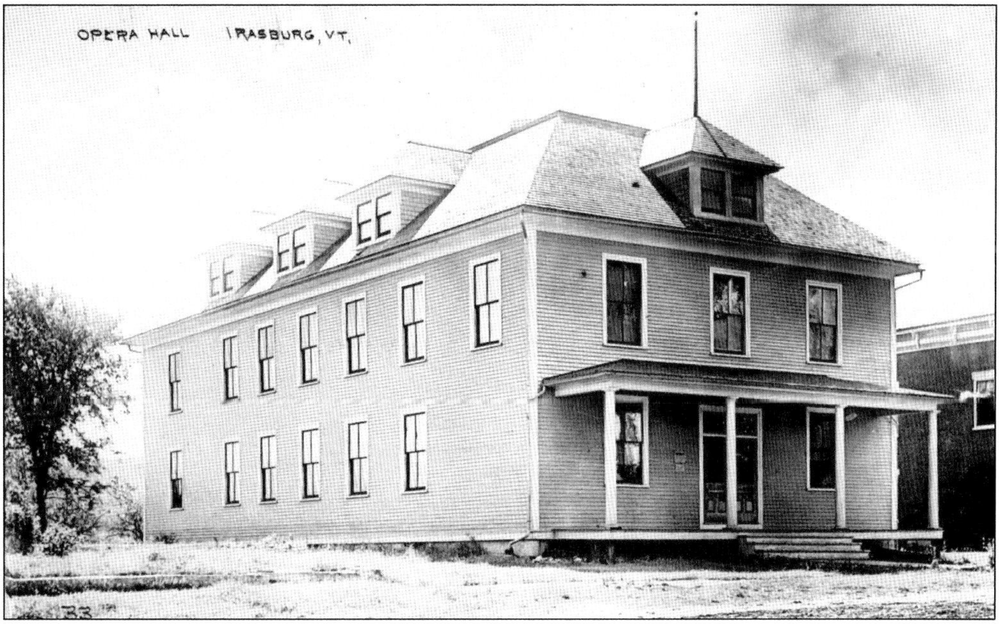

This town hall building in Irasburg, also used as an opera house, was built in 1912, about a year after the first town hall burned down in the Irasburg fire of 1911. The upper hall of the building boasted 17-foot-high ceilings, a stage, dressing rooms, and a back stairwell to the kitchen. (APC.)

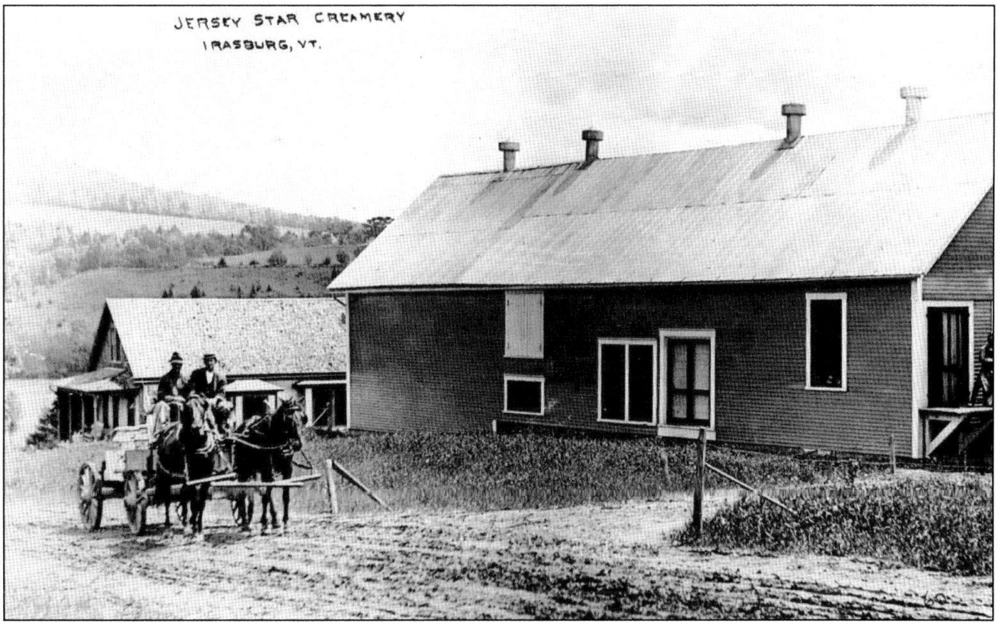

In 1912, the Jersey Star Creamery Association bought land from H. Chamberlain to build a creamery for Irasburg. They were in business two years later, with butter as their main product. During the years of the Great Depression, many of the local farmers who had supported the creamery were financially ruined, so its time in Irasburg came to an end. The creamery was bought out and moved to Orleans. (APC.)

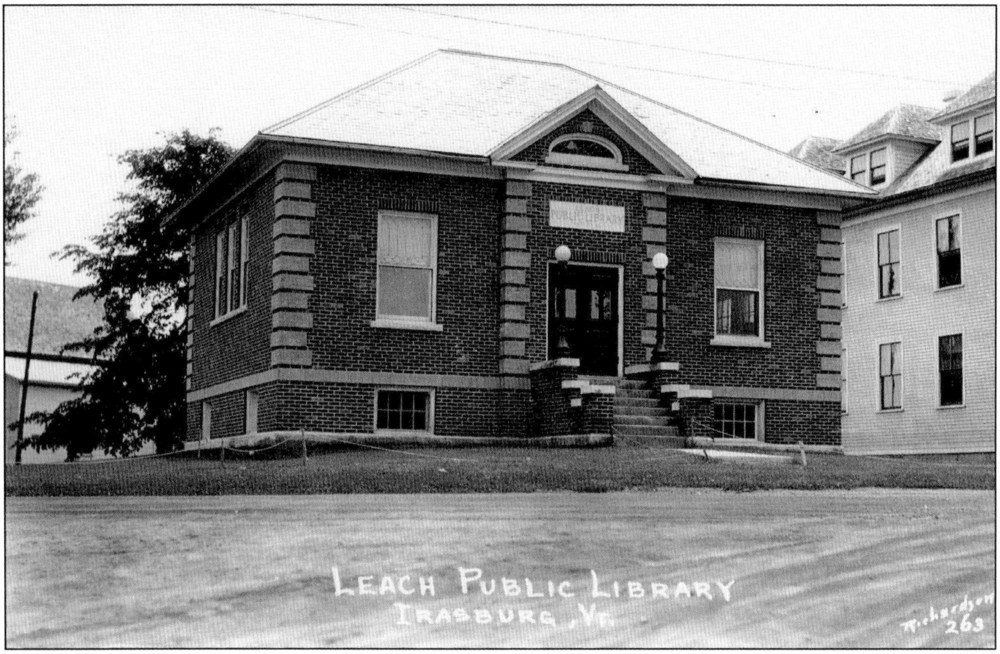

Leach Public Library was built in 1926 on the common in Irasburg. Orrin and Cora Leach of Wahpeton, North Dakota, donated the funds for the building if the town would provide the building site. Orrin was an Irasburg native. The Leaches donated funds to Wahpeton for a library, so one will also find Leach Public Library in that town. (APC.)

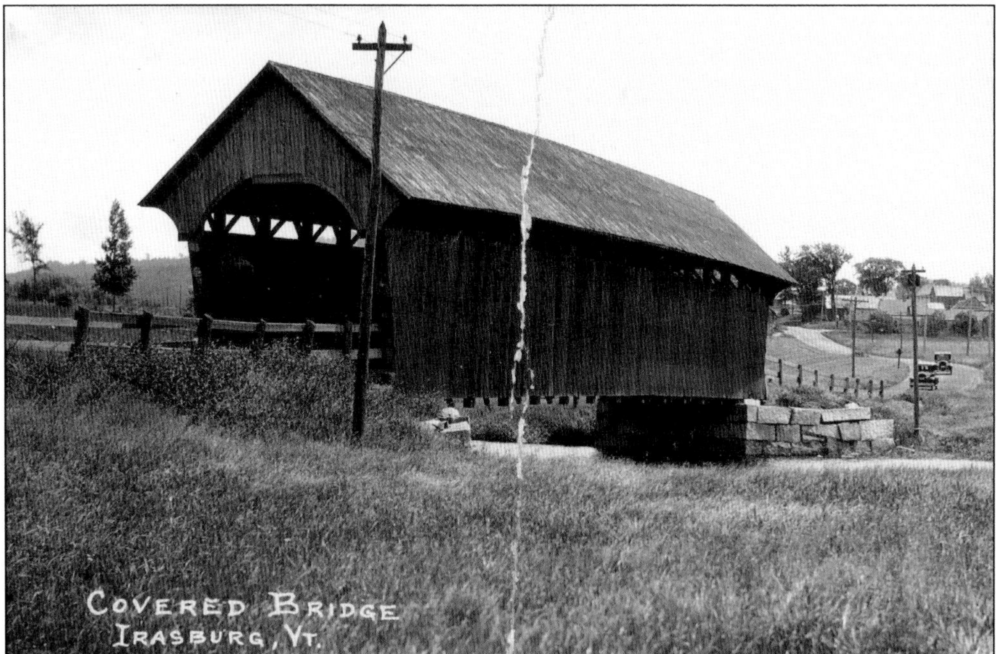

This covered bridge north of Irasburg Village on Route 14 was called the Kennison Bridge after a local family who lived close by. During the flood of 1927, this bridge remained on its foundation, but the Kennisons' house floated away in the overflowing Black River. (APC.)

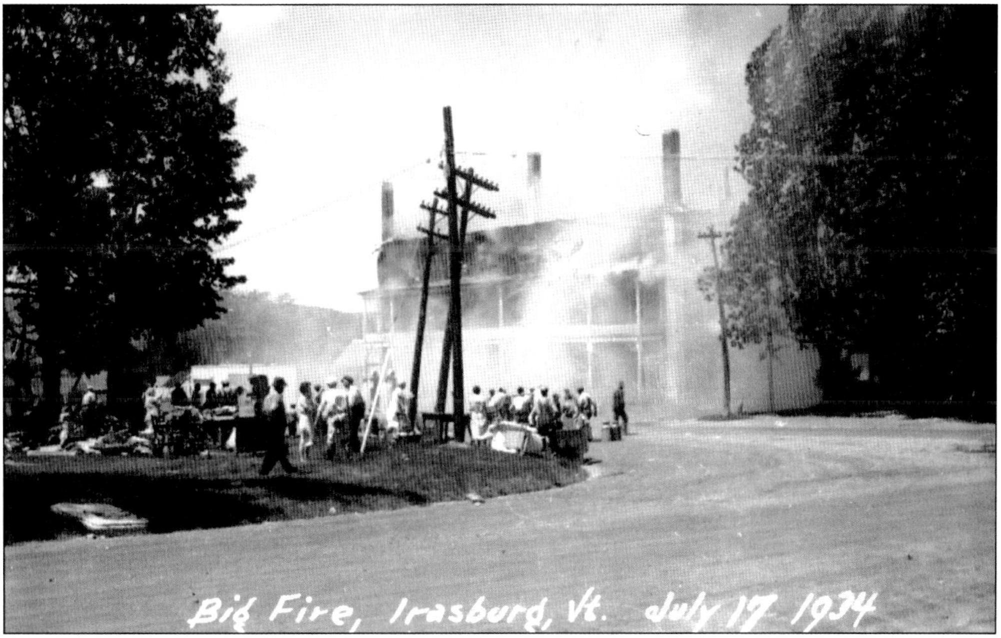

On July 17, 1934, in Irasburg, men at a nearby mill noticed fire and smoke rising from the roof of this old hotel. When they ran to investigate, they noticed the entire back side of the roof was on fire, and people were already trying to put it out. Because of high wind, the fire was spreading too quickly. Houses, the Masonic temple, and an empty church were destroyed. (APC.)

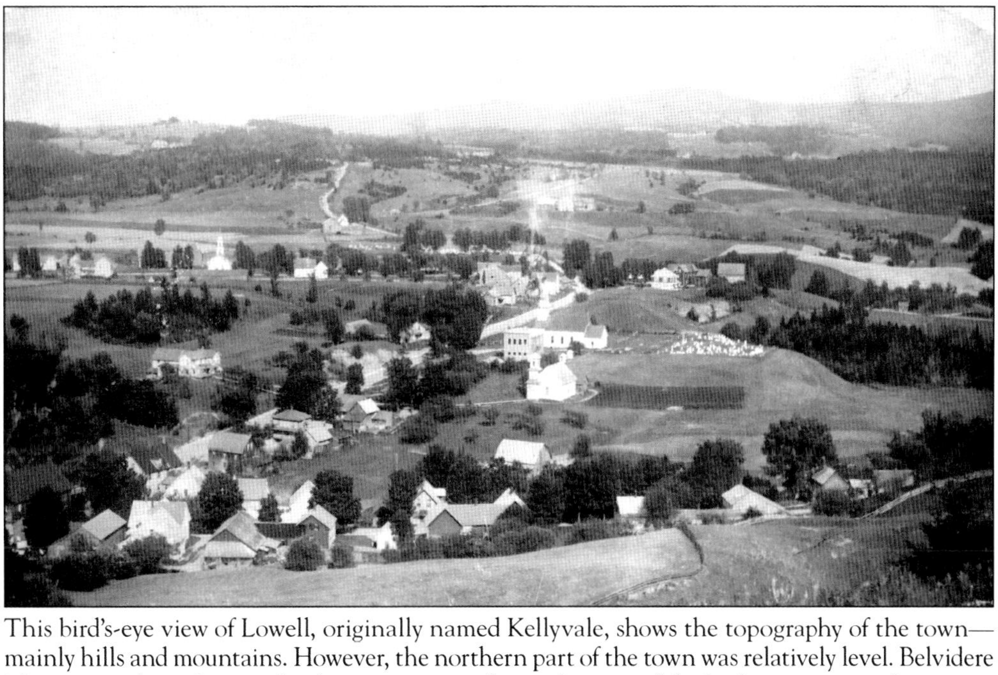

This bird's-eye view of Lowell, originally named Kellyvale, shows the topography of the town—mainly hills and mountains. However, the northern part of the town was relatively level. Belvidere Mountain, where the town's asbestos mine was located, is one of the highest points in the county at 3,360 feet. (OCHS.)

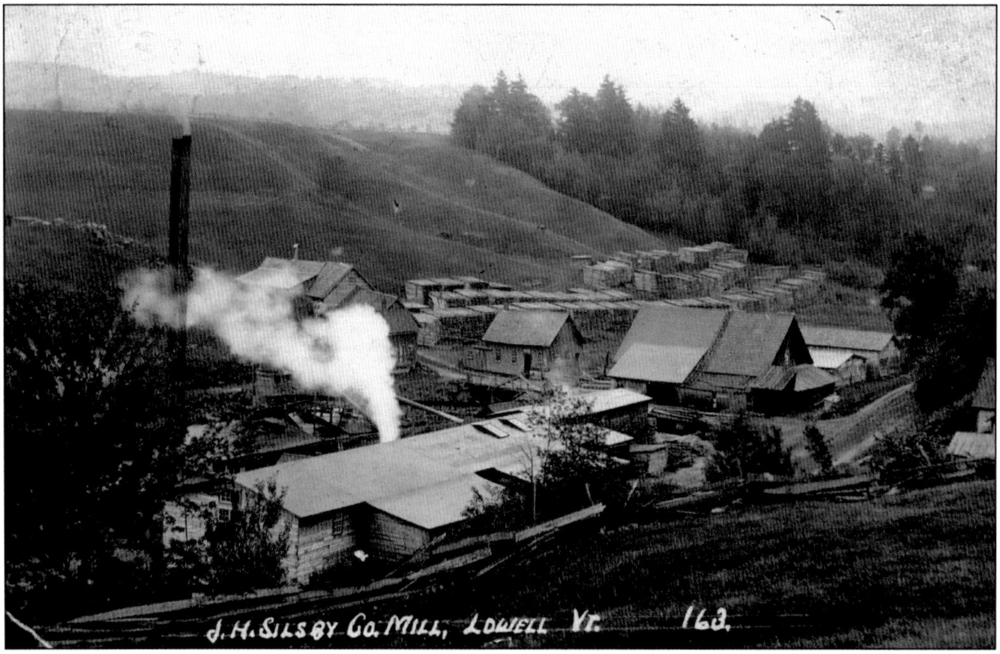

The large quantities of standing timber brought about the construction of numerous mills in Lowell. The Silsby Mill, headquartered in Connecticut, operated in Lowell for 30 years. It closed in the 1920s, mainly due to the depletion of the surrounding forests because of lumber operations. (APC.)

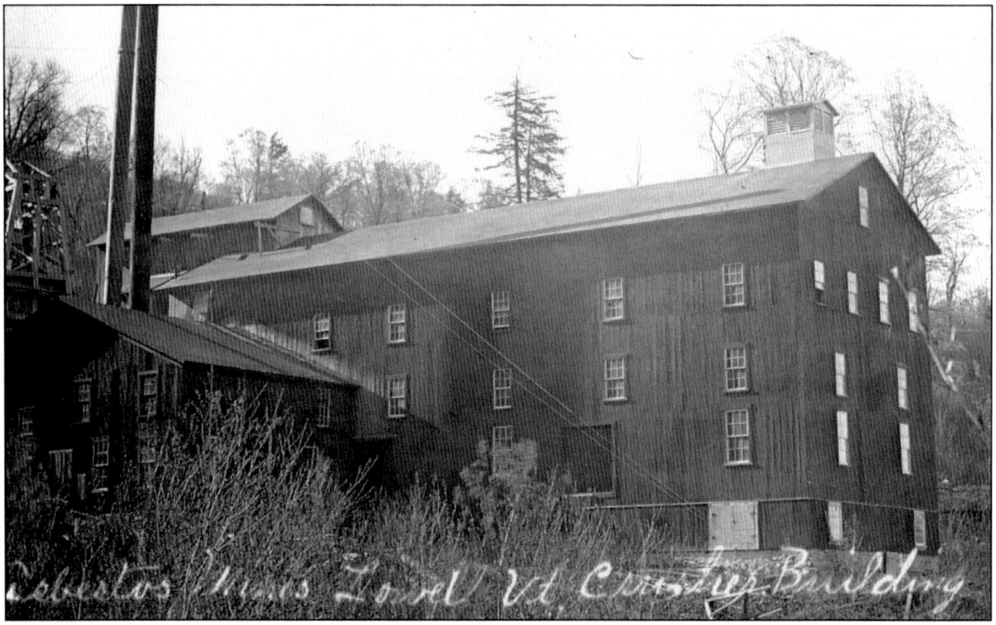

Asbestos was discovered in Belvidere Mountain in 1824. However, production was not successful until the early 1900s. Asbestos fiber from the mines was used to make fire retardant house siding. In 1975, the employees bought the company to save it from going out of business. The next year, the mine was producing 96 percent of the asbestos manufactured in the country. The mine closed in the 1990s. (APC.)

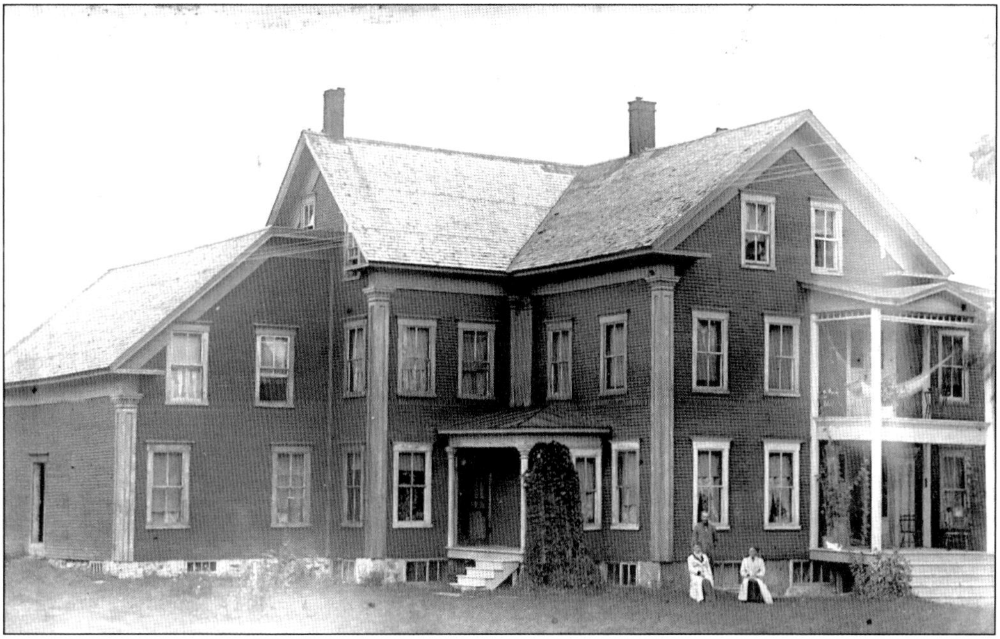

This hotel was one of two in Lowell in the early 1900s. The other hotel, called the Chase Hotel, burned in 1933. Seen here sitting in front are Thomas Patterson and his wife, May, with an unidentified lady. The hotel in the picture became rental apartments in the 1950s and then was vacant for years before it also burned in the late 1960s. (Lowell Historical Society.)

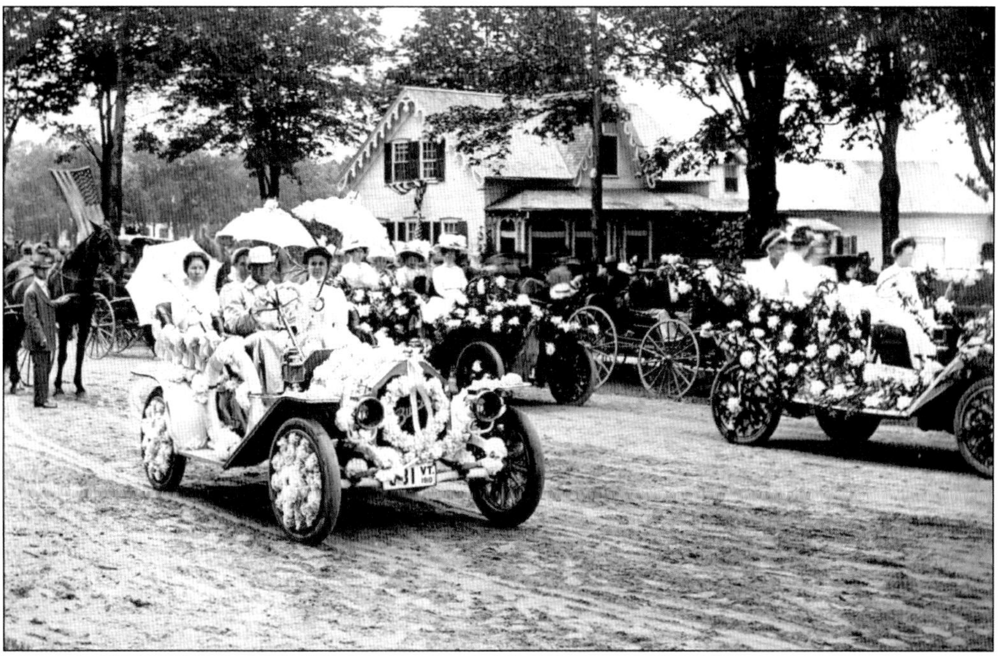

Thousands turned out to help Lowell celebrate the centennial of the town's organization and the dedication of the Bayley-Hazen Road marker on July 4, 1912. Floats with themes from Lowell's history paraded down Main Street to start the day. F.W. Baldwin was one of many who gave a speech, and then the band played, followed by a town baseball game. (APC.)

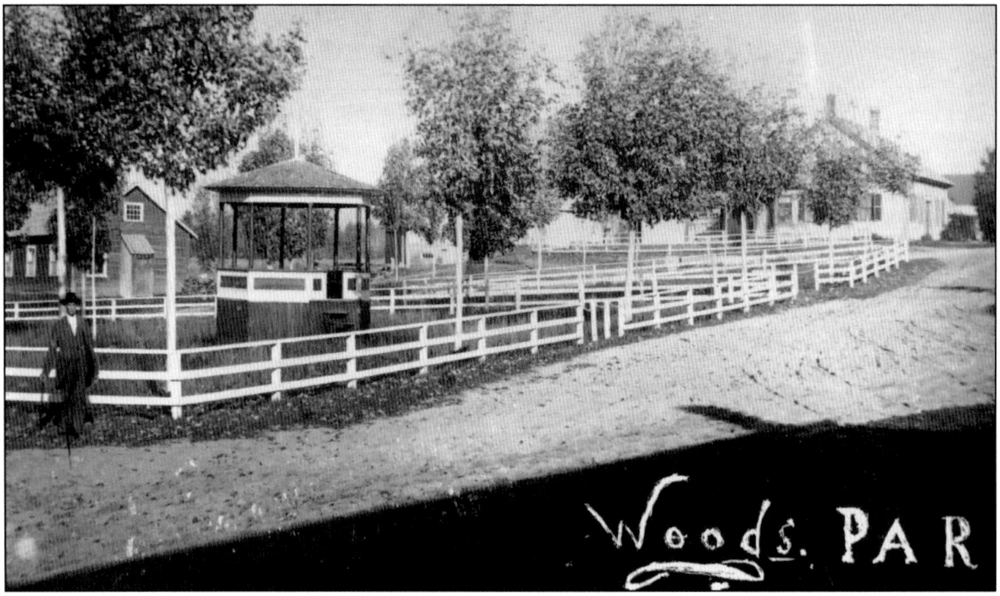

Near the center of town, this park served the community of Lowell and special town events. Concerts, music, and town gatherings happened here in the early part of the 20th century. Today the gazebo still stands, though it was replaced with a newer structure in 2004. (Lowell Historical Society.)

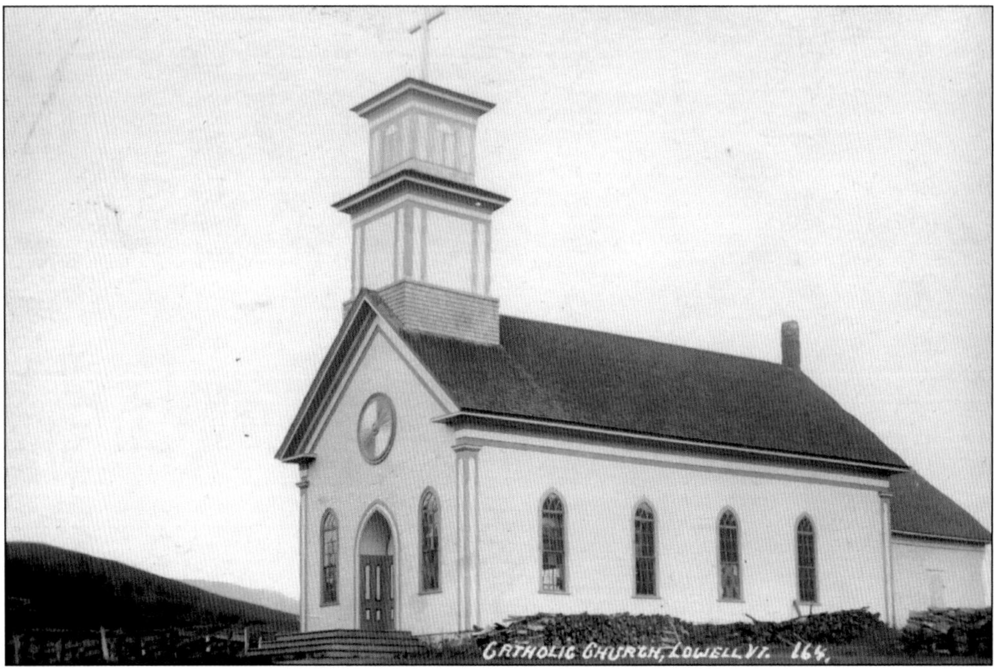

St. Ignatius Catholic Church in Lowell was one of the earliest Catholic churches established in the county. In 1843, Fr. Jeremiah O'Callaghan from Burlington led the first mass, held in the McGinty home on West Hill. In 1854, the church lot was purchased, but the structure was not finished until 1875. In 1878, there were 70 families attending mass in Lowell. (Lowell Historical Society.)

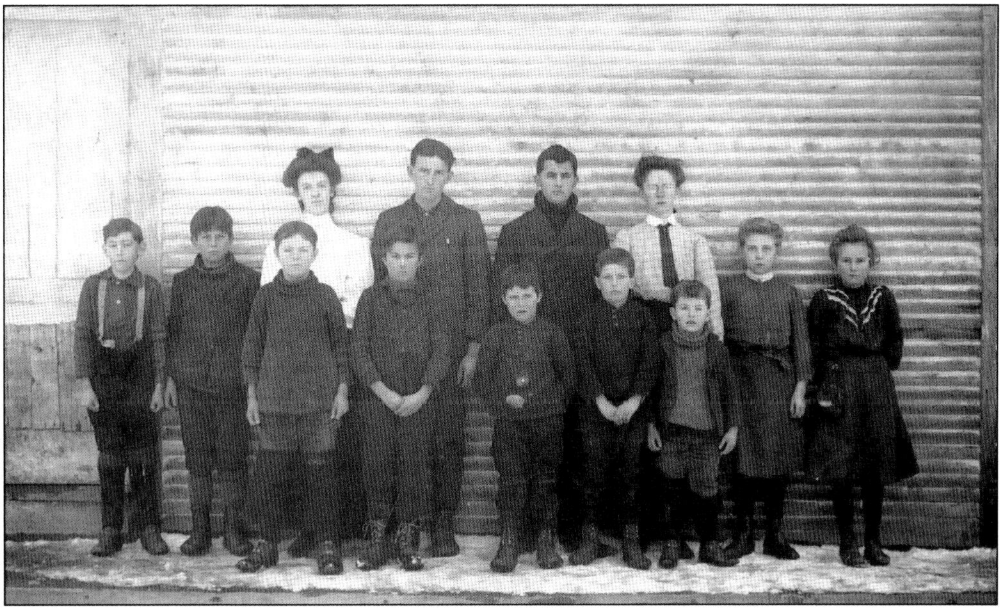

It was a cold winter day for the students and teacher of Lowell School District No. 6 to be outside posing for a picture. There were nine school districts in town. This picture was taken around 1909. (Lowell Historical Society.)

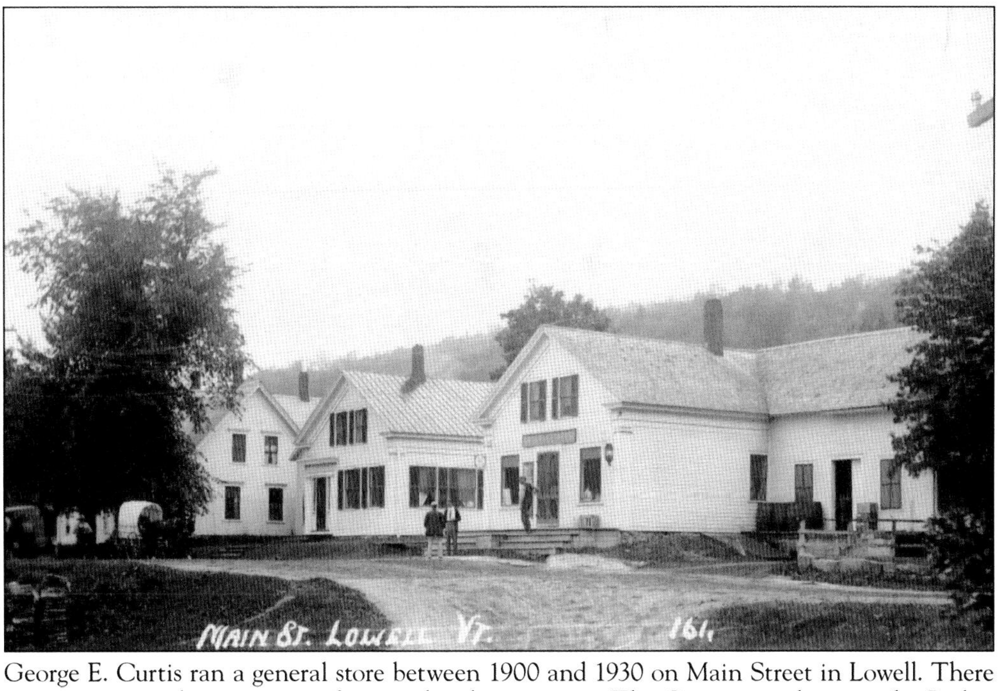

George E. Curtis ran a general store between 1900 and 1930 on Main Street in Lowell. There were two general stores across from each other in town. The Curtis store became the Parker store in the 1930s and continued through two other owners before the building was destroyed by fire. (APC.)

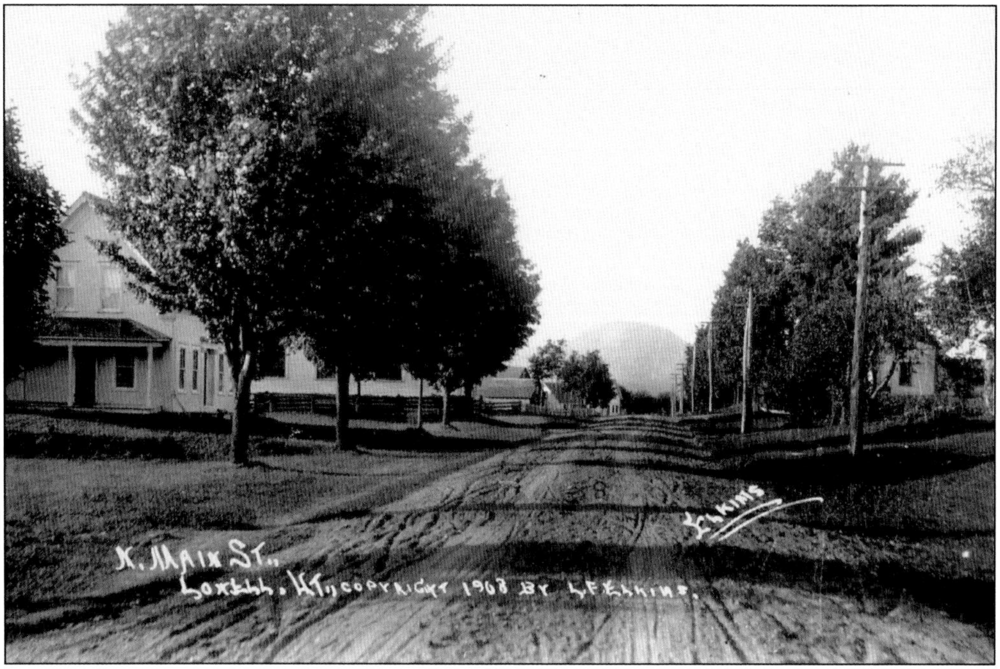

This is North Main Street, Lowell, looking towards Brown's Ledges. (APC.)

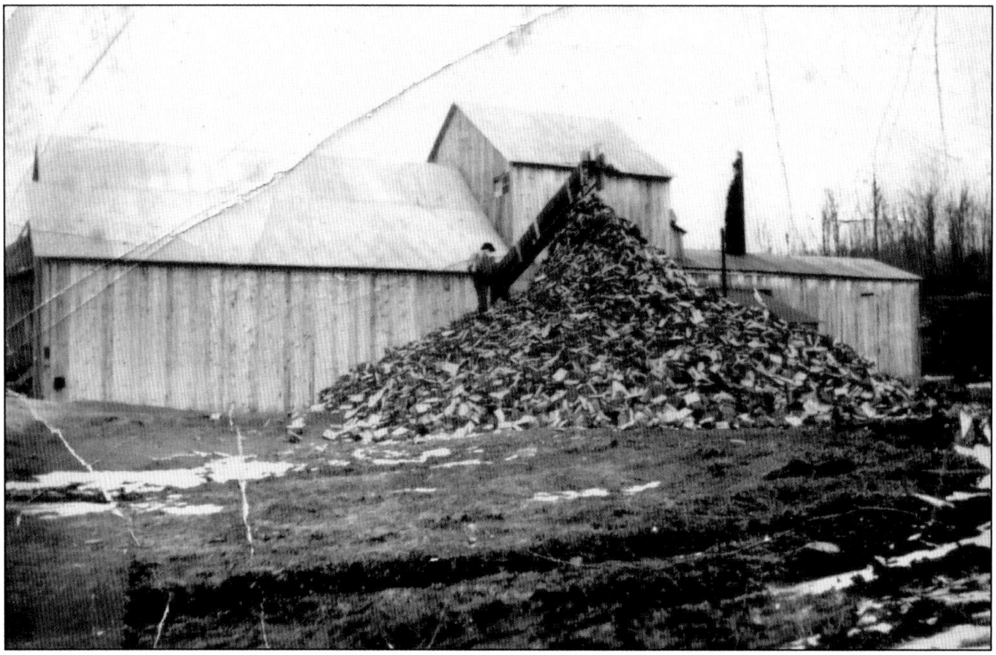

On the road up Lowell Mountain heading east was an all-in-one bobbin mill, sawmill, and planer mill owned by Bertrand Powers. His first sawmill burned in 1919, destroying $5,000 worth of bobbins waiting to be shipped. When he rebuilt in 1927, his mill could plane lumber for building construction, create bobbins for the textile industry, and cut logs from nearby forests. He sold the mill in 1939. (Lowell Historical Society.)

Seven

Jay, Westfield, and Troy

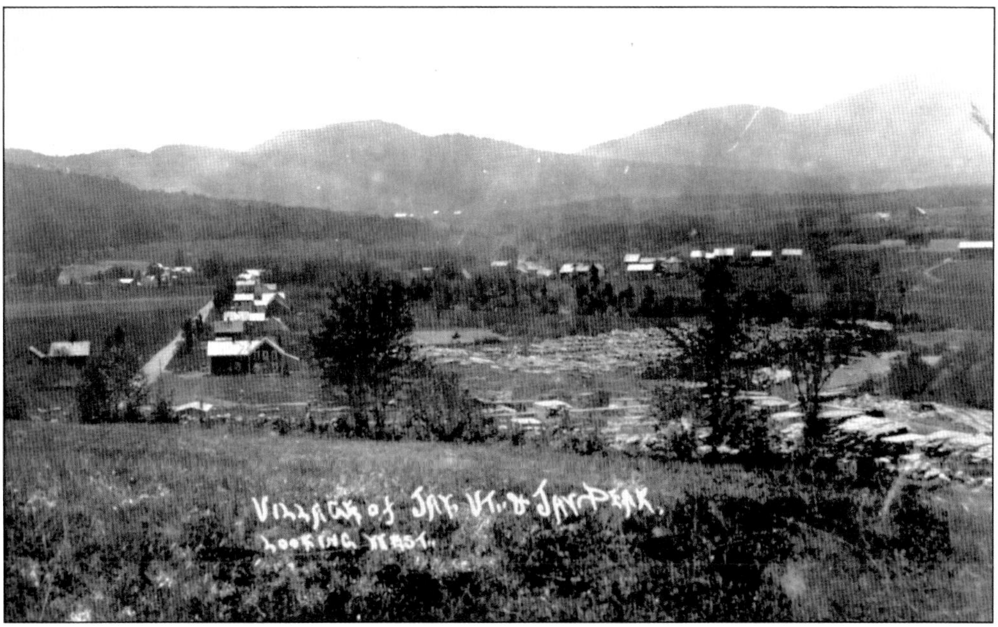

The town of Jay was originally called Carthage. In 1792, the legislature issued a charter to John Jay and John Cozine, which renamed the town Jay. The western side of town is dominated by the Green Mountains, particularly Jay Peak. The mountainous terrain hindered much settlement. As seen from the timber in this early picture of the village, Jay's main industry was logging. (APC.)

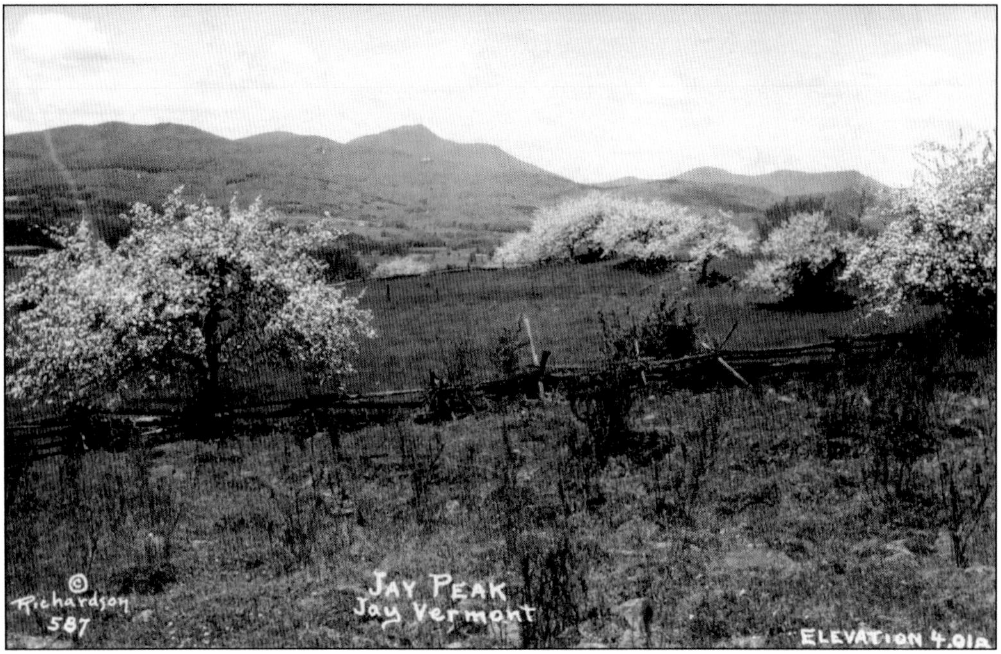

Apple trees in bloom mark the edge of a farmer's fence in the shadow of Jay Peak. The third settler in the community, Robert Barter, remained in town with his family during the scare of 1812. Barter's wife had just put the web on her loom, so she refused to leave her weaving until it was finished. By that time, the scare was over. (APC.)

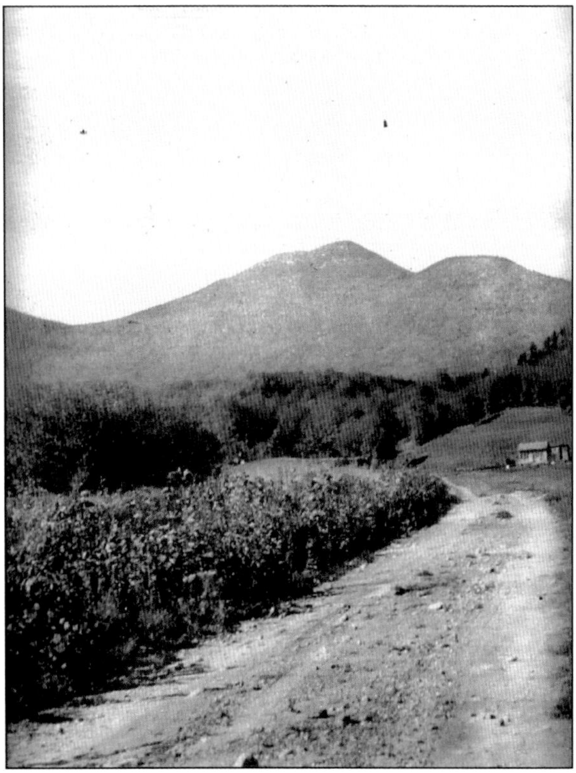

This mountain road on Jay led up to the grassy knoll just beyond the house in the right of the picture. There was no road leading over the mountain until 1955, so anyone who wanted to travel that way had to hike the distance. The settlement of Western Jay had to drive north through Canada and back south into Jay in order to vote in town meetings. (Emeline Harmon.)

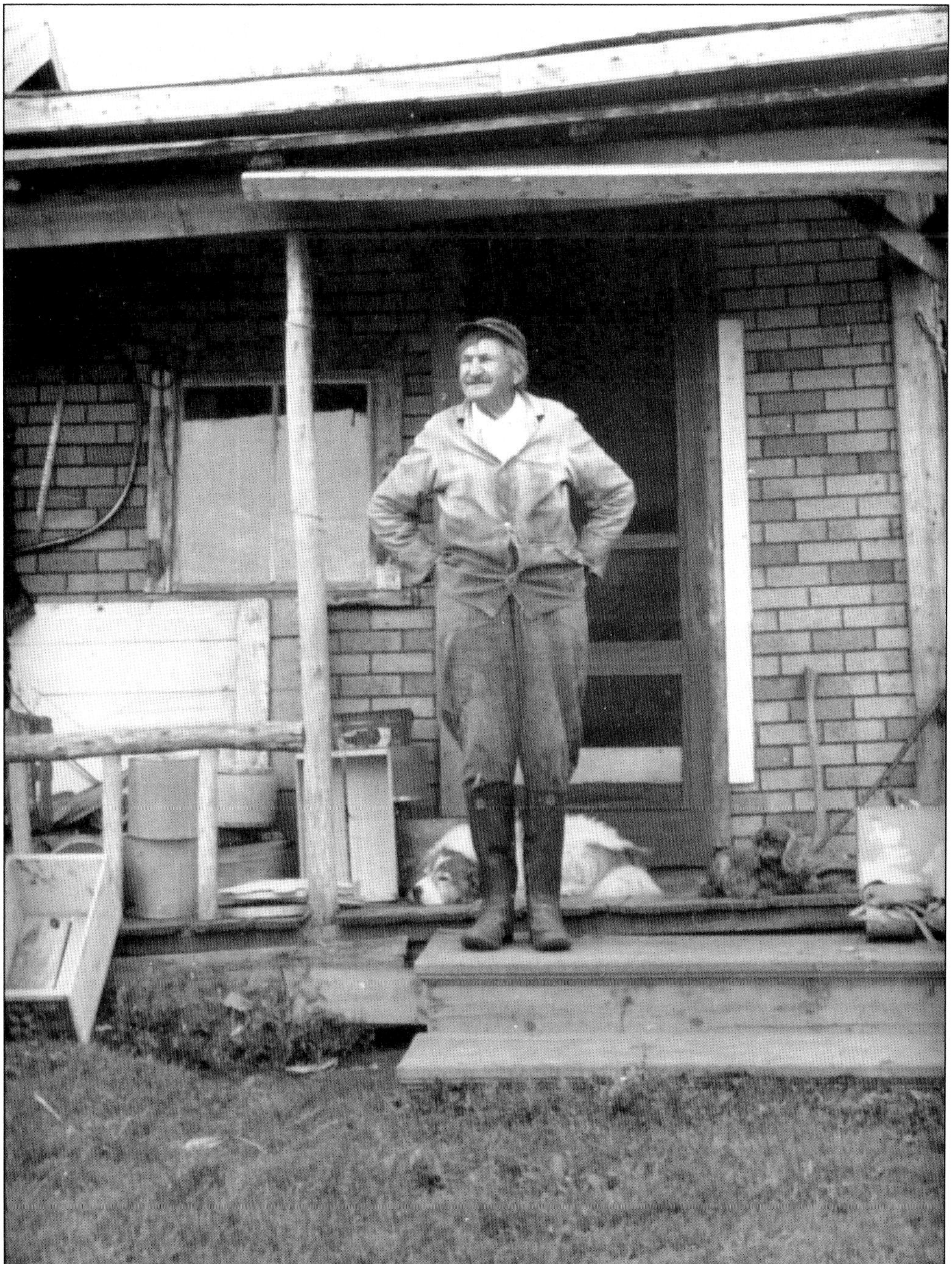

Known as the Old Indian, David Kennett was a longtime resident of Jay. Born in Montgomery Center in 1875, he lived on the mountain road in Jay for years. His house was built where the road ended going up the mountain. (Emeline Harmon.)

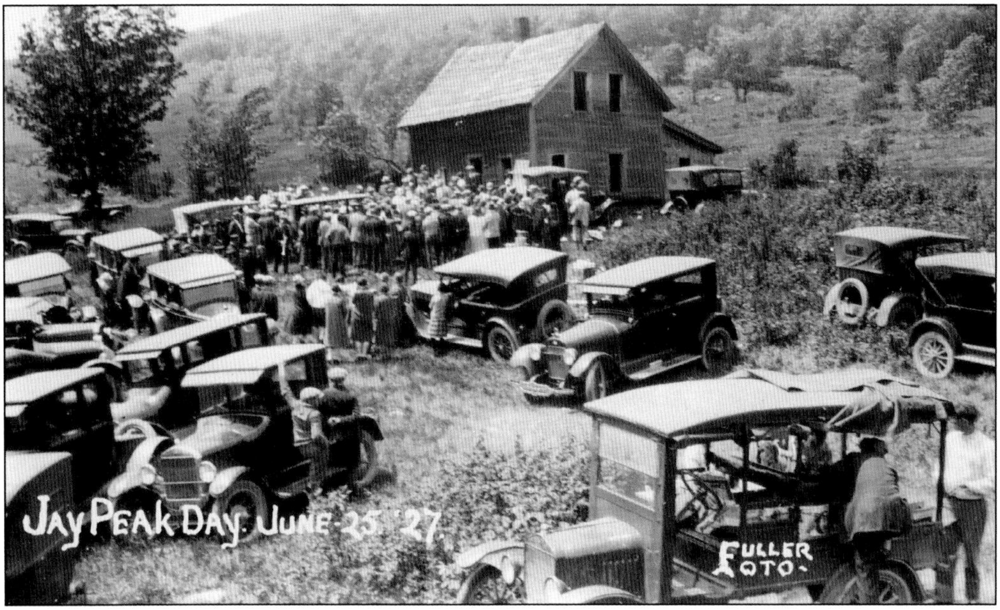

Annually at the end of June, before the road was built over the mountain, people came from far and wide to celebrate Jay Peak Day. The men would play horseshoes, the women socialized, and children hiked the mountain. In 1927, the road over the mountain was improved. Here, the crowd is listening to an address by James P. Taylor, secretary of the Vermont State Chamber of Commerce. (APC.)

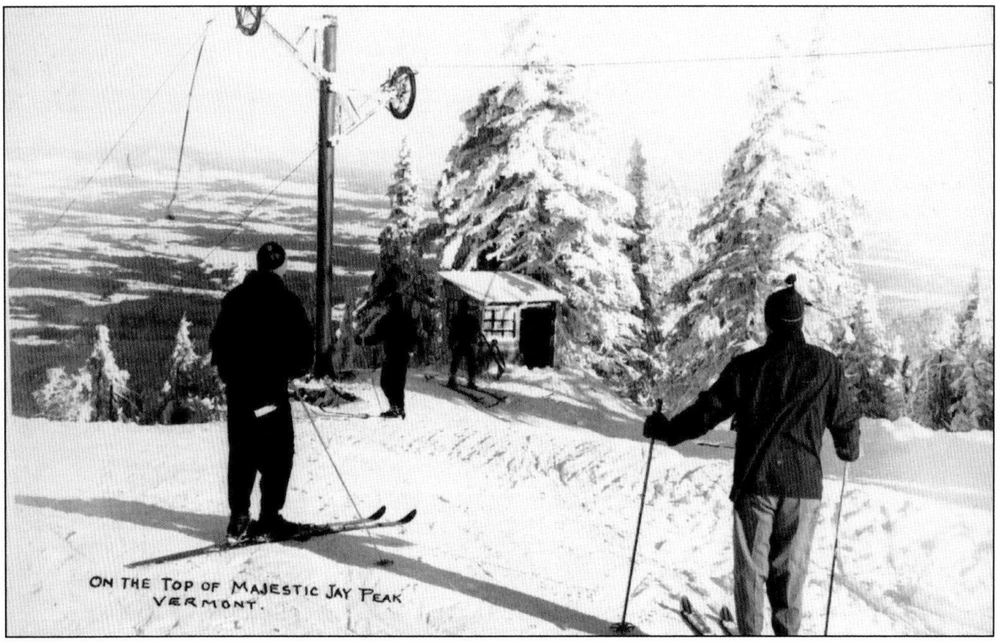

The North Troy Kiwanis Club and Harold Haynes began promoting skiing Jay in the early 1940s and into the 1950s, but it did not become popular until Walter Foeger arrived in the area in 1956. Foeger was well known for his *Natur Teknik*, a quick and easy technique for downhill skiing. In 1964, Jay Peak was one of the largest ski schools in the state, thanks to Foeger and his instructors. (RCC.)

Jay Peak Ski Area opened in 1956. Jay Peak's first lift was a French-made Pomalift, which was installed in 1956. The lift was 8,000 feet in length and served two trails on Little Jay, the Open Slope and the Sweetheart Trail. The lift was powered by diesel generators provided by Citizens Utilities in Newport. In 1967, the ski area constructed an aerial tramway for year-round use. (RCC.)

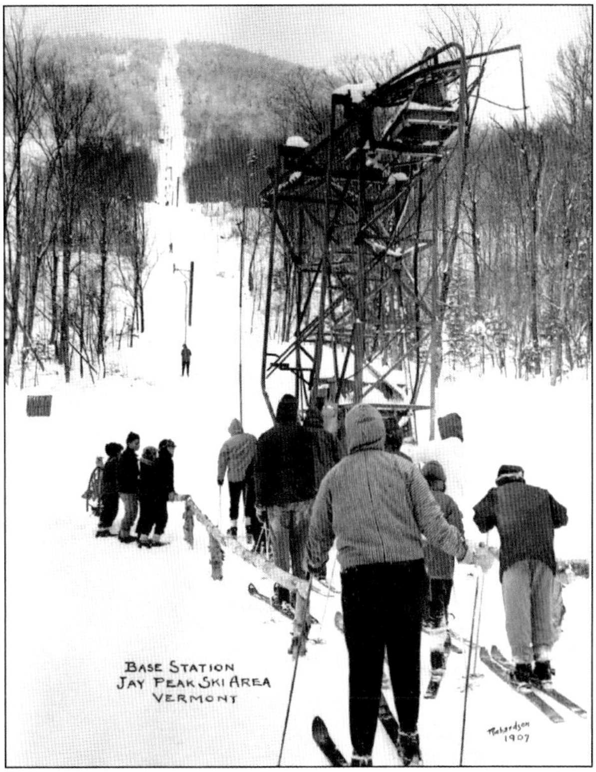

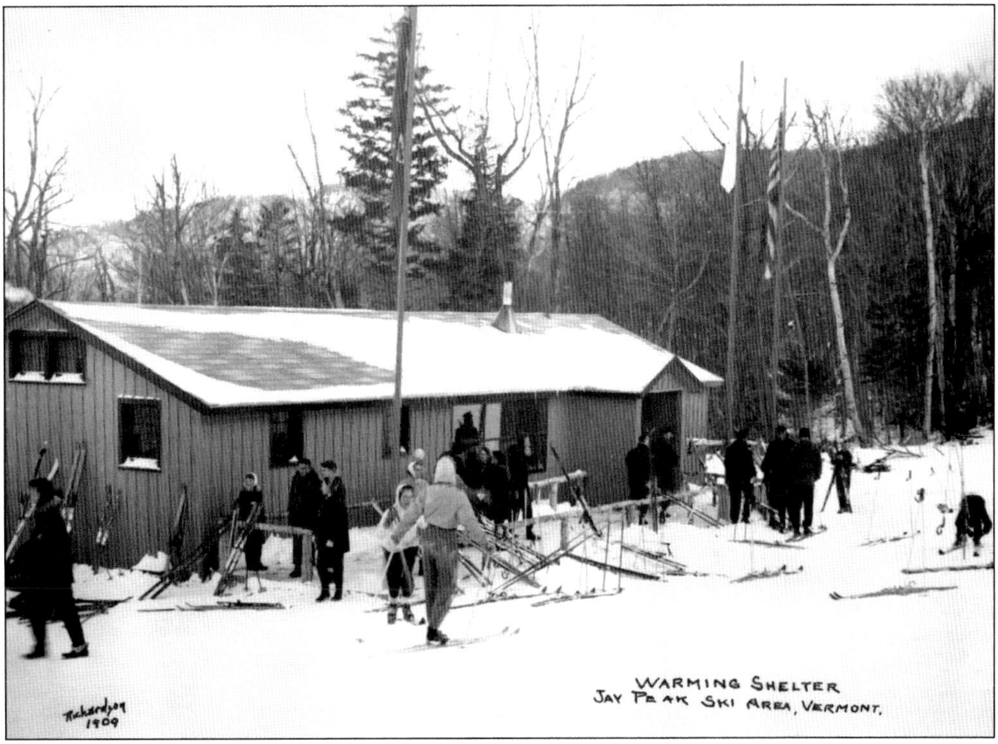

Jay had a warming shelter for the skiers when they needed to get in from the cold. (RCC.)

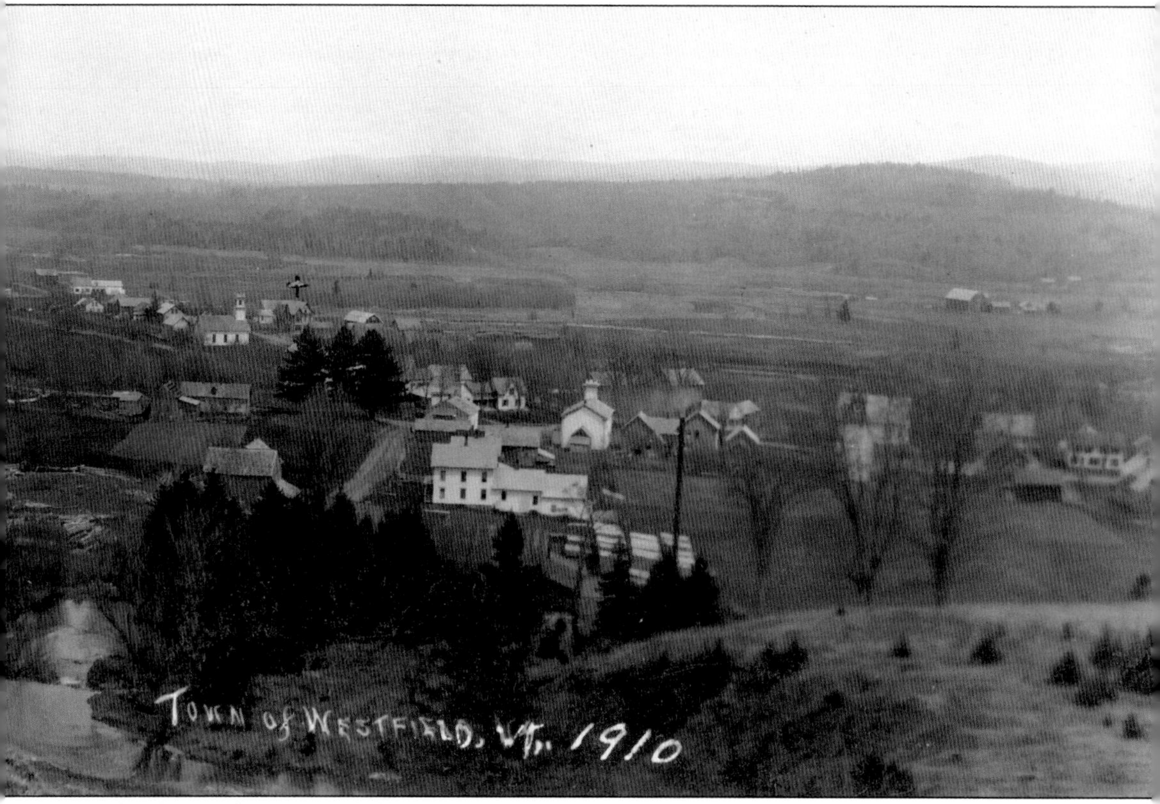

The first settler in Westfield was Jesse Olds, who moved into town on West Hill in 1798. Most of the early settlers lived on the western hills, which were more lightly timbered and easier to farm. The road through the village was a main route to Burlington from the Northeast Kingdom, which helped in its growth. (APC.)

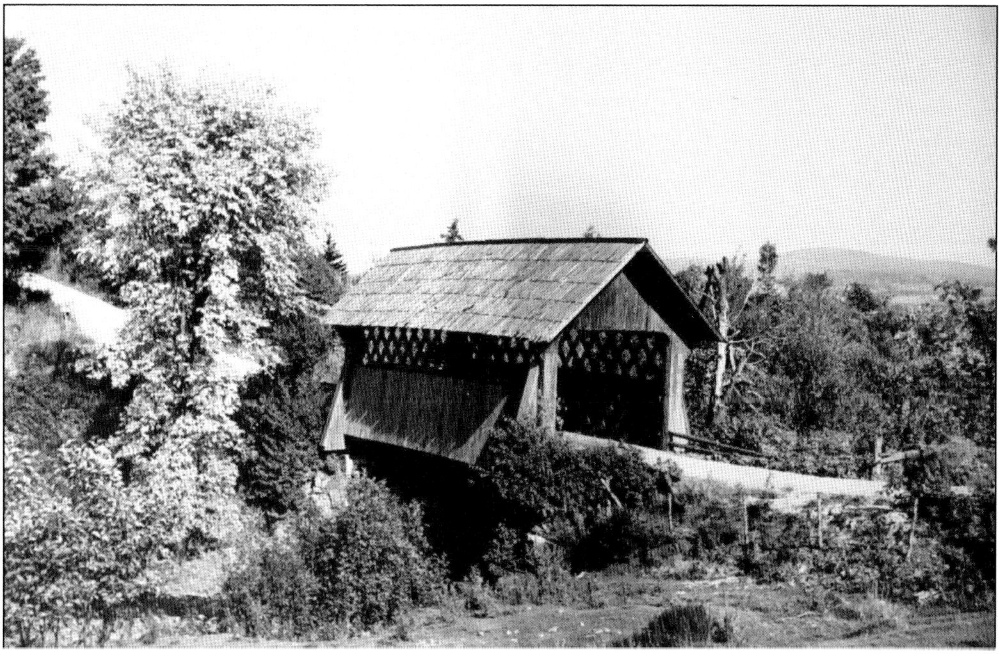

This covered bridge spanned the Taft Brook in Westfield. One of the main tributaries to the Missisquoi River, Taft Brook was the site of the town's first mill, built by early settler Lyman Taft. The Taft Brook Bridge was constructed using a light lattice truss, the most popular design used in Vermont bridges. (OCHS.)

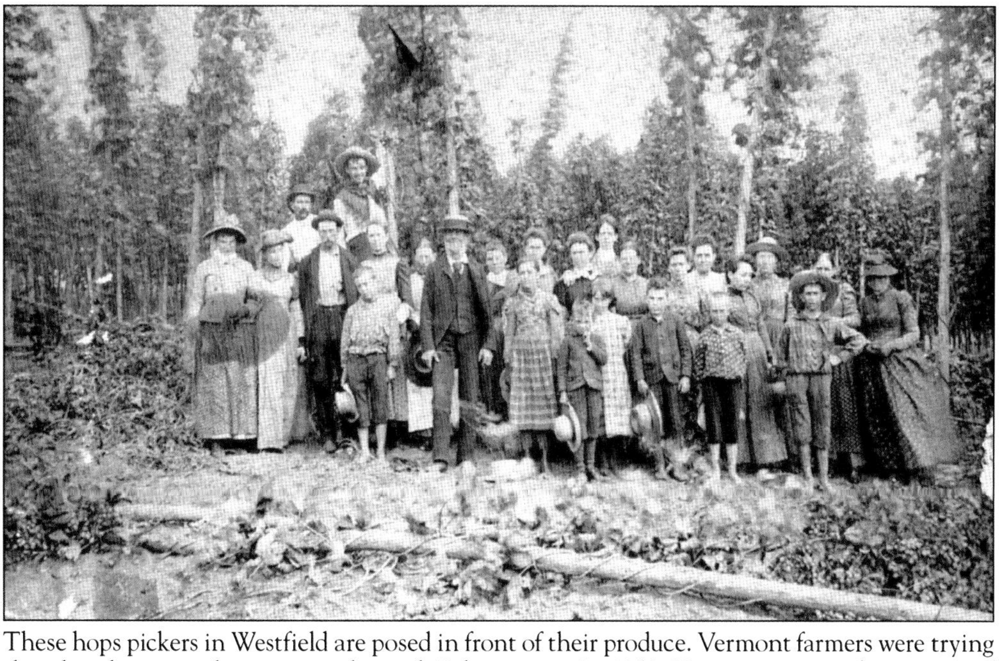

These hops pickers in Westfield are posed in front of their produce. Vermont farmers were trying their hand at specialty crops in the mid-19th century. In 1850, Vermont grew eight percent of the nation's hops crop, and for 20 years, it was second only to New York in production amounts. However, by 1870, competition from the west hurt Vermont's hops crop, and by 1900, it was gone. (Hitchcock Memorial Library.)

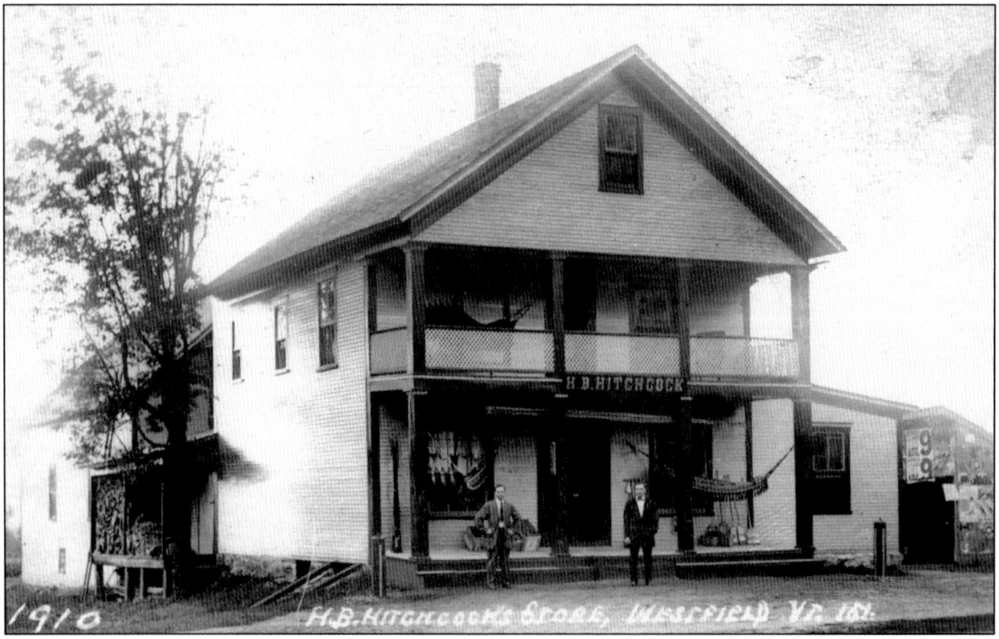

Homer B. Hitchcock (standing at left), the owner of this store, was born in Westfield, Vermont, in 1871. He went away to Rhode Island for schooling and remained there for three years, working as a clerk before returning home to Westfield in 1897. He opened a general store, which was successful for many years. (Hitchcock Memorial Library.)

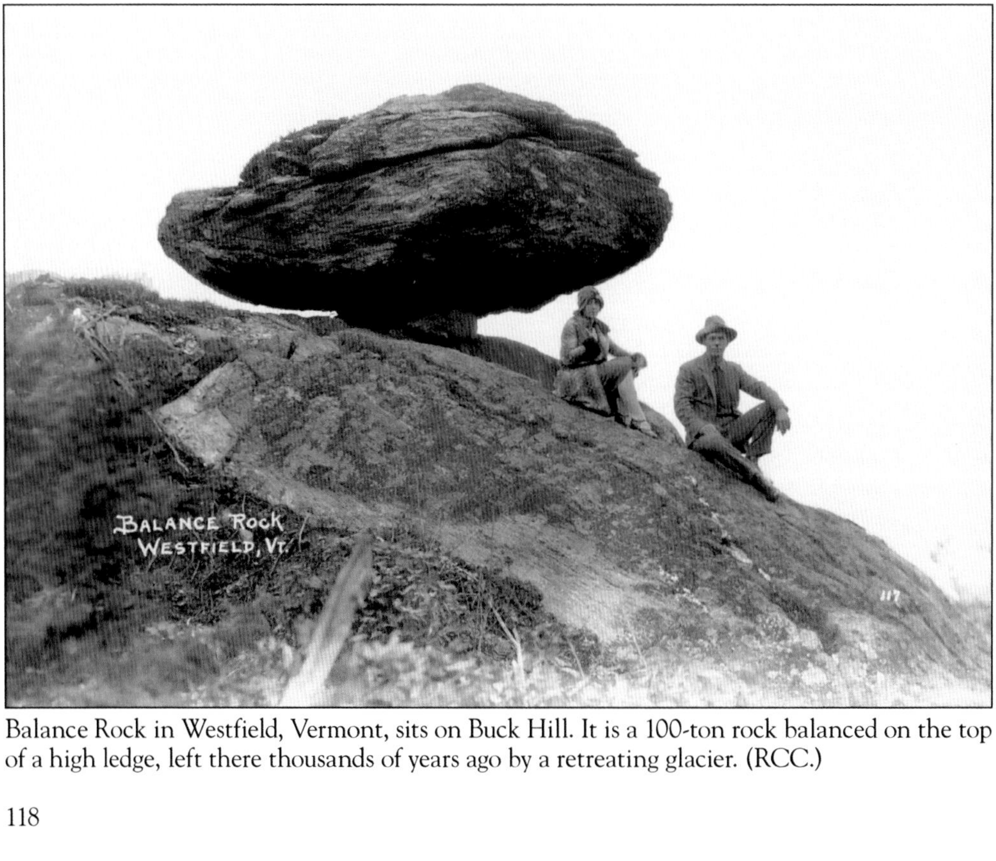

Balance Rock in Westfield, Vermont, sits on Buck Hill. It is a 100-ton rock balanced on the top of a high ledge, left there thousands of years ago by a retreating glacier. (RCC.)

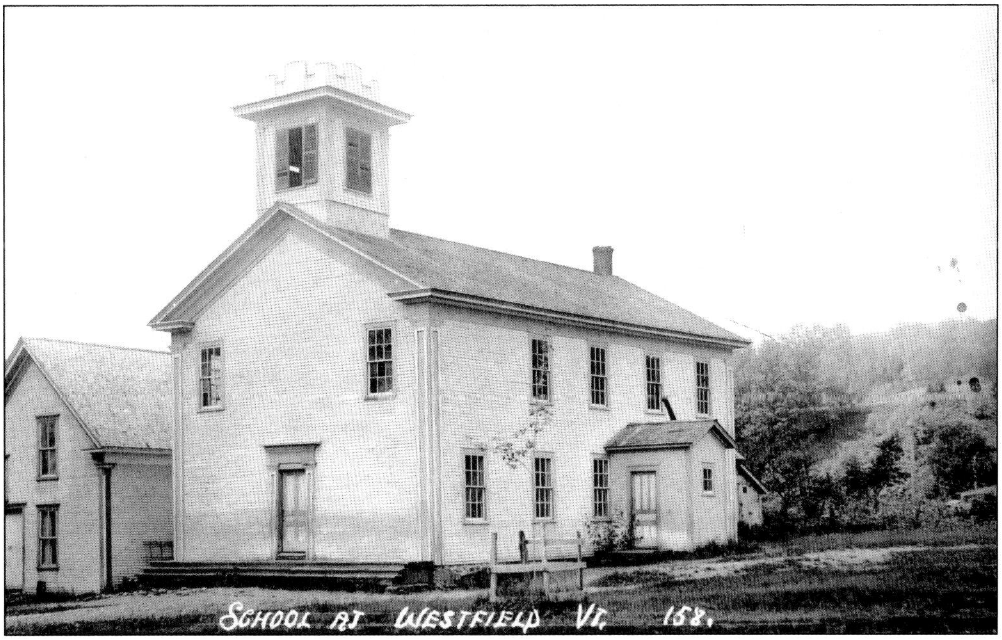

The first grammar school in Westfield started in the home of its teacher in 1857. Three years later, the first school building completed in the village had two floors. The first was used for the school, the second for town meetings. (APC.)

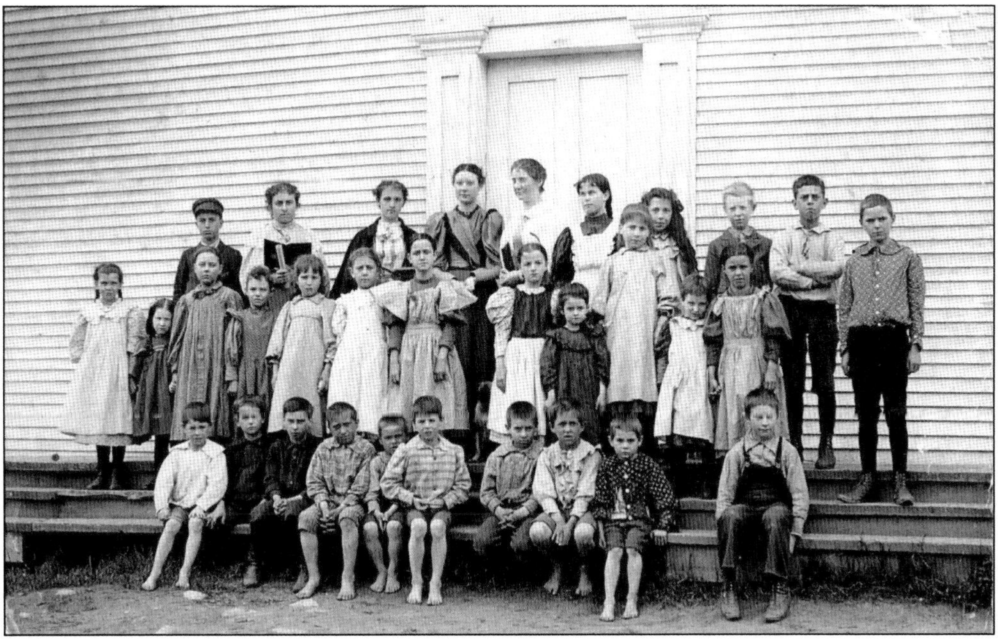

Westfield Village School poses for a picture around 1897. Note that the boys in the front are not wearing shoes. (Hitchcock Memorial Library.)

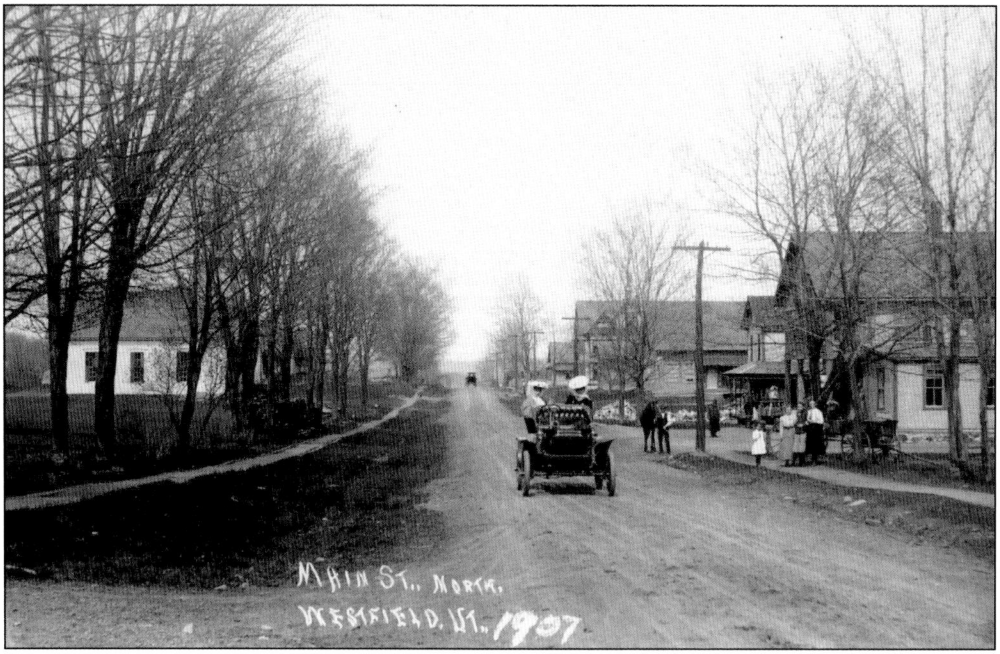

This is a picture of Main Street in Westfield in 1907. (APC.)

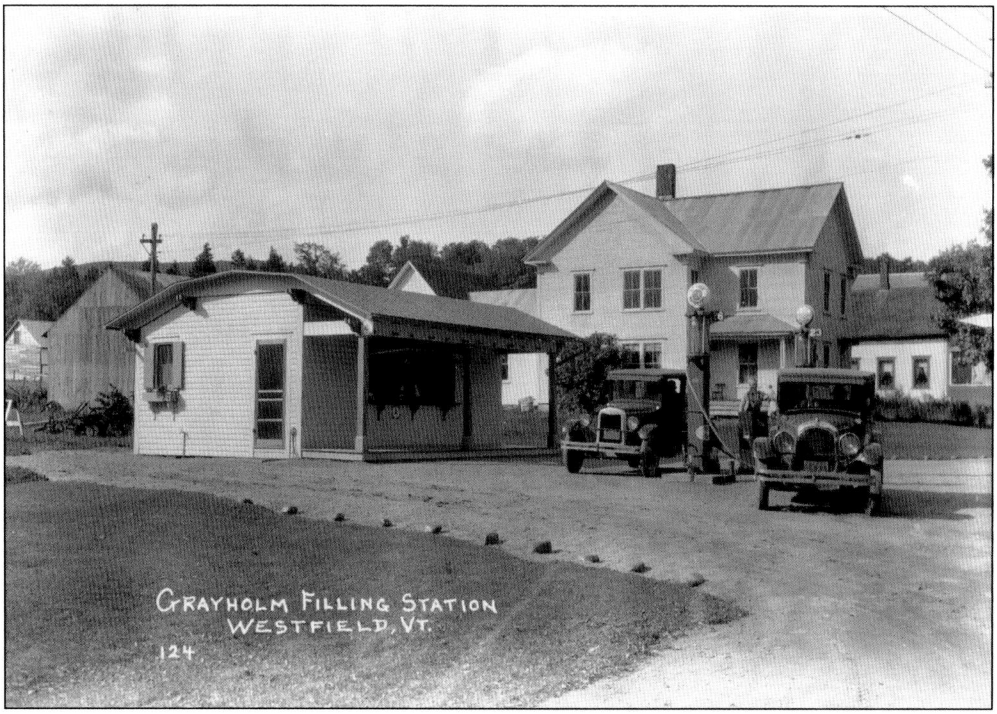

The Grayholms in Westfield opened this shop and filling station across from their house in the 1930s. They sold food, such as hot dogs, and gave visitor information to travelers. (RCC.)

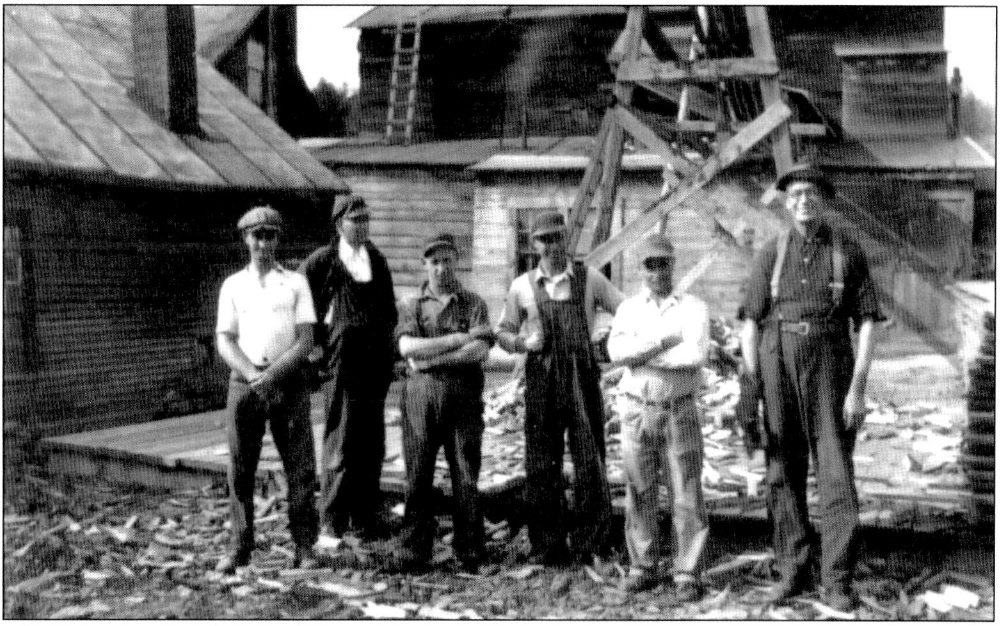

These men were workers in the Bowen and Hunter Bobbin Mill in Westfield. The mill produced bobbins for the cotton weaving industry from maple, birch, and beech wood. Over 8,000 feet of lumber were processed every day using steam power. It opened in the 1940s and closed as a mill in the 1970s. In 1993, the building became the Old Bobbin Mill Restaurant and Pub. (Hitchcock Memorial Library.)

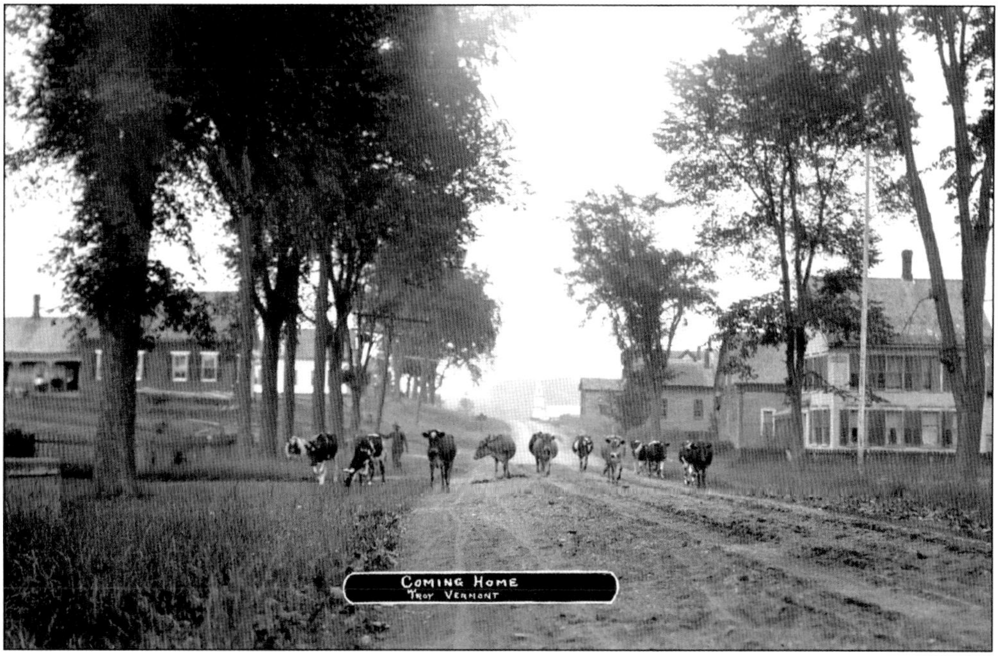

The town of Troy was originally named Missisquoi, after the river that winds through the northwest region of Orleans County. As the source of power for many mills and factories, the river and its tributaries proved to be important factors in the area's development. The town's name was changed to Troy in 1803. The farmer in this picture is bringing his cows home from pasture. (RCC.)

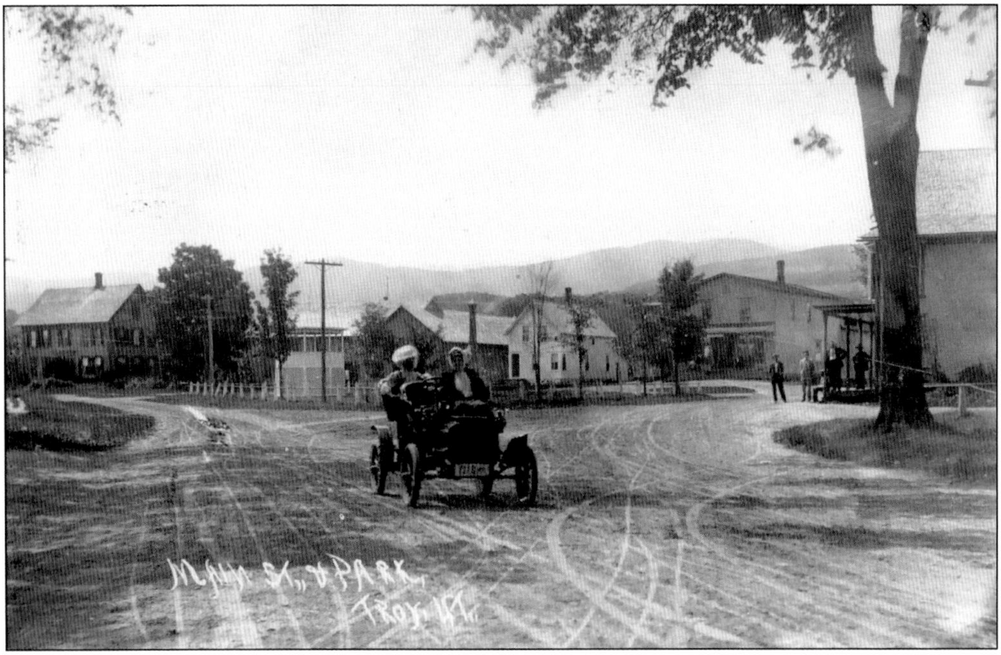
Main Street runs through what was called South Troy, the first well-settled village in Troy. The road that traveled through here was a main route from Newport to Burlington, which was especially important during the days without railroads. When the railroad went to North Troy in 1871, some of the businesses traveled north. In the center background of this picture is a triangular-shaped common with a bandstand. (APC.)

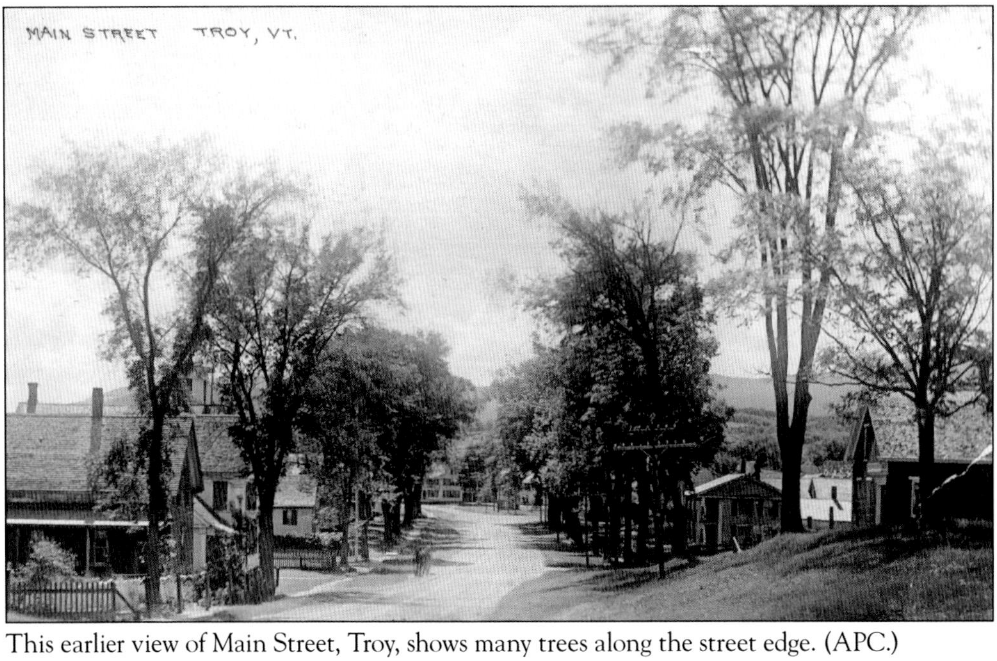

This earlier view of Main Street, Troy, shows many trees along the street edge. (APC.)

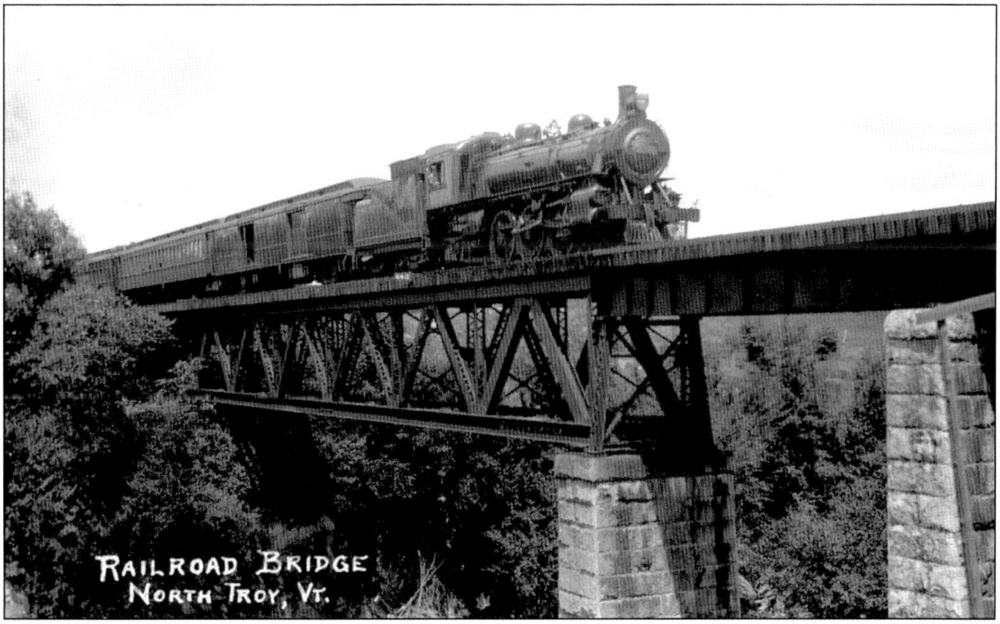

In 1871, the railroad came through North Troy. The Canadian Pacific Railroad, which also stopped in nearby Newport, arrived and departed from town six times a day, even on Sunday. The mail arrived by train and was delivered to the post office every morning. The combination of rail transportation, water power, and raw materials led to the growth of the town into a bustling industrial center. (RCC.)

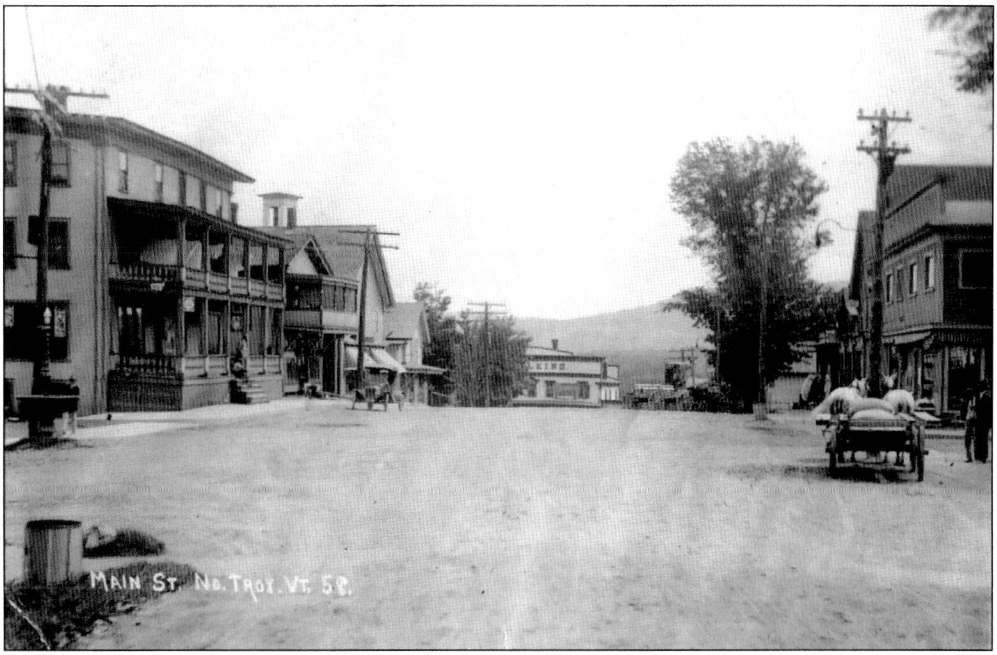

This picture of Main Street in North Troy was taken when both automobiles and horse-drawn carriages were in use, as seen in the image. In 1884, Charles Ramsdell ran the Frontier Hotel (front left) and also managed a livery and feed stable. The Frontier Hotel offered formal dances. Next door was a hardware store run by Clive Seaver and the Gardyne general store. (APC.)

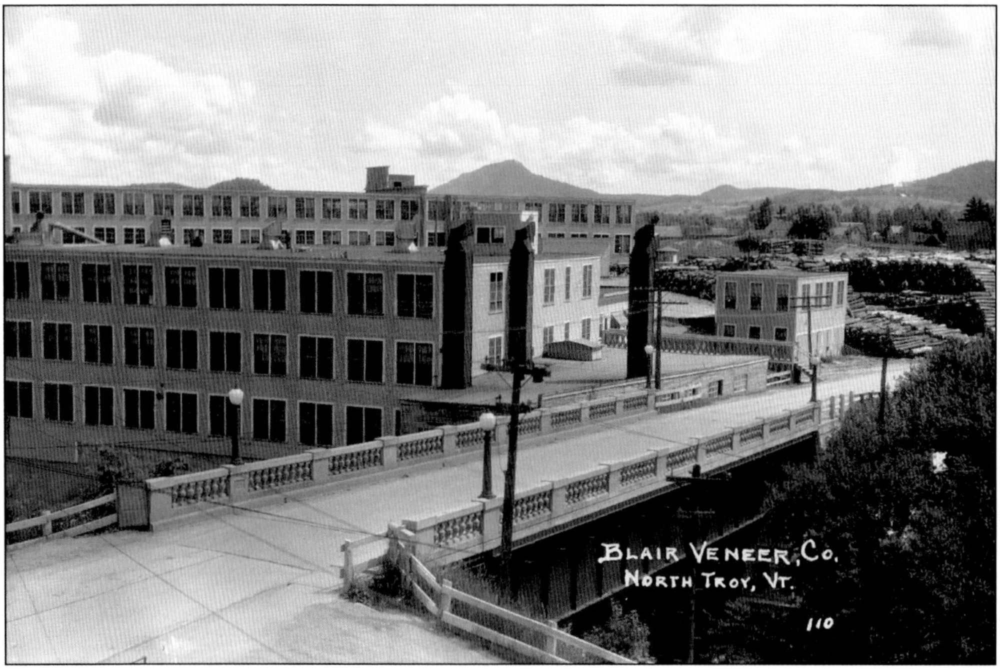

In 1903, brothers Myron and Enos Blair of Jay organized the Blair Veneer Company, which manufactured plywood panels, chair seats, and piano sounding boards. During the Great Depression, the company ran almost full-time, with a workforce of approximately 200. In 1939, the total properties were valued around $1 million. The plant suffered from two fires in 1910 and 1924. It closed for good in 1970. (RCC.)

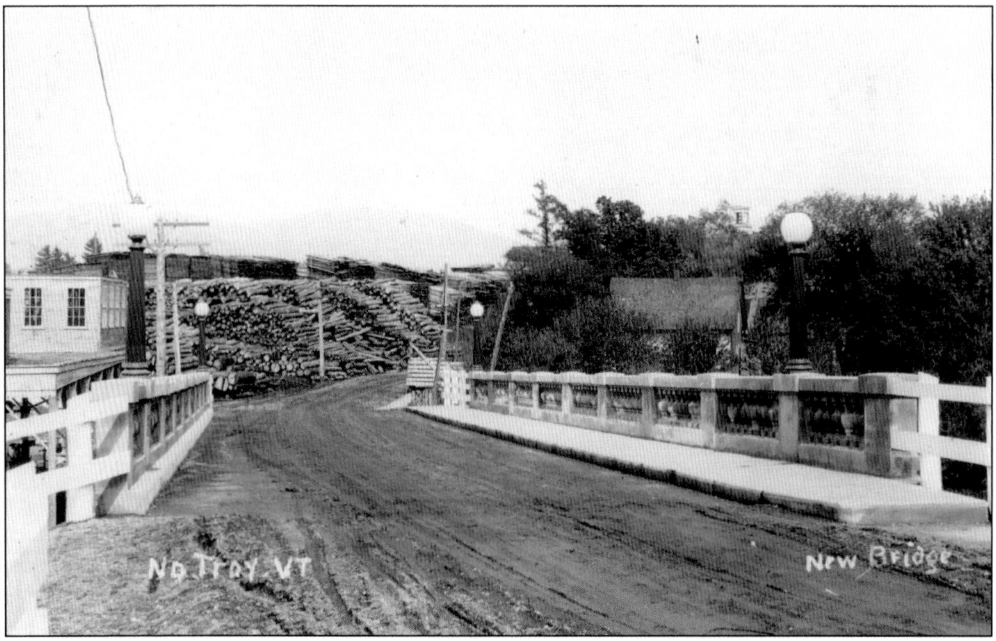

This was once a covered bridge merging Pleasant Street and East Main Street over the Missisquoi River. Situated close to the Blair Veneer Mill, it burned during a fire at the mill in 1924. It was replaced with this cement and steel bridge later that year. (APC.)

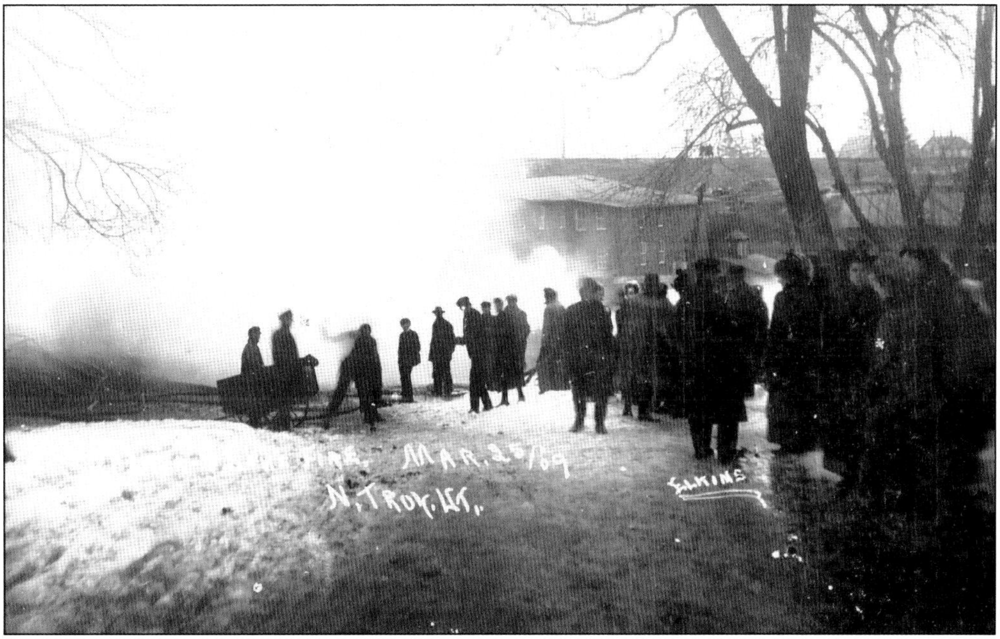

One of the buildings used by H.B. Parker and Son—a factory in North Troy that created sounding boards for stringed instruments, sashes, doors, and butter tubs—burned on March 25, 1909. (APC.)

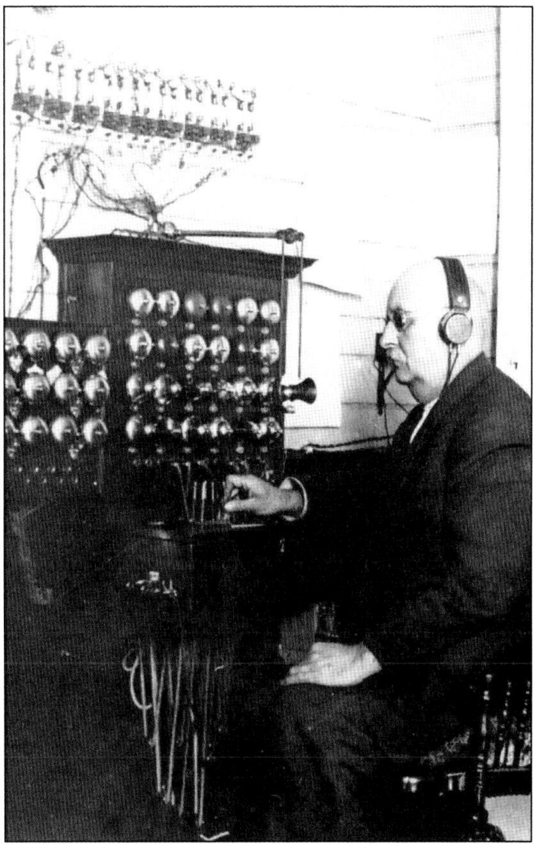

William Hodsden, a blind man from Troy, served as a telephone operator and helped to bring telephone service to the towns of Westfield, Troy, and Lowell. He had a special switchboard with bells that had different sounds for the various lines. He died in 1917. In 1961, the towns that he helped bring telephone service to converted over to the dial system. (Hitchcock Memorial Library.)

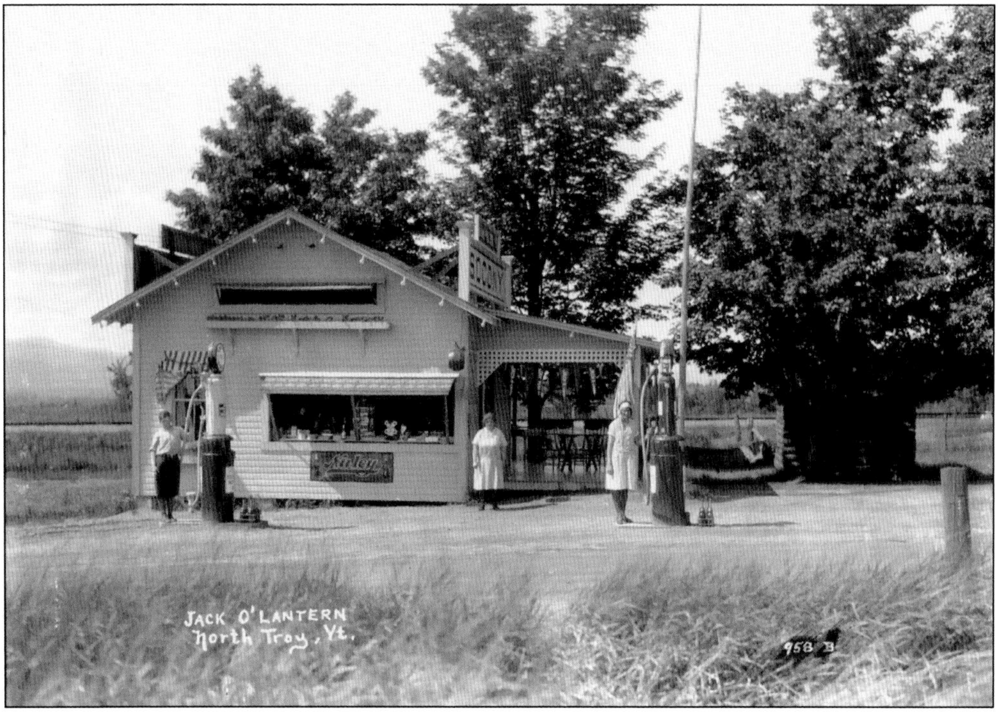

The Jack O'Lantern was a diner and gas station in North Troy. (RCC.)

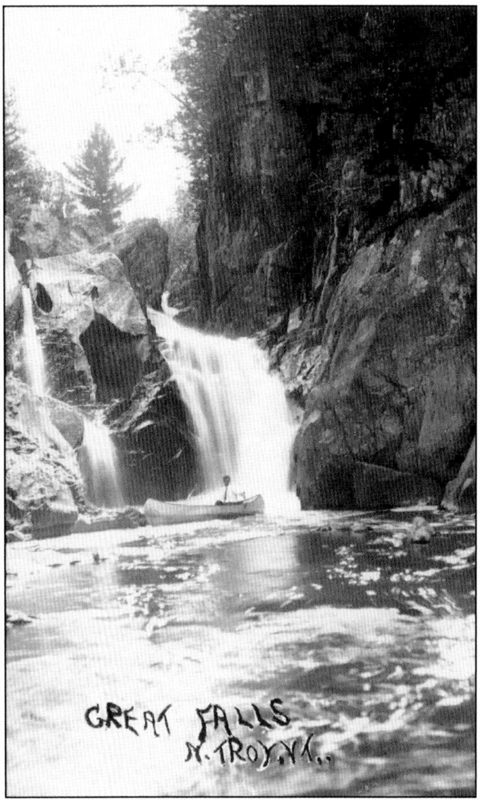

The Falls at North Troy are a mile and a half south of the village. An overhanging cliff and high rock formation lead to a grand waterfall on the Missisquoi (once called Missisco) River. It is a favorite place for swimming and diving. (APC.)

About the Organization

In 1853, the Orleans County Historical Society (OCHS) was founded by a group of prominent local men as the Orleans County Natural and Civil History Society. When the Old Stone House Museum was purchased in 1916, the name was changed. The mission of the OCHS is to foster understanding and appreciation of the regional history and culture of Orleans County and 19th-century life in a hill village. This includes the preservation of artifacts, buildings, skills, and landscapes. There is a special emphasis on the Brownington Historic District, the Orleans County Grammar School, and the lives of Alexander Lucius Twilight and Samuel Read Hall. The OCHS owns the Old Stone House Museum and is responsible for maintaining the building, as well as five other historical buildings and 55 acres of working farmland.

The OCHS offers educational programs for children and adults both at the museum and off-site during the spring, summer, and fall. Some of these programs are tours of the museum, youth education days like Spring Field Days, Time Travelers Camp, adult craft classes, and a collector's fair. Youth programs combine hands-on training and factual history of 19th-century life. Local artists, performers, musicians, poets, historians, and researchers frequently are part of programs at the museum. The biggest event of the year is the annual Old Stone House Day, which celebrates local history with demonstrations of traditional skills, heritage crafts, farm animals, a farmer's market, and a museum open house.

A free research facility for genealogy and local and state history is available with archived photographs, journals, and rare books. A new archival building houses these collections in a temperature-controlled environment. There is a small research library on-site with books like *Walton's Vermont Register* from 1836 to 1959 and the *Foxfire* volumes. The museum's website, www.oldstonehousemuseum.org, has online historical resources like biographies, poetry, town histories, and 19th-century maps.

There are six staff members who run the day-to-day museum business and organize the assortment of events with the help of many volunteers. Events take place every month of the year except December and January, and the museum is open May 15 to October 15.